A Rugged Nation

Marco Armiero

A Rugged Nation

Mountains and the Making of Modern Italy:
Nineteenth and Twentieth Centuries

The White Horse Press

Copyright © Marco Armiero
First published 2011 by
The White Horse Press, 10 High Street, Knapwell, Cambridge, CB23 4NR, UK

Set in 11 point Adobe Garamond Pro
Printed by Lightning Source

British Library Cataloguing in Publication Data
A catalogue record for this book is available from the British Library

ISBN   978-1-874267-64-5 (HB) 978-1-874267-70-6 (PB)

But memory is not only made by oaths, words and plaques;
it is also made of gestures which we repeat every morning of the world.
And the world we want needs to be saved, fed and kept alive every day.
It is enough to give up a little while and everything is ruined forever.

Stefano Benni, Saltatempo, 2001

To Stefania and Giulia
And to the memory of Marcello

Contents

Pictures and Tables

Note

Unless otherwise stated, translations from the Italian are the author's own.

Biographical Note

Marco Armiero (Ph.D. in Economic History) is an environmental historian, currently working as a Senior Researcher at the National Research Council, Italy. He was among the founders of the environmental history field in Italy, co-authoring with Stefania Barca the first Italian textbook on the subject, *Storia dell'Ambiente. Una Introduzione* (2004). His main topics of study have been the history of environmental conflicts over property rights and access to common resources (forests and sea), the politics of nature and landscape in Italian-nation building and the environmental history of mass migrations. In English, he has published several essays ('Seeing Like a Protester'; 'Enclosing the Sea'; 'Nationalizing Italian Mountains'; 'The Tree and the Machine'), co-edited with Marcus Hall the book *Nature and History in Modern Italy* (2010) and edited *Views from the South. Environmental Stories from the Mediterranean World (19th–20th cent.)* (2006).

After two short periods of research at the University of Kansas and Brown University, in recent years he has worked at the Program in Agrarian Studies, Yale University; at the Environmental Science, Policy and Management Department, UC Berkeley; and at The Bill Lane Center for the Study of the American West, Stanford University.

Since February 2010 he has been a Marie Curie Fellow at the L'Institut de Ciència i Tecnologia Ambientals (ICTA), Universitat Autònoma de Barcelona, working on a project about the political ecology of garbage in contemporary Naples, Italy.

Acknowledgements

To have people and institutions to acknowledge is for me the best part of writing a book. In all probability, the acknowledgments could stand as a partial substitute for the introduction to this book because they express the true reason why I have written it – to enjoy the company and friendship of the very many people who have marked my path through this project. Meeting all of them has been the best result of my research on Italian mountains.

I want to thank the Italian colleagues with whom I shared my first steps on this journey: Piero Bevilacqua, Giuseppe Civile, Paolo Macry, Duccio Scotto di Luzio, Marco Viscardi and Wilko Graf von Hardenberg. With Wilko I recently started an international network on Nature&Nation studies and my thoughts have been influenced by our common work; therefore, thanks to all the members of the Nature&Nation group.

Without the valuable support of the Istituto di Studi sulle Società del Mediterraneo – CNR I could never have accomplished my research.

Recently I have moved to the ICTA at the UAB in Barcelona, Spain thanks to a Marie Curie Grant (for a project entitled 'LARES – Landscapes of Resistance'); therefore my gratitude goes to them for their unending support. In particular, I want to thank the colleagues at ICTA who have talked with me in seminars, on the metro and at lunch and parties, discussing mountains, memory and history: Joan Martinez Alier, Giorgos Kallis, Christos Zografos, Giacomo D'Alisa and Federico De Maria. They will be relieved that this book is finally done.

I also want to express my gratitude to the US institutions which have supported my research: the Agrarian Studies Program at Yale University (which would not be as it is without Kay Mansfield), the Department of Environmental Science, Policy, and Management at UC Berkeley and the Bill Lane Center for the Study of the American West at Stanford University. In particular, I had the opportunity to discuss my project with Nancy Peluso, Jim Scott, Richard White, Carolyn Merchant and Martin Melosi. I could not have been luckier! To all of them, my thanks for their suggestions, thoughts, support and, first and foremost, their friendship.

In Berkeley I had the opportunity to present my research at a seminar in the Italian Studies Department; I hope I have been able to include in this book something from that wonderful discussion.

In the past few years I have had the opportunity to work with Marcus Hall, gaining advantage from his extensive expertise on Italian environmental history; in addition, he is a wonderful friend – and this helps a lot.

Special thanks to John McNeill who inspired this book and who believed in it when it was more or less just one page long.

I am extremely fortunate to have an extraordinary friend in Donald Worster; meeting him in Kansas when I was only a young postgraduate represented for me the liberating discovery of environmental history and of a good friend. It is Donald's fault if, since our meeting, I have always confused the passion for environmental history with the need to be a better human being.

Many people have helped me in my journey through the Italian mountains. Il Nucleo Bibliotecario di Geografia has been my home for several years; I owe so much to its director, Rosa D'Elia, for having facilitated my research in every possible way.

My travels around the US, Spain and Portugal, while enriching my life and my scholarship, have also made this research difficult to accomplish. On those occasions, I have come to appreciate some very good friends in Italy. Valeria Rucco has done an incredible job for me in providing many materials from the library of the Nucleo Bibliotecario di Geografia; surely, she has done for me much more than was required by her job. Giovanni Salvietti has been a most instrumental helper on this project. Without his nose for research and his passion for history and mountains, this book would have been much weaker.

My friends in Longarone, Tiziano Dal Farra and Ivan Pollazzon, made possible the section on the Vajont; our friendship is only beginning and I know that it will deepen in the future. Once you meet the Vajont, it will stay with you forever.

Mark Walter and Veronika Fukson have been instrumental in the language revision of this manuscript. I owe special thanks to Veronika who has always helped me generously, patiently tolerating me and my language.

An earlier version of Chapter 3 has already been published in the book *Nature and History in Modern Italy* (Athens, Ohio UP, 2010); I want to express my appreciation to Ohio University Press (www.ohioswallow.com) and especially to Jim Webb for allowing me to publish the essay again.

This book would never have been published without Sarah Johnson; her work at the White Horse Press has made everything smooth and enjoyable.

I am particularly lucky because I share my life with Stefania Barca; I know that I have pilfered ideas, readings and other materials from her. I always feel that my work is not mine alone but co-authored with her. In fact, I am happy to be in that position.

My eleven-year-old daughter Giulia has seen me working on this book for years while she was completing page after page of her own books, stories, poems and scripts. She will be relieved that I have finally finished something after all.

My father Mario was not a historian; nevertheless, he was a great story-teller. He transmitted to me his love for words and his passion for narration. He would have preferred to see me as a judge but I am sure that, wherever he is now, he is enjoying my stories.

∿ Introduction ∿

Italy is only a geographical expression.

Klemens von Metternich

It has never been easy to explain the reasons why I decided to write a book like this. People keep asking me, 'A book on the Italian mountains?' with the same dubious expression as if I were presenting a project on fishery communities in the Sahara or pastures and shepherds in New York City.

Italy is the country of art, the Mafia, good food and political scandals; nature does not have a remarkable place in its public representation. In addition, if we want to discuss nature, then we should look for a hybrid version rather than one based on mountains, because the Italian landscape is well known to be human-made, filled with memories and traces of culture. The Tuscan hills are probably the emblem of the stereotypical Italian landscape: olive groves and vineyards with a bell tower in the background are what everyone expects to see and the amount of human agency is rather high in this 'natural' scene. Mountains do not fit very well in this canonical representation; too wild and too 'northern', they seem to lack the typical ingredients of *Italianness*. In the international division of nature's work, mountains are everywhere but Italy, as the encyclopaedia of all landscape fantasies – that is, the Tourist Catalogue – authoritatively states. Maybe, for Italy, a book on the sea or, even better, one on cities and their surroundings would have worked better. After all, beaches and historic centres are what everyone wants to see in Italy. If you consider that I myself am not a mountain-climber, the motivation for writing a book like this becomes even more puzzling.

And yet, Italy is indeed one of the most mountainous countries in Europe, with 35 per cent of its territory covered by the Alps and the Apennines and 42 per cent by hills. Therefore, if one looks at a geographical map of Europe, writing a book like this should be self-explanatory; an environmental history of Italy must deal with its rugged terrain. Is that all? Is just an ordinary physical map, one of those that was on the wall of every classroom in an Italian primary

2

Physical Map of Europe.

school when I was a child, what I need to make my point? Is it that physical geography dictates our history, or at least our narratives about history? This is not a deterministic book and I will not suggest that the orography of the country can explain its history or the basic character of its inhabitants. Nonetheless, the prevalence of mountains in Italian physical geography may explain several aspects of its history, including the distribution of population and settlements, some economic patterns and even some geopolitical issues. However, I have not chosen those topics for this book. My faith in physical maps does not go so far. In fact, I believe that a physical map makes explicit many aspects that may be hidden in the public memory and can also be deceptive. By definition, it is fixed in time and space, appearing as the immobile background of historical dramas. Clearly mountains are fixed and quite immobile, as are plains and other physical features; nevertheless, as I argue in this book, they have been more dynamic than we think. The making of the nation has been interlaced with the shaping of the national landscape in terms of both culture and ecology. Mountains did not move, but their place on the map of the nation did change. They entered into and exited from the political representation of the national landscape in a dialectical relationship between nature and culture. The physical map cannot relate any of those movements; it is unable to show the mutual constituency of the natural and the political; the hierarchies that draw distances and inform our knowledge of space stay hidden in it. Looking at the map is not enough; if we want to understand these issues, we need a narrative that blends nature and history. Practically speaking, we need *this* book.

Historiographically, this book can be considered part of recent scholarship on the making of national landscapes. It is not by chance that those studies come especially from Europe – that is, from a continent where the discourse of wilderness has never been particularly strong. On the contrary, the concept of landscape seems always to have been the lens through which we have understood European nature, a concept carrying an extraordinary measure of nation in it. As Thomas Lekan and Thomas Zeller have written in their introduction to *Germany's Nature*:

> For all its conceptual ambiguity and perhaps because of it, landscape offers one of the best tools for conceptualizing and narrating the messy, dynamic interaction between these different elements. It enables scholars to move beyond simple dichotomies between use and abuse, materialism and ideology, representation and reality.[1]

Although, for a long time the English landscape has been the main subject of such studies, representing, according to John Agnew, the 'paradigm case of the significance of a certain idealised landscape as symbolic of national identity', lately Germany has been taking the leading role in the field.[2] Actually, John Agnew was advocating new studies that could go beyond the English paradigm, proposing as possible examples Germany and Italy. While studies on Italy remain meagre,[3] Germany has inspired several such books, showing the particularity of European environmental history as it engages with cultural, political and social history. Thomas Lekan's and David Blackbourn's books are excellent examples of this scholarship on nation and nature;[4] they deliberately aim to go beyond the borders of environmental history, challenging other his-

---

1.   Lekan and Zeller 2005, p. 5.
2.   Agnew 2011.
3.   On Italian environmental history, in English, see Armiero and Hall (eds.) 2010.
4.   Lekan 2004; Blackbourn 2006.

torians and historical narratives to take nature into account. It is not by chance that Lekan's point of departure is Hobsbawm and his studies on nationalism, which Lekan wants to extend to the natural world.[5]

My research on mountains and the making of modern Italy is part of that scientific effort, aiming to understand the connections between nature and nation. Raymond Williams once wrote:

> 'Nation' as a term is radically connected with 'native'. We are *born* into relation-ships which are typically settled in a place. This form of primary and 'placeable' bonding is of quite fundamental human and natural importance. Yet the jump from that to anything like the modern nation-state is entirely artificial.[6]

Rather than denying Williams' point, I have tried to explore the ways in which that 'jump' has historically occurred, merging the artificial with the natural. Concretely, my aim is to investigate the nationalisation of Italian nature, us-ing mountains as a case-study. Hence, this is a book not on mountains *per se* nor on the making of the nation. Rather it is an exploration of the mutual constituency of both.

Nationalising mountains implied imposing meanings, appropriating resources, enforcing the authority of the State, redefining boundaries between wild and tamed, wise and irrational, beautiful and ugly; it also meant trans-forming mountaineers into citizens, and sometimes citizens into mountaineers to make Italians out of soil and rocks. The mix of nature and nation is a dan-gerous concoction to manage. As David Blackbourn has recently written, no scholar in Germany can be comfortable in speaking of 'people and land' or of 'roots in the land'; these metaphors which connect nature and nation provide a bitter memory of the tragic experiences of European totalitarian regimes.[7] Racist theories, deterministic approaches and nationalistic chauvinism seem to be below the surface of any discourse on nature and nation. At the turn of the twentieth century, several historians tried to dismiss the naturalist approach to nations: according to Renan, nation was an 'everyday plebiscite'; and Febvre and Toynbee criticised the idea of natural frontiers as the 'natural' features of homeland. Nations are historical rather than ecological products; mixing the two has brought anything but good.[8] Nevertheless, precisely the fact that we

---

5. Lekan 2004, p. 5.

6. Williams 1983, p. 180.

7. Blackbourn 2006, p. 18.

8. 'However, when it is not accompanied by serious critical analysis, an emotional link between landscape and nation can be politically suspect. The search for rootedness in

are managing an explosive potion is evidence that nature did have agency in the invention of nations; there would be no imagined communities without a place to be transformed into the Fatherland. The mutual constituency of imagined communities and constructed natures is at the very core of this book. I speak of 'constructed nature' and not just of imagined nature because I want to stress again the hybridity of that process; nature is socially constructed in the sense that it has been made by generations of people working, living and narrating it but the social, blending with nature, bonds itself to environmental materiality.

Therefore, I reject the dichotomist approach that seeks to divide culture and nature, narratives and environments. As I will show in the following pages, the Italian mountains have been shaped by words and bombs, by the narratives of modernisation and the tonnes of concrete which brought that modernisation to life through dams, roads and railways.[9] The result is a hybrid landscape and, therefore, a hybrid book. Undoubtedly, purists will be disappointed by both: those who want a cultural history of nature will find too much 'stuff' in it, while, according to hard-core materialists, the nature I present in this book will have too many extra doses of narratives to be true. Hopefully, there will be readers who, like myself, are more at ease with hybridity than with purity, unafraid of blending approaches and sources; after all, the world does not turn around our scholarly disputes and rules. Using Richard White's words, we need to deal with a 'mixed and dirty world in which what is cultural and what is natural become less and less clear and as hybrids of the two become more and more common'.[10] Nonetheless, in my understanding, hybridity is not the simple victory of the cultural or social; otherwise, it would not be hybrid. Therefore, although I have built a large part of this book on narratives about mountains and their place in the national discourse, I share Donald Worster's preoccupation with the risks inherent in discursive reductionism. My point is not to deny the existence of a mountain nature outside narratives and this book. Monte Bianco and a forest, a war memorial and a glacier, a pasture and

place, in other times and places, has led to politically unpleasant consequences: the German conception of *Heimat* is an obvious case in point'; in Johnson 2007, p. 177.

9. This is David Blackbourn's approach to the German landscape. As he wrote, 'There are two different ways of saying that history occurs in space as well as time. Real space and imagined space. The landscapes that feature in the title of this book come in two kinds. There is the cultural construct framed by the observer; and there is the physical reality of rock, soil, vegetation, and water … When I write about the making of the modern German landscape, it is in this double sense. The two meanings complement each other. They represent two halves of a single history'; in Blackbourn 2006, p. 15.

10. White 1999, p. 223.

6

Introduction

a reservoir represent very different combinations and percentages of nature and artefact. As Worster argues, nature is at once independent from us and created by us.[11] Rather than striving to measure how much of a given landscape is natural or artificial, I am interested in analysing how nature and culture have interacted in shaping the landscape and the social practices of looking at it and using it. It seems to me that the Italian experience, with its rich and ancient stratification of memories in a relatively tiny and crowded environment, offers an excellent case-study for understanding the incorporation of nature into the construction of the nation through both political discourse and social practice. In other words, rather than looking at nature as discourse, I am intrigued by the opposite perspective – that is, by the fact that nature has always been significant in the discourse about national identity and the practice of nationalising space, memory and people. One could say that in this book I am striving to 'materialise' discourses rather than 'dematerialise' nature.[12] In the following pages I propose a journey through those narratives that have incorporated mountains into Italian national discourses, showing how nature and national narratives have embodied one within the other.

Discourses about wildness/wilderness are one of the main threads of this book. Starting from Chapter 1, I will analyse the ways in which the nation has incorporated the wildness/wilderness of mountains into its narrative; of course, this process has implied some form of appreciation of their natural beauty, even if soon commodified into goods for the tourist market. Nevertheless, the Italian version of wild/wilderness was basically a declensionist narrative about ruined landscape and degraded people, which called for reclamation and taming rather than appreciation. The extensive hydrogeological instability affecting all of Italy needed a narrative on taming the wilderness based on the categories and practices of ordering chaos and regimenting natural forces. Forestation policies

---

11. Worster 1989, p. 302.

12. From this point of view, I completely share the approach proposed by Linda Nash, who expresses this idea better than I: 'Any environmental history must confront the idea that the environment about which we write is, inevitably, something that we always under-stand through language and certain cultural practices ... But like most environmental historians, I remain committed to a materialistic view of the world. I am interested not only in how people talked about environment and disease, but also in what happened on the ground, the changing pattern of disease, the changing use of the land, the changing qualities of air, water, and soil. Consequently, I do not hew to either a materi-alistic or a cultural approach, nor have I tried to separate out the two. That is precisely the point. Our understandings of environment and disease are shaped simultaneously by culture and by material realities of the world. These stories need to be told together'; in Nash 2006, p. 10.

and hydroelectric imperialism were the faces of these discourses on the Italian mountains; both imposed meanings and rules on places and local people, generally shifting from the wellbeing and interests of local mountain communities to the health of nature and the interests of nation. In Chapter 2 I explore how the taming and ordering of mountain nature also included the taming and ordering of its inhabitants; the continuous transfer of qualities from nature to humans is the other leading thread in national narratives about mountains. Mountains have always been places of rebellion where the State struggled to impose its rules and institutions. Heretics, bandits and smugglers – these were the mountaineers, according to the inhabitants of the plains; and evidently, just like streams and landslides, they also needed to be tamed. In particular, in Chapter 2 I will use the peasant uprising in southern Italy, following the 1860 political unification of the country, as a case study showing the nationalisation/ taming of both people and mountains. In the narrative about wild mountains I also include the discourse on common property, the basic way of organising the social appropriation of nature in these environments, showing how the imposition of private property was another face of the nationalisation process. According to these narratives, the wilderness of mountains somehow passed from nature to people and to their social relationships. The results of this hybridisation were different and even contradictory; while the wilderness of the southern Apennines produced savage rebels, people from the Alps seemed to preserve a sort of genetic patrimony ready to be used as the nation needed. As I argue in Chapter 3, this kind of narrative was promoted during World War One in celebrating the *Alpini* (the Italian Alpine Corps). The rhetoric of the stubborn and fierce mountaineer defending the Fatherland along the sacred borders of the Alps became a fundamental narrative of the war. During the Great War this process of nationalisation of people and of places reached its acme. Regarding places, the war annexed the Alps into the nation in two ways, obviously through the military conquest of territories that had been part of the Austrian Empire but also through the inclusion of otherwise out-of-the-way places in the emotional map of the nation. In Chapter 3 we will see this politicisation of war's landscape as a repository of the collective memory of the nation. The exaltation of mountaineers as the genuine prototype of the 'Italian race' became the basic ingredient of the fascist discourse on mountains. In Chapter 4 I will analyse these fascist narratives in the context of the regime's more general discourse on ruralism vs. urban environment and culture. I will uncover the patent contradictions between the celebration of mountaineers and repressive policies against them which became clear with the militarisation of ranger corps and the 'battle against goats'. While historians have accepted Anna Bramwell's arguments and generally dismissed any environmental reference in Italian Fascism,[13] I argue here that fascists did indeed have their environmental narrative, which became environmental politics and policies. Improvement rather than conservation was the keyword in fascist discourse and practices about nature; in turn, as I explain in Chapter 4, in the process of being politicised, mountains *naturalised* fascist narratives about the nation. In the Epilogue I end this book with two stories about nation and mountains in contemporary Italy. In the first I show the links between democracy and mountains in Italian history, covering the Resistance against Nazi-Fascist occupation in 1943–45. The experience of Resistance was deeply rooted in mountains, the embodiment of freedom; a Copernican revolution reversed the political and moral geography of the nation, placing mountains at its core and leaving cities on the periphery. But it lasted only during that extraordinary historic period; in fact, the second story offers a tragic and eloquent parable about the strange mix of marginalisation and centrality of mountains and mountaineers in the aftermath of World War Two. The highest arched dam in the world, a reservoir with 150 million cubic metres of water capable of producing 800 million kwh annually, 2,000 people dead—these facts can effectively summarise the story of the 'Great Vajont', which tells of the inclusion of remote alpine valleys in modernity and, more precisely, provides proof that the modernisation of the nation passed through those remote valleys. Although placed at the centre of the modernisation process, becoming the powerhouse of the nation, these valleys still remained marginal, included in the national narrative in a subaltern position. In the Epilogue we will see that the 'genocide'[14] of 2,000 people was the predicable effect of this inclusion of the Alps in national modernisation.

In summarising this book, I realise how many topics are missing; as Eugene Weber wrote about his own book on the making of peasants into French citizens, there is no way that a study like this can be exhaustive.[15] I do not offer a section on the creation of Italian national parks, although they were largely placed in mountain areas. The connections between the creation of these parks and national discourses were less meaningful in Italy than in other

---

13. Bramwell 1989, pp. 169–171

14. Even though I am aware that the use of this word in this context is very controversial, I have decided to employ it to make explicit the connection between my own interpretation of the event and the one expressed by the lawyer Sandro Canestrini, who, defending the interests of the survivors, spoke of a 'genocide of the poor' (Canestrini 2003).

15. Weber 1989, p.12, from the Italian translation.

countries where nature embodied the very essence of the Fatherland. In addition, James Sievert's excellent book, *The Origins of the Italian Conservationism*, has already thoroughly covered this issue[16] and Wilko Graf von Hardenberg is in the process of releasing his research on fascist policies regarding national parks.[17] Emigration is also largely missing from this book, but not from the Italian mountains. I am convinced that it deeply affected the socio-ecological relationships in the mountains and actually also on the plains; furthermore, national and local identity has been moulded into the experience of migration, as Donna Gabaccia has shown.[18] Isn't it true that the environmental history of Italy has been deeply affected by these movements of people from mountains to the industrial cities on the plains? Although I recognise these deficiencies, I am also aware that a book can, if allowed, be a never-ending process; an encyclopaedia is tempting.

I envisioned this project as an attempt to engage environmental history with political, cultural and social history. Wolves and fascists, hydroelectric companies and mountain climbers, war memorials and scolytid beetles cohabit in the pages of this book. I know that this will seem odd to some. Never mind. Mountains have never been places for conformity.

16.　Sievert 2000.

17.　Graf von Hardenberg 2010.

18.　Gabaccia 1999, p. 1116.

～ 1 ～

Wild Mountains

Nowadays forests are cut, sometimes properly, other times inaccurately; wide roads have tamed the most remote regions; hermits have learnt how to live among humans; the mould from which killers were cast has been lost; wolves and bears can be admired, stuffed in the museums; and now that we can go through the Alps by train, even Saint Bernard dogs will be fired… Oh what a century without poetry.

Antonio Stoppani, *Il Bel Paese*, 1876

Which Wilderness?

Looking at mountains from a ski resort, comfortably sitting on a chairlift or enjoying hot chocolate in a coffee shop, one can easily think about them as anything but wild. Probably, a good wireless connection will link us to the rest of the world, while the invisible network of airwaves that nowadays wraps around everyone and everything will convey our words wherever we want, invading the silence of mountains with the creative rings of our mobile phones.

Nevertheless, the invasion of mountains started precisely with the promise of a wild nature waiting to be discovered, a wilderness still possible in the middle of the least 'natural' continent thanks to the remoteness of mountains. Far removed from cities and main routes, mountain ranges appeared isolated worlds and, like every enclosed habitat, seemed to have maintained some of their original ecological and socio-economic features. This was both an empirical fact and a cultural construction. Nowadays, as in the past, there are more wolves and bears in the mountains than in city streets or fields; but for a long time the wilderness of mountains amounted to much more than this obvious consideration. Mountains were, or were perceived as, the place of ecological and socio-economic endurance. They were wild places because the rules of the plains did not work there; common property and moral economy survived in the mountains longer than in the lowlands; any kind of resistance found its ultimate hideout or its starting flashpoint in the mountains. As we will see in the course of this book, according to this narrative, mountains' wilderness shaped not just landscapes but also souls, producing outlaws, heroes, saints and healthy citizens. The wildness of mountains had not always been synonymous with beauty; on the contrary, it is well known that mountains were long places to be avoided. No one has told the story of the shift from 'mountain gloom to mountain glory' better than Marjorie Hope Nicolson. As William Cronon has written in the introduction to a recent republication of her book:

> Who would have imagined that people four hundred years ago could have looked at a landscape we would today regard as surpassingly beautiful – the Matterhorn say, or Yosemite Valley – and feel none of the emotions we experience in such a place? What has happened in the interim is not that nonhuman nature has changed, nor even that people have somehow awakened from a dream and realised the 'truth' that mountains are beautiful. It is rather that our language and our culture give us the vocabulary through which we experience the world around us. The nature inside our heads is as important to understand as the nature that surrounds us, for the one is constantly shaping and filtering the way we perceive the other.[1]

With his *Eloisa*, J. J. Rousseau was the mastermind of this narration of the Alps as the ultimate refuge for freedom and honesty.[2] Switzerland, with its mountaineer hero William Tell, became the epitome of another Europe, historically resistant to any kind of imperial power. The story of the Romantic reinvention of the mountains, and specifically of the Alps, has been told many times; it is a tale of redemption, from the condemnation of mountains to their celebration, a tale in which artists, intellectuals and alpinists, generally British by nationality, played the role of heroes rescuing the queens of the earth from the dragons of oblivion.[3] One could argue that this is an imperial version of the story that hides the true contribution of local people and knowledge; beyond the heroes of the British Alpine Club, we should also include the Italian alpine guides, mountain climbers and excursionists who contributed significantly to the cultural shift in appreciating mountains. Nevertheless, even this kind of enhanced narrative still depends on wilderness as beauty to be discovered, while what is truly at stake is the very definition of wilderness and, therefore, of its qualities. What was wild for Italians and what did this mean?

---

1. Cronon 1997, p. xii.
2. On Rousseau's contribution to the 'Western awareness of mountains' see Rudaz 2009, p. 149.
3. Enhel 1950; Fleming 2000.

Which Wilderness?

In this chapter I will explore the representation of wild mountains, analysing the contradictory meanings of 'wild', suspended between the appreciation of pure nature's beauty and the condemnation of its chaotic effects. Slopes of mountains, windblown and drenched by rain, can be beautiful and dreadful at the same time; peaks covered by ice and snow allude to peaceful excursions, sources of hydropower or gigantic avalanches; streams can gladden the scene or overwhelm everything. Different observers see different things, of course; mountain climbers and artists will be more inclined to look positively at the wilderness of mountains, while this approach is much more difficult for economists and agronomists, focusing essentially on the problems deriving from an untamed nature. Nevertheless, as I will show in the following pages, in the Italian case, rather than a passion for pure science, a patriotic effort at understanding and controlling the Fatherland's resources was the mountain climbers' and excursionists' lure. We might say that Italian alpinists went to the top with the tools of engineers and sociologists rather than with those of glaciologists and meteorologists. I will focus mainly on those kinds of mountain explorers.

If the observer was crucial, the observed also deeply affected the narrative. Looking at the southern Apennines or the Alps generated different visions and narratives about mountain wilderness and beauty and in this chapter we will see that the discovery of the beautiful mountain focused mainly on the Alps while the discourse on wildness as chaos referred basically to the Apennines.

Dragons and Other Evils

Before becoming the peaceful landscape of Heidi and her sheep, mountains were believed to be populated by a quite different kind of inhabitants. Dragons and witches, demons and ghosts, wildmen and wildwomen filled the Italian mountains and, of course, not just the Italian ones; they were the folk translation of natural phenomena, ancestral fears and social dissent, personified in these supernatural figures.[4] In this way uneducated mountaineers gave an explanation to things they could not understand; but this is just part of the story. In fact, for a long time, they shared those beliefs with well-educated people who used these same categories to describe mountains and to repress any kind of unconventionality. I will return to this issue in the second chapter, which is entirely devoted to the taming of mountains and therefore to the stories of rebellion embodied in these landscapes. Here, we might start by quoting the physician Ortensio Lando who, in the 1550s, listed the witches of the Lombard

---

4.   On the symbolic meanings of forests see the classic Harrison 1992.

Alps in his curious repository of Italian oddness but the list of scholars crediting the presence of some form of supernatural in the Alps was much longer, including Johann Jakob Wagner (1680), Johann Jakob Scheuchzer (1716–18), Abraham Ruchat (1714) and Moritz-Anton Kappeler (1767).[5] Hence, these beliefs circulated much more widely than simply among poor mountaineers and extended far beyond the period predating progress and modern science. As Simon Schama has pointed out, it was in the Age of Reason that Johann Jacob Scheuchzer, a professor of physics and mathematics at the University of Zurich, member of the Royal Society and correspondent of Newton, included a detailed description of dragons in his treatise on the Alps.[6] When the first mountain climbers and travellers started to frequent the Alps, they found a landscape completely filled with these beliefs; the mountains they were discovering were made by rocks and tales. In 1860, for instance, Edward Whymper could not find any guide willing to join his expedition to the Matterhorn because of the demons living on that peak.[7] Arnold Lunn confirmed that the Matterhorn was an off-limits zone for local people, even if not demons but only wildmen were the frightening inhabitants he mentioned.[8] According to the president of the Italian Alpine Club (CAI), Paolo Lioy, in 1870 a Swiss alpinist could still die in the *Unterwald* because his cries for help were mistaken for the whispers of evil spirits.[9] The belief that the dead were trapped among the glaciers to expiate their sins was popular; to prove it, Paolo Lioy told the story of a woman from the village of Alagna who was caught cutting some steps into the ice of Monte Rosa, so that her dead mother could climb more easily to heaven.[10]

It is clear that those popular traditions were also becoming part of the lure of mountains; this was evident in Paolo Lioy's narrative about the Alps, which blended tales and natural descriptions. A good example was found in a 1930 guidebook to Courmayeur which, in a section covering accommodation, excursions and naturalistic information, included a dark local tale about a procession of the dead who were believed to climb Monte Rosa every night.[11] The procession of the dead was a staple in this folk narrative about the Alps; it seems that everywhere lines of ghosts ascended the mountains by night. They might

---

5.   Bartaletti 2004, p. 75.

6.   Schama 1995, p. 421; Colli 1986, p. 245.

7.   Ring 2000, p. 1.

8.   Lunn 1914, p. 150.

9.   Lioy 1889, p. 270.

10.   *Ibid.*

11.   Nebbia 1930, p. 3.

have been the virgins martyred with St. Orsola marching from the Monviso to the Church of Superga on the night of 7 September or perhaps the souls of heretics haunting the Susa Valley where they had found their extreme refuge and tragic end;[12] or they might just have been 'regular dead' leaving their graves every night for a strange round-trip to Monte Rosa.[13]

Those stories gave meanings to places, noises and fears, drawing maps of the mountains which became visible not just in the narratives but also on the ground. The Bridge of the Devil, the Rock of the Witch, the Nefarious Way, the Tooth of the Giant or the Hell Valley were common toponyms in the Alps, as the Italian geographer Fabrizio Bartaletti has pointed out.[14] For a long time, Monte Bianco was known to the people of Chamonix as *Mont Maudit*, the Accursed Mountain.[15] Folktales have preserved the memory of this imaginary geography connecting feelings and places. The roar of dragons or the whimper of the dead must have been a concrete experience for those who lived close to mountains and dealt daily with the strange signs and noises coming from the heights. Anthropologists and ethnographers have analysed the ways in which rural communities in the mountains have rearranged their experiences of nature and social relationships into tales and myths.

Sometimes the supernatural was much closer and more real than one could imagine. Witches and heretics have always found their way to the re- mote Alpine valleys, looking for refuge from persecution, as we will see in the following chapter. According to Burckhardt the Alpine Valleys, and especially the Camonica Valley, became the ultimate hideout for women persecuted as witches;[16] Carlo Ginzburg analysed rural rites in the Alpine region of Friuli, proving the existence of witchcraft beliefs in the sixteenth and seventeenth centuries, while Carolyn Merchant has explored the connections between the feminisation of nature and the quest for its domestication with the prosecution of women as witches.[17] Although the great season of the witch-hunt had already ended in the eighteenth century, witches were nonetheless still present in the rural society of the mountains. In 1828, in the Valsesia Valley, an angry mob killed an old woman accused of being a witch;[18] and it happened again in 1911

12.   Savi Lopez 1889, pp. 21, 114.

13.   *Le cento città d'Italia illustrate – Biella* 1930, p. 3.

14.   Bartaletti 2004, p. 74.

15.   Beattie 2006, p. 109.

16.   Burckhardt, p. 209.

17.   Ginzburg 1985; Merchant 1980, Ch. 5.

18.   Triglia 1986, p. 429.

when an old woman was killed in Perugia because she was believed to be a witch.[19] Even in the twentieth century, witches and wizards were part of rural society in the Apennines. During his exile in a remote village in Lucania,[20] the Italian anti-fascist Carlo Levi had a chance to meet several of them; actually, his maid was said to be a witch and introduced him to some secret formulas. As Levi explained in his masterpiece, *Christ Stopped at Eboli*, witches were believed to be mediums able to communicate with the supernatural presences filling the world of the peasants:

> This old woman was a witch and she often conversed with the souls of the dead, met goblins and talked to real devils in the cemetery. She was a thin, clean, good-natured peasant. The air over this desolate land and among the peasant huts is filled with spirits. Not all of them are mischievous and capricious goblins or evil demons. There are also good spirits in the guise of guardian angels.[21]

This was the imaginary landscape of the southern Apennines into the 1930s. And it was, without a doubt, a wild one.

If witches, demons and ghosts were the supernatural marks signalling the passage between the anthropogenic world and the wild, there is no doubt as to why they were so popular in the mountains; it was there that these two worlds continuously met, often through special figures who travelled between the wild and the community. Loggers, poachers, smugglers, charcoal burners even shepherds lived at the periphery of the community; they always shifted between both worlds, negotiating the meanings of their survival with the wild and its personifications. It was said, for instance, that ibex hunters practiced cutting their hands so that their blood could help them adhere to the vertical walls of mountains. Living in the common place of all magic, the forest, and managing fire for their work, charcoal-burners embodied this merging of natural and supernatural; they were often accused of having some kind of agreement with demons or other fantastic creatures living in the wild.[22] Special jobs required special skills to thrive in an otherwise hostile environment; what else if not magic could explain this existence? After all, the transformation of poachers and smugglers into alpine guides was precisely the ultimate form of exploitation of their magical knowledge of mountains.

---

19. Ankarloo and Clark 1999, p. 141.

20. Lucania is the ancient name for the Basilicata region.

21. Levi 1947, p. 151.

22. Fagioli, pp.10–11.

Hunt in the Riccia Forests, Fortore Valley.
Five wolves were killed (four appearing in the picture).

Hence, these special people moved across the borders separating the community from the wilderness but they were not alone. There would not have been any wild without the presence in the mountains of animals that had disappeared from tamed spaces. Again, even more than witches, wolves and bears were not just stories in the Italian mountains; for a long time they were living figures in fur and blood, both metaphorically and materially trespassing the frontiers between tamed and wild. Similar to the human trespassers, these wild animals suffered strong persecution in Italy and elsewhere. In his studies on the Italian fauna Fulco Pratesi has offered an idea of this war against dangerous animals. Of course, the expansion of farmlands and the increase in human population were the most powerful agents in the extermination of wildlife, specifically wolves.[23] Nonetheless, the destruction of these animals was not only the collateral effect of changes in ecological patterns but also the result of a deliberate plan to eliminate them. In regard to wolves there has been a political and cultural continuity in Italian history; regional states, such as the Vatican

---

23.   Pratesi 2001, pp. 139–161.

Hunt in the Campobasso Forests. The hunter in the picture is Corradino Guacci.

State, the Kingdom of Naples[24] and that of Piedmont shared the same policy of supporting the elimination of wolves by awarding special prizes to hunters. The political unification of the country in 1860 did not improve conditions for those wild animals: in 1887 the prize for a dead wolf varied from five *lire* for a cub to fifty *lire* for a pregnant specimen. In their studies of the war against wolves both Fulco Pratesi and Nicola Farina have stressed that, compared with the level of salaries in nineteenth-century rural Italy, the profit derived from the hunting of wolves was more than attractive. Prizes and special hunts promoted by the government were the answers to a diffuse culture of fear.[25] Even zoologists and conservationists shared this hatred of wolves. The Italian conservationist Erminio Sipari, founder of the Abruzzo National Park, clearly stated in 1923: 'the wolf is the enemy of the park';[26] and, in fact, that same park offered prizes to wolf hunters, even when the prizes were abolished by law.[27] While generally

---

24.   With the expression 'Kingdom of Naples', I am referring to the southern part of Italy under its different political denominations.

25.   On the fear of wolves in the French mountains see Whithed 2000, p. 43.

26.   Pratesi 1978, pp. 32–43, but here cited from the website http://www.storiadelafauna.it

27.   Altobello 1924.

Which Wilderness?

Poisoned wolf, Mount Matese.

devoted to the promotion of natural and artistic beauties of the country, in 1924 the journal of the Italian Tourist Association (TCI) hosted an article by the naturalist Giuseppe Altobello unequivocally entitled 'An Enemy to Fight: The Wolf'.[28] Of course, the wolf did not need either scientists or conservationists to spread its bad reputation; this was deeply embedded in popular culture and extensively diffused. The most popular magazine of nineteenth- and early twentieth-century Italy, *La Domenica del Corriere* [The Sunday Courier], devoted several of its artistic covers to bloody depictions of wolves attacking people.[29] In the 1950s and 1960s Italian culture still expressed a strong hatred of those animals. In 1956 the famous director Giuseppe De Santis produced *Uomini e lupi* [Men and Wolves], a movie on the *lupari*, wolf hunters, and their lives on the Abruzzo Apennines.[30] Whereas this was only fiction, in 1963 a well-known Italian naturalist, Alessandro Ghigi, wrote that the persistence of wolves in the southern Apennines was an indicator of 'a backward economy and civilisation'.[31]

28. *Ibid.*

29. See, for instance, the covers of *La Domenica del Corriere* of 17 Feb. 1907, 7 Feb. 1915 and 3 Jan.1937.

30. The plot is available at the website of the cultural association dedicated to De Santis: http://www.assodesantis.com

31. Pratesi 1978, but from http://www.storiadellafauna.it

These discourses against wolves produced very tangible results: in 1970 the wolf population was estimated to be only about one hundred.[32]

Witches and wolves embodied the wildness of mountains; they were frightening presences in both the natural and narrative landscape. Modernisation in the mountains also meant the eradication of foolish beliefs and deadly predators, even if it might have left some space for a revaluation of them under a folkloric agenda.

But witches and wolves were simply the personification of the universal wildness pervading the Italian mountains; and as we have seen, this wildness did not always have the positive value inherent in the US vision of nature. As it referred to the Italian mountains, the very meaning of wildness was quite ambiguous: of course, it referred to untamed nature, sometimes pristine beauty, but more often it had a different connotation. Wild did not describe the state of nature but rather, and paradoxically, it was a mark of human interference; we may say that Italian mountains ran wild more than they simply were wild. According to this narrative, the human mismanagement of mountains produced their wildness in terms of chaos and disequilibrium. It was through deforestation that Italian mountains ran wild, out of control, resulting in a chaotic landscape of disruption and danger. For the American and, more generally, for the Anglo-Saxon public, George Perkins Marsh is the matrix of this narrative.[33] Marsh wrote his masterpiece on environmental degradation and restoration while he was a US ambassador to the Kingdom of Italy and therefore deeply affected by the natural surroundings in which he was living.

> The historical evidence is conclusive as to the destructive changes occasioned by the agency of man upon the flanks of the Alps, the Apennines, the Pyrenees and other mountain ranges in central and southern Europe and the progress of physical deterioration has been so rapid that, in some localities, a single generation has witnessed the beginning and the end of that melancholy revolution.[34]

Marsh analysed the effects of deforestation in the Mediterranean mountains, connecting the destruction of forests with climate change, erosion and hydrogeological instability – in other words, mountains running wild. Marsh did not have any doubt about the agency of humans in the degradation of mountains; as he wrote, 'the clearing of the woods has … produced within two

---

32.   Bocedi and Bracchi 2004, p. 406.

33.   On George Perkins Marsh see Lowenthal 2000; Hall 2005.

34.   Marsh 1864, p. 232.

or three generations effects as blasting as those generally ascribed to geological convulsions'.[35]

Although in the Anglo-Saxon world Marsh has been credited as the first to connect so clearly human agency and environmental degradation, several Italian writers before him had actually used the same narrative, focusing precisely on mountains. In the 1830s Carlo Afan de Rivera, director of the Neapolitan Bridge and Road Corps, published his four hundred long page *J'accuse* on deforestation in the Apennines.[36] According to de Rivera, the southern Apennines were completely devastated by human activities, which spoiled them of their forests, exposing them to water erosion and hydrogeological instability. His book abounded with dark descriptions of naked slopes marked by torrential watercourses and landslides; this was the wild face of mountains. As a matter of fact, without the natural cover of trees, the water became wild, untamed, carving the face of mountains and affecting even life in the plains.

> The waters depriving the slopes of the vegetative soil made them barren and unable to produce anything… an army would have not been able to produce as extensive and durable damage as that procured by the unceasing expansion of agriculture to the mountains.[37]

Afan de Rivera's analysis of the disruption of the southern Apennines connected ecological, political and historical factors; due to malaria and invasions from the sea, the inhospitable coastal plains pushed the population up to the mountains, increasing deforestation and tillage. But if initially the virgin soil had offered abundant harvests, soon it started to be eroded by water; without the cover of forests the slopes became unstable, a lunar landscape of naked rocks. The metaphor of wildness referred here to the untamed power of water creating a peculiar opposition between nature and wildness. Forests were the natural cover of mountains but it was with their destruction that mountains ran wild, out of control.[38] This negative interpretation of wildness as a consequence of human agency was extremely clear in de Rivera's narrative; much earlier than Marsh he and other writers denounced the systemic effects of deforestation on mountain and plain environments. As the Italian geographer Bruno Vecchio demonstrated in his path-breaking 1974 book, awareness of the connections

---

35. *Ibid.* p. 262.

36. Afan de Rivera 1833. Several scholars have studied Afan de Rivera; among others, see Bevilacqua 1996, especially chapter 3.

37. *Ibid.* pp. 274–5.

38. The same kind of narrative about the 'anarchic, disorderly nature of mountains and their inhabitants' was employed in France: see Whited 2000, p. 3.

between deforestation and hydrogeological disorder was widespread among writers and intellectuals at least from the eighteenth century, becoming even stronger during the Napoleonic age (1800–1815).[39]

Stefania Barca has recently demonstrated that the incorporation of rivers in the capitalistic system needed the counter-narrative of what she strikingly called the 'disorder of waters';[40] in short, the lack of secure property rights over both land and water led to overexploitation and deforestation which could have been stopped only by transforming nature into natural capital, through massive land enclosures and the incorporation of rivers into factory systems. Unfortunately, as her book shows, the environmental effects of this appropriation of nature were rather different from those expected.[41] Nevertheless, the declensionist narrative of the ruining of the mountain landscapes was extremely popular.

Just to quote a few examples, in 1835 the geographer Attilio Zuccagni-Orlandini described the Genoese Apennines as a landscape made of horrid landslides and deep precipices;[42] in 1844 the well-known Italian philosopher Carlo Cattaneo, the most vocal advocate of the wise management of Italian farmers in the Po Plain, could not avoid critically commenting that the disorder of the Alpine watercourses was the effect of mountain deforestation;[43] in 1817 the inspector of forests Giuseppe Gautieri published a book on the environmental services of forests, focusing, obviously, on the negative effects of their destruction: in his words, the soil, exposed to any kind of natural agents, 'decomposes, liquefies, falls into pieces and erodes'.[44] There was no doubt, according to these narratives, that the Italian mountains were disintegrating due to the unwise management of humans, which, instead of controlling them, unleashed the hidden forces of nature, mainly water. Things did not change after the political unification of the country. In 1890 the *Nuova Rivista Forestale* [New Forestry Magazine], the official journal of the Italian Forestry School, announced that 'the deforested mountains were falling piece by piece towards the valleys'.[45] Actually the military unification of the country in 1860 was a special occasion to recast the narrative about the southern Apennines; as we will see in chapter two, Italians met those mountains through the violent experience

---

39. Vecchio 1974 and 2010.
40. Barca 2010, p. 36–48.
41. *Ibid.* pp.111–16.
42. Zuccagni-Orlandini 1838.
43. Cattaneo 1844, pp. 87–8.
44. Gautieri 1817, p. 57.
45. Herzen 1890, p. 107.

Tagliamento Valley: Lavareit's slide.

of a bloody civil war with rebels opposing the regular army. And wildness was the main category employed by the nationalistic elites to describe not only the battlefield, the interior mountains where these rebels found their hideouts, but also the entire southern society, unifying nature and people in one narrative.

While the nation arrived in the southern mountains through the army, the Italian mountains also moved towards the rest of the country through the work of several intellectuals, politicians and technicians who were revealing the conditions of the southern Italy to the public. They were called *meridionalisti*, from *meridione* which means South, and their main aim was to analyse the causes of the backwardness of that part of the peninsula, evidently assuming that there was such a backwardness needing to be addressed. It is not my focus here to discuss the accuracy of their analysis and far less of their assumptions; rather, I want to stress that they frequently, in trying to explain the reasons for southern woes, ended up with a kind of environmental determinism, stressing the agency of climate, orography, water and malaria over this part of the peninsula. The *meridionalisti*'s discourse was not basically about mountains of course but since mountains were so physically relevant in the South, they became an important part of their analysis. The key was still the disruption of mountains and their growing wild due both to human activities and natural preconditions. One of the most influential *meridionalisti*, the deputy and historian Giustino Fortunato, defined the southern Apennine chain as an immense disintegrating mass of rocks [uno sfasciume pendulo], thus evoking its unstable hydrogeological equilibrium. The destruction of mountains was also at the core of the analysis of several other *meridionalisti*; in a book entitled *Il Mezzogiorno agrario quale è* [The Agrarian South as It Is] the agronomist Eugenio Azimonti wrote:

> The destruction of the territory started with the tillage and then the abandonment [of the mountains]; the little furrows became abysses, then the abysses became slides of materials flushed away from the slopes. Today, it is impossible to find ten hectares of integral land, conserved in one piece.[46]

No image could have been more powerful than this; in the southern Apennines the territory was simply falling to pieces due to the combination of natural and social factors. The 1909 Parliamentary Committee on the conditions of the rural population in the South stressed the same issue; Francesco Saverio Nitti, one of the researchers of the Committee who later became an important politician and even Prime Minister, wrote that deforestation and malaria were the most relevant agents in the history of the South:

> On the slopes of the Apennines, the widely diffused deforestation makes water incredibly powerful and chaotic, causing severe and continuous ruin.[47]

While the *meridionalisti* tried to establish the distinction of southern Italy from the rest of the country, other politicians and intellectuals viewed mountains as a unifying tract between northern and southern poor regions. The deputy Luchino dal Verme, among the most vocal advocates of mountain interests, expressed this concept clearly in a speech in the Parliament in 1902:

> If some southern provinces are in such a miserable situation, the mountain regions of the North are also in the same condition ... It is not an issue of North vs. South; rather the problem is mountain vs. plain. The conditions of agriculture in the mountains are despondent everywhere, in the Alpine as well as in the Apennine regions[48]

At the turn of the nineteenth century this perception of the 'mountain problem' was at the root of the Friends of the Mountains Parliamentary Com-

---

46. Azimonti 1921, p. 67.

47. This quotation is from the report Nitti wrote for the Parliamentary Committee on the Conditions of Southern Italy as cited in Azimonti 1921, p. 71.

48. Cited from Gaspari 1999.

Which Wilderness?

Illustration by Achille Beltrame, La Domenica del Corriere 13–20 December 1908.

mittee, a sort of bipartisan lobby to support measures in favour of mountain areas. As the Italian historian Oscar Gaspari has explained, the foundation of this committee represented a new approach to the problems of mountains; in fact until that time, deputies, technicians and opinion-makers had preferred to speak about a national forestry question, choosing to identify the problems of mountains with those related to forests. There was no difference between mountain and forest; they were synonyms in the public discourse. Without question the focus was indeed on hydrogeological disorder; from 1860 to 1922 Italy experienced more than 1,400 landslides and floods and practically no Italian province was immune from this problem.[49]

On this basis the Italian associations interested in mountain excursions and climbing also shared these contradictory feelings towards the wild; of course, they contributed to constructing a narrative about the beauty of the wild but they also subscribed to the discourse about the inherent risks of 'nature going wild'.

Saving the Dying Mountains

> Only the mountain climber can understand the great purpose of the tree in nature because he is the only one who can see and admire it in the high mountains. The mountain climber only can defend the tree from profane rapacity and stop the desires of humans who often destroy a significant common good for an insignificant individual profit. The mountain climber is the knight of the tree; this is his social mission.[50]

With these words the professor of arboriculture Luigi Savastano defined the purpose of the Italian Alpine Club in an article published in 1899 in the journal of the association's Naples branch. No definition could have been more appropriate. Professor Savastano stressed the connection between mountain climbing and the protection of nature through scientific knowledge; exploring high altitudes, alpinists were able to look at trees in their natural environment, acquiring what we may today call an ecological understanding of their functions.

It is well known that the first explorations of the Alps were strongly motivated by scientific impulses. For geologists, mountains were the archives of the Earth; their rocks were believed to preserve the history of the creation

---

49. Data from the Sistema Informativo sulle Catastrofi Naturali [Informative System on Natural Catastrophes] of the Italian National Research Council; the online database is available at http://sici.irpi.cnr.it/

50. Savastano 1899, p.109.

or, less theologically thinking, of the formation of the world. Benedict De Saussure, for instance, was a scientist before becoming a passionate admirer of mountains.[51] In his book on the Alps, Arnold Lunn clearly stated that the dichotomy of 'pure' mountain climbers versus academic mountain climbers was fictitious:

> The distinction is important; but it is often forgotten that scientists, like De Saussure, Forbes, Agassiz and Desor, were nonetheless mountaineers because they had an intelligent interest in the geological history of mountains. All these men were inspired by a very genuine mountaineering enthusiasm.[52]

John Ball, the first president of the British Alpine Club, linked the increase of a taste for travelling and the growing interest in physical science, a connection he saw especially evident in Alpine journeys.[53] Although aiming to criticise the idea of mountain climbing as a scientific activity, Douglas Freshfield, the editor of the *Alpine Journal*, furnished a precise description of it through an unknown professor's words:

> The Alps are not a playground for idle boys, but a store-room full of puzzles; and it is only on the understanding that you will set to work to dissect one of these that you can be allowed to enter. You have free leave to look on them, according to your taste, as a herbarium, or as a geological, or even entomological museum, but they must be treated, and treated only, as a laboratory.[54]

This was so true that for several years no alpinist would ever ascend a mountain without a sackfull of scientific instruments; according to Lunn, Bourrit's ascent of Monte Bianco without even a barometer ought to be considered a turning point in the history of alpinism.[55]

The scientific roots of mountain climbing have been explored by so many historians that I would prefer not to insist on this issue.[56] Obviously, the Italian Alpine Club also connected its activities to the development of science; in his thoughtful history of the Club, Alessandro Pastore asserts that from 1874 the father of the Italian association, Quintino Sella,[57] bonded his creation to

---

51. Gribble 1904, pp. 37–9; Fleming 2000, pp. 26–37.

52. Lunn 1914, p. 112–13.

53. Ball 1863, p. v.

54. Freshfield 1875, p. 91.

55. Lunn 1863, pp. 56–7.

56. Engel 1950; Fleming 2000.

57. Quintino Sella (1827–1884) was a prominent Italian politician, several times Minister of Finance. In that role he was able to balance the State budget through strict control of

the progress of scientific knowledge.[58] In 1885 an Italian handbook listed the equipment needed to be a perfect mountain climber; it was clearly written that 'the basic scientific tools could not be missed'.[59] We could list here several other examples and the result would be the same; the Italian Alpine Club linked itself to the progress of science. Actually, the situation was the same for other alpinist associations; everywhere geology, glaciology and meteorology were the scientific substrata for the first explorations of mountains. Nevertheless, forest coverage and its influence on the hydrogeological stability of mountain slopes were a specific focus of the Italian associations and had to be linked to the nationalistic discourse about knowledge and wise management of the country's natural resources. It was not by chance that Professor Savastano spoke about a 'social mission' of mountain climbers rather than just about their scientific duties. After all, for them the Alps and the Apennines were not an antiseptic laboratory for improving their geological knowledge; these mountains were 'nation' and according to this nationalistic vision the climbers shared with them a common destiny and not just a few weeks of vacation. Founded in 1863, the Italian Alpine Club had in its bylaws the patriotic mission to introduce Italians to their mountains (art. 2). The knowledge the club proposed was both scientific and emotional; Italians needed to learn the beauty of their mountains as well as the practical employment of their resources. According to Lorenzo Camerano, CAI president in the 1910s, the 1863 ascent of Monviso, which was considered the starting point of the association, clearly expressed its patriotic–scientific agenda; as a matter of fact, Mount Monviso is the origin of the River Po, the most strategic watercourse in the entire country. It was not a coincidence that Quintino Sella and his friends started thinking about an Italian society of mountain climbers precisely during the quest for the source of the Po.[60] A clear synthesis of this emotional and scientific approach to mountains is found in a long-lived best seller, published in 1876 by Antonio Stoppani, one of the central figures of Italian alpinism and geology – a combination which confirms the scientific mission of mountain exploration:

> We grow up without knowing anything about our country, worse than if we were strangers newly arrived. We do not know anything about the natural

---

expenses. His interest in mountains was both scientific and passionate; in fact he was a professor of mineralogy and a mountain-climber. Biographical information from http://en.wikipedia.org/wiki/Quintino_Sella

58.   Pastore 2003, p. 21.

59.   Corona, Pini, De Castro, E. Bassi, R. Bassi, Abbate 1885, p. 99.

60.   Pastore 2003, p. 20.

beauties of our Italy, even if we are so proud when someone calls it a garden; anything about the varieties of physical conditions which are so relevant to science; anything about the many advantages which Italy offers to industry[61]

Appreciating mountains and their resources – this was the basic mission of the Italian Alpine Club, which produced a special typology of mountain climber, a blend of tourist, sportsman, scientist and patriot.

But returning to Savastano's quotation, the CAI's mission was beyond aesthetic and scientific appreciation; the Italian alpinists were supposed not only to observe mountains but also to change or, better still, to restore them. During the 1874 CAI congress, Quintino Sella celebrated the creation in the Italian Parliament of a bipartisan lobby among members of the club to support any law for the preservation of the Alpine environment, quoting as an example the new regulation on the reforestation of municipal lands. According to Sella, that law should have been named after the CAI, due to its members' special effort to enact it. Without a doubt the forest issue was at the core of the CAI's concerns; as Sella stated in 1874, deforestation was the most important problem Italian alpinists needed to address.[62] The commitment of the association was not limited to the scientific analysis but became political through the laws it supported in Parliament and practical through several experiments with voluntary reforestation. The CAI directly reforested several areas in Verbano, Falterona, Oropa and Faito, starting a collaboration with the same Professor Luigi Savastano, who wrote a book on the reforestation of the southern Apennines, published in 1893 by the association.[63]

Even more committed to the preservation of forests was the Italian Tourist Association (TCI), created in 1894 in Milan, which aimed to join the newly emerging middle-class passion for out-doors with patriotic effort to unify the country. The TCI's main mission was to reveal Italy to Italians, promoting the beauty of the country and supporting any initiative to improve access to it. So, yes, the Touring Club could support the construction of a road as well as publicising the magnificence of a virgin landscape; apparently the leaders of the association could not see any contradiction between promoting progress and preserving nature. The concept and practice of improvement was their middle ground or point of mediation; according to the TCI, improvement was not a radical transformation of nature but rather a means to help nature express itself at its best. Obviously, the TCI worked at improving tourist infrastructures,

---

61. Stoppani 1915 [1876], p. 25.

62. Sella 1874, p. 603.

63. Clementi 1980, pp. 18–20.

making Italian mountains more comfortable and accessible through roads, hotels, cableways and other means of this sort, but the TCI's idea of improvement was much grander. It concerned the natural infrastructure and not just the tourist one. Starting in the first decade of the twentieth century, the TCI decided to deal with the decay of the Italian mountains and specifically with their hydrogeological instability. In 1909 the association gathered a special committee dedicated to the study of mountain problems, with a strong focus on the burdens caused by deforestation.[64] Although the TCI gathered technical experts to be part of this panel, its main goal was to go beyond the scientific arena, raising public concern about the destiny of forests and mountains. According with the general mission of the association, this panel was meant to popularise the issue of deforestation and the need for a forestry policy. As the TCI stated, the aim was to create awareness of forest conservation among the general public, which could then support the experts' wise but isolated view. Presenting the association's main goals in respect to forests, Luigi Vittorio Bertarelli, the TCI's founder, stated in 1915:

> We aimed to destroy the apathy towards forests and stop the ineffectual whimpers for every falling tree. We wanted to popularise the true function of the forest and support the right economy for mountains.[65]

The committee promoted a series of popular conferences about deforestation and forest conservation;[66] nevertheless, its most durable contribution was the publication of two books dedicated to the hydrogeological instability of the Italian mountains: *Il bosco, il pascolo, il monte* [The Forest, the Pasture and the Mountain],[67] edited by Arrigo Serpieri, and *Il bosco contro il torrente* [The Forest Against the Stream],[68] written by the inspector of the national forest agency, Giuseppe Di Tella. According to the TCI, just like the alpinist, the excursionist also had socially significant duties:

> A serious fruit sprouts from the traveller; it is the comprehensive knowledge of the country, which is the basis ... of everyone's love for the Fatherland, political consciousness and intellectual activity. National problems, as only the traveller can see, cannot be understood deeply without knowing the environment

---

64. Bertarelli 1909. On the TCI Committee, see Piccioni 1999 and Meyer 1995.

65. Bertarelli 1915, pp. 37–8, cited here from Sulli and Zanzi Sulli 2002, p. 387.

66. On the conferences promoted by the TCI with the financial support of the T. Borsalino Fundation see Sulli and Zanzi Sulli 2003, pp. 378–79.

67. Serpieri, Azimonti, Di Tella, La Fauci, Scalcini, Scrittore, Taruffi, Trotter, Voglino n.d. [1911].

68. Di Tella 1912.

Which Wilderness?

where they take place; the topographic and social environment are connected reciprocally.[69]

How did the mountain environment look to these nationalistic excursionists? Well, first and foremost, it appeared as a decaying landscape where the destruction of forests compromised the geological equilibrium of the entire system. The Italian mountains were described as a crumbling landscape, 'a sea of spoiled hills, fractured by deep ravines, or covered by rocks, like the beds of streams, alpine regions cluttered with landslides and avalanches'.[70] According to the TCI experts, the cause of such destruction was undoubtedly the human mismanagement of the mountain environment, of which deforestation was the most visible feature. In *The Forest, the Mountain and the Pasture* the TCI provided its view of the dramatic extent of deforestation through a series of snapshots; in the Lucania region, for instance, the privatisation of common and Church properties and the war against the rebels in 1860s–70s led to the destruction of about 30,000 hectares.[71]

Table 1.1. Data on deforestation collected in The Forest, the Mountain and the Pasture, *p. 17.*

Provinces	Hectares
Cagliari (Sardina)	91,446
Sassari (Sardina)	125,070
Torino and Alessandria (Piedmont)	82,000
Palermo (Sicily)	12,000
Brescia (Lombardy)	3,489
Mantova (Lombardy)	3,287
Cremona (Lombardy)	5,600

(Since the TCI did not translate those numbers into percentages, they can only offer a rough idea of the area of destroyed forests.)

Although the book offered a series of quantitative data on deforestation such as those on Lucania (see Table 1.1), the TCI experts preferred to embody them in concrete case-studies, more suitable for the purposes of the association. After all, the TCI was a society of travellers and therefore travelling had to be the tool for their discovery of mountains. From Valtellina to Calabria, crossing the Tuscan and Abruzzo Apennines, the TCI researchers covered every mountain

---

69. Serpieri *et al.* 1911, p. 7.

70. *Ibid.*

71. Data from Savastano, quoted by McNeill 2002, pp. 226–27.

environment of the country, describing it in the book. It was a meeting with mountains, forests, rivers and streams but also with the people living there; the 'patriotic' traveller the TCI aimed to shape needed to look at the landscape in a holistic way, learning to listen to nature and humans together.

> We think that we have better understood the intimate life of mountains since we listened to both the voices of humans and nature.[72]

This does not mean that the TCI was sympathetic to mountaineers; its narrative was the usual declensionist one about improvident peasants and ruined landscape. As was clearly stated in *The Forest, the Mountain and the Pasture*, listening to mountaineers' reasons offered an inventory of extenuating circumstances which helped in understanding the nonetheless destructive nature of mountaineers' relationships to mountains;[73] in fact, according to the TCI's experts, poor and ignorant mountaineers were destroying forests and mountains in a peculiar dynamic of taming and 'wilding' nature. Cutting forests and planting crops and pastures, while generally considered the main tools for taming the wild, became the evil instruments of allowing nature to run wild in the sense of absence of order and useful purpose. To tame the wild mountains it was necessary that the tree reappeared on the slopes, protecting the soil and controlling the water. In the second of the two volumes produced by the TCI committee, the author Giuseppe Di Tella spoke explicitly of wild waters, which only extensive reforestation could discipline. Forest was the answer to the environmental decay but the TCI propaganda tried to support reforestation and forest protection also in terms of economic, and not only ecological, advantages; once again, the association chose to navigate a course between economic progress and environmental protection. Merging profit and protection in forests was the TCI ideal. The association aimed to demonstrate the profitability of having trees beyond their environmental utility for the stability of the mountain–plain system. In *The Forest, the Mountain and the Pasture*, for instance, the authors stressed the positive role of the tannin industry in the conservation of chestnut woods. According to this thesis, the factories were forced to exploit those trees in a sustainable way; otherwise, they would have lost the basic raw material for their production. Nevertheless, this was only a theoretical hypothesis since, in reality, the tannin industry contributed to the destruction of forests rather than to their conservation[74]. It was in the

---

72.   Serpieri *et al.* 1911, p. 25.

73.   *Ibid.*

74.   *Ibid.* pp. 74–75.

hydroelectric field that the TCI sought to find the common ground between conservation and progress.

Electric Mountains

Hydroelectric plants reshaped the landscapes of mountains, creating artificial lakes and consolidating their slopes with reforestation. As Francesco Saverio Nitti, the most influential scholar and politician to support the hydro-electrification of mountains, had repeatedly stated, hydroelectric production implied a holistic vision of the water–forest problem:

> Reforestation, reclamation, struggle against malaria, management of rivers and streams are many faces of the same prism; these are problems which cannot be solved separately but need a unifying vision[75].

Neither industrial nor agricultural exploitation of water could ever occur without an extensive program of reforestation that safeguarded the infrastructure and the regular flow of water from the decay of the Italian mountains. According to the electrical engineer Angelo Omodeo, reforestation was the necessary tool to transform the potential energy of Italian mountain water into power; as he wrote in 1906:

> To make useful for industrial development the immense quantity of energy that is wasted now, we need to implement the hydraulic restoration of mountains and first and foremost we need to reforest them.[76]

Even the TCI included the hydroelectric exploitation of watercourses among the four pillars of a correct plan for the restoration of mountains – the other elements were intensive selviculture, livestock farming and a good network of communications.[77] The TCI's trust in the progressive/protective virtues of the hydroelectric companies was more than just an intellectual attitude; as James Sievert has pointed out, the hydroelectric industries were among the most generous donors to the association.[78] They had a remarkable role in particular in the committee for the restoration of mountains: seven large hydroelectric companies were listed among the members of the committee, contributing about 26,000 *lire* (see Table 1.2).

---

75.   Nitti 1905, p. 368.
76.   Omodeo 1906, but quoted here from Saba 2005, p. 198.
77.   Serpieri *et al.* 1911, p. 50.
78.   Sievert 2000, p. 144.

Wild Mountains

Table 1.2. List of hydroelectric companies sponsoring the TCI Committe for Forest Protection. Source: Serpieri et al., Il bosco, il monte, il pascolo, pp. 5–6.

Name	Contribution (in *lire*)
Associazioni esercenti imprese elettriche Milano	6,000
Società forze dell'Adamello	6,000
Società lombarda distribuzione energia elettrica	6,000
Società imprese elettriche Conti	4,500
Società idroelettrica ligure	3,000
Società anonima elettricità Alta Italia	300
Società anonima forze idrauliche Moncenisio	300

The TCI did not betray its donors and in *The Forest, the Mountain and the Pasture* stated clearly:

Today the protection of existing forests and the creation of new ones are supreme public interests; they mean defending the Fatherland's soil; they mean giving life to mountains which were killed and depopulated by mismanagement; they mean furnishing an element which is as vital to our economy as bread is for people, that is, an abundant provision of 'white coal' coming from the richness and regularity of waters.[79]

James Sievert was obviously right in stressing the conflict of interest on hydroelectric issues inside the TCI; as a matter of fact, although the association gave voice to opponents of the hydroelectric revolution, its official position was basically in favour of it, at most supporting some forms of mitigation of its environmental impacts.

Nevertheless, the TCI's positive vision on hydroelectricity did not reveal merely the economic linkages between the association and the electric corporations. Rather, the TCI shared a general passion for hydroelectricity that was increasingly mounting in the first decades of the twentieth century. Lewis Mumford was not on the payroll of any hydroelectric company when he celebrated the arrival of this new form of power as the victory of the neotechnic age, far away from the dust and pollution of the industrial revolution.[80] In Italy the age of hydroelectricity had a special patriotic meaning, which overcame any discourse about its ecological virtues, in any case not so central in the Italian debate on energy: it promised to free Italy from its servitude to coal and other fossil fuels, imported from abroad. Francesco Saverio Nitti published in 1905 *La Conquista della forza* [The Conquest of Power], the manifesto of the

---

79.   Serpieri *et al.* 1911, p. 117.

80.   Mumford 1934, pp. 222–23.

hydroelectric revolution, which, according to him, Italy desperately needed in order to achieve full industrial development. The starting point of Nitti's analysis was the geographical basis of Italian economic life:

> Italy, due to the current forms of production, is one of the poorest countries in Europe and surely the poorest among the largest countries … Its natural features, celebrated by poets who live on traditions, and by politicians, who live on exaggerations, are generally bad.[81]

Nitti's pessimistic vision of the natural poverty of the country was typical of the *meridionalisti*'s narrative and, in particular, of his mentor, Giustino Fortunato, who, as we have seen, had rooted his analysis of the South in its environmental conditions, focusing explicitly on mountains. According to this narrative, the backwardness of southern Italy came from its natural characteristics; the disequilibrium between mountains and plains, which ended in a malarial environment, was viewed as a curse for the South and therefore for the whole country. Nevertheless Nitti overcame this pessimistic vision through faith in technology; hydroelectric engineers could change the face of the country and with this its destiny, transforming the rugged aspects of the landscape into the main source of its prosperity.[82] Actually, hydroelectricity changed much more than the pessimistic tones of the *meridionalisti*'s narrative; once again, the landscape embodied the discourses in concrete features, this time particularly visible as dams, reservoirs and conduits. In 1905 Italy occupied third place in the world production of hydroelectricity with seventy per cent of its energy produced by water;[83] between 1898 and 1914 the hydraulic power produced in Italy shifted from 40,000 kWh to 850,000 kWh.[84] These numbers did not exist only in the statistics about energy production; they represented million of tonnes of concrete, iron and dirt, making artificial lakes, diverting rivers, changing the face of mountains. According to Sievert's data, by 1921 Italy had 91 artificial lakes, while another 41 were under construction.[85]

Hence, hydroelectricity was the great chance for Italian industrialisation but it was more than a source of power for factories. The hydroelectric revolution implied a general transformation of the mountain landscape and a reorganisation of the plain–mountain relationships. Putting the mountain water to work became

81. Nitti 1905, p. 11.

82. *Ibid.* p. 23.

83. Ciarlo 1993, p. 61.

84. Barone 1993, p. 205.

85. Sievert 2000, p. 90.

the dream to tame forever the wildness of that landscape; dams, reforestation, and reservoirs would impose a modern order on water and rocks. Landslides and inundation were no longer to be allowed on the Fatherland's mountains. This was the Italian version of the scheme of high modernism proposed by James Scott – the mystical combination of faith in scientific and technical progress and indisputable central power all aiming toward unlimited economic growth.[86] That holistic approach to the production of hydroelectricity as a major agent in the reshaping of mountains was extremely strong in the southern Apennines; there, the combination of malaria, seasonal aridity and landslides called for a radical rearrangement of water, which was at the centre of this geographical drama. In the South hydroelectricity did not mean exploiting rivers rationally; rather it meant creating rivers, as Angelo Omodeo wrote in 1916.[87] Therefore, at the turn of the twentieth century, the South became the open laboratory for the new technocratic approach to the economic and ecological problems of the country. Following the messianic 1902 trip through the Basilicata region made by Prime Minister Giuseppe Zanardelli, in 1904 the government issued a special law for the development of that area, which, among other measures, provided a unifying policy for the restoration of mountains and reclamation of plains. Significantly enough, speaking in a crowded assembly at the end of his tour Mr. Zanardelli committed himself and the government to fight against the adversities of nature in order to end poverty in Basilicata.[88] The law was based on what we might today call an environmental vision of Basilicata's problems, which found a coherent expression in the technical survey accompanying the legislation. In that report Eugenio di Sanjust, an engineer from the Public Works Office, described the hydrogeological ruin of the region as the critical cause of its backwardness and prescribed a consistent policy of reclamation involving both mountains and plains.[89] Two years later, in 1906, it was Calabria's turn; a new law addressed the problems of that region, starting once more from their geographical basis – that is, the reclamation of plains and the reforestation of mountains. The Italian historian Giuseppe Barone has thoughtfully analysed the generation and outcome of these laws; as he has argued, in spite of their limitations, these policies represented a remarkable innovation both in terms of institutional tools, providing the massive intervention of the State, and

---

86. Scott 1998, pp. 88–89.

87. Omodeo 1916, pp. 28–29, quoted from Barone 1993, p. 225.

88. Rinaldi 2002, p. 65.

89. On this report see Giura Longo 1992.

holistic vision, connecting economic policies to environmental restoration.[90] With more than 26 million *lire* allocated for reforestation in Basilicata and special incentives for waterworks furthering irrigation or energy production, these laws prepared the way for the development of hydroelectric transforma-tions.[91] It was especially through Nitti's direct participation in politics[92] that these special measures for mountain restoration joined with the hydroelectric development plan. Between 1908 and 1916 the South was home to several hydropower projects, such as the Volturno River power plant, the Muro Lucano reservoir and plant and the starting of the artificial lakes system in Calabria. As Barone explains, the Calabria case was an example of the tensions between technocratic understanding of environmental problems and social resistance to the kind of changes technocrats were supporting: specifically, the policy of reforestation and forest protection proposed for the Sila area, on top of the Calabrian Apennines, encountered the staunch opposition of the mountaineers who felt penalised compared to the rich landowners of the plains.[93] Neverthe-less, in the 1920s, the system of artificial reservoirs of the Sila area was built, producing about 750 million kWh annually, the largest producer of energy in the entire South; but the national park, which was planned together with the hydroelectric reservoirs would be realised only in the late 1960s, existing for a long time on paper alone. Nevertheless, the Sila case confirmed the existence of a strange mix of hydroelectric revolution and environmental conservation; in transforming mountains, the hydroelectric industry claimed to be also their redeemer. Of course, while reforestation was easily seen as a good thing for mountains, reservoirs, dams and conduits were more controversial; after all, according to several scholars, the Italian conservation movement was ef-fectively born on the banks of La Marmora Falls, trying to defend them from their transformation into a hydroelectric machine.[94] Hence, conflict was the basic outcome of the arrival of hydroelectric engineers at the top of the Italian mountains; the landscape of artificial lakes and new forests they brought with

---

90. Barone 1986, pp. 14–20.

91. *Ibid.* p. 16.

92. Nitti became a deputy in 1904 from the Radical Party; then he served as Minister of Agriculture, Industry and Trade under Prime Minister Giovanni Giolitti (1911–14). In the following years Nitti was appointed Minister of Finance (1917–19) and Prime Minister (1919–20). Biographical information from http://en.wikipedia.org/wiki/Francesco_Saverio_Nitti; for his exhaustive biography, see Barbagallo 1984.

93. Barone 1986, p. 243–76.

94. Fontana 1981, p. 24.

38

them was anything but peaceful;[95] even their promise to tame the wild forces of nature by millions of cubic metres of concrete did not work properly. The story of the hydroelectric mountains is full of disasters, some almost inconceivable, as we shall see in the epilogue, created rather than solved by the new arrangement of water and rocks.

The resistance of mountaineers to the hydroelectric companies is largely obliterated; those stories are dispersed in a wide range of archives, surfacing only on extreme dramatic occasions when local communities paid a blood price for the modernisation of their mountains. Generally speaking, the construction of reservoirs implied the submersion of large portions of land dedicated to farming and grazing; hydroelectricity brought with it reforestation and a stricter level of control over access to mountain slopes that was unappreciated by mountaineers, not to mention the huge burden of living under the permanent threat of gigantic dams.

While mountaineers fought for their freedom to access and use their land and resources, preservationists had mixed feelings towards hydroelectric corporations; of course, they represented a huge transformation of natural landscapes but they also promised clean energy and restoration of mountains. For sure, there was no room for an alliance between conservationists and local mountain communities. In 1925 the TCI magazine published an article by well-known Italian geographer Olinto Marinelli, who dismissed any concern about the hydroelectric exploitation of an alpine lake and stated unequivocally that mountaineers should be grateful to hydroelectric companies investing in their remote valleys; no harm would come to the local environment from them.[96] Of course, an attentive policy of sponsorship was crucial in the greenwashing of those hydroelectric corporations; for instance, in 1928 they offered half a billion *lire* to the fascist Committee for the Protection of Forests, thus accrediting themselves as the most generous sustainers of trees. In the same year, the TCI magazine expressed the association's opinion about the development of hydroelectric infrastructure: the author of the article recognised that the hydroelectric industry, 'bringing new economic activities and modern machinery into the remote valleys', could cause massive transformations in the landscapes, often not with the best results. Nevertheless, the author added:

> Now we think that between the advantages coming from these activities for the whole nation and the even regrettable disfigurement of the landscape, the

95. Caravaggi 1998.
96. Marinelli 1926.

prevalent interest must come first.[97]

This article was essentially ambiguous but it fitted well with the TCI's compromising approach to the issue; according to the author, technology offered positive solutions to the conflict between the protection of nature and the needs of production. And this conflict was not at all a theoretical possibility but rather a concrete experience. This 1928 article came, in fact, at the conclusion of a long struggle over the construction of two artificial lakes in the Abruzzo National Park; on that occasion the conservationists won their battle and the fascist regime revoked its permission from the hydroelectric corporation.[98] Apparently, the TCI wanted to stress its softer position on the matter. After all, the conservationists won, but their leader, Erminio Sipari, father of the Abruzzo National Park, lost a lot in the struggle and would soon be removed from any political position, including the directorship of the park he had created. The association's magazine reflected this tendency to compromise: the majority of articles concerning hydroelectric projects proposed a vision of lack of conflict between them and the conservation of nature. Several of the articles were employed to support this vision but all of them collapsed under the same basic narrative; with hydroelectric power the frontiers between natural and artificial became porous, calling for a new appreciation of hybridity instead of purity. The association celebrated hybrid landscapes in which wild and tamed merged in these 'electric' mountains. The geographer Carmelo Colamonico, writing in 1928 for the TCI magazine, unequivocally stated that Matese Lake (Naples area) was no longer a natural element of the Apennines, since an artificial bypass regulated its level and its very existence.[99] According to the writer Giuseppe Isnardi, the hydroelectric corporations had actually completed the Sila landscape, putting into it what was missing:

> Until this year the tourist coming from the north felt that Sila lacked an essential element for the beauty of the region. Looking at the Arvo and Ampollino valleys, everybody expected to see the blue spots of the Alpine lakes. But now what was just a dream has become a reality. A lake … has been created by humans in the Ampollino Valley.[100]

Outdoing God, who evidently did not do a good job in the Sila, hydroelectric engineers shaped the landscape as it was supposed to be, putting

---

97.   Bognetti 1928, p. 200.
98.   Sievert 2000, pp. 177–179; Piccioni 2000, p. 994.
99.   Colamonico 1928, p. 538.
100.   Isnardi 1927, p.783.

the right thing where everybody expected it. If a mountain landscape needed a lake to be 'authentic', the construction of a reservoir would make it more natural; the perception between artificial and natural blurred. According to the TCI's mainstream narrative, hydroelectricity improved mountain landscapes, thus humanising otherwise too-wild environments. With this argument the association's magazine supported a dam on Monte Rosa:

> The works undertaken on the mountain by mechanical man – works which seem pharaonic to the man who does them – do not bother the beauty and power of the mountain. Ceding some particle of its strength to human ingenuity, Monte Rosa does not suffer ... Actually, its majesty as an indifferent god appears more humanised.[101]

Although these were the general tones of articles published by the TCI, some isolated voices expressed concerns and even open opposition to the hydroelectric revolution. Luigi Parpagliolo, responsible for the Antiquities and Fine Arts Agency, expressed this minority vision in several essays published in *Le Vie d'Italia* [Roads of Italy]. While in 1926 Parpagliolo included the over-exploitation of water for economic purposes among the main environmental problems of the country, in 1927 he explicitly attacked the hydroelectric corporations; he blamed them for the destruction of forests, especially in constructing infrastructure, uncovering the intrinsic contradiction of thinking of them as possible allies in the protection of forests.[102]

> It is necessary that the concept of public interest in protecting natural beauty becomes the basis and the aim of all laws regarding the exploitation or transformation of places. It is necessary for everybody to understand that this public interest is not less important than the industrial, agricultural and hygienic one; in analysing public works and concessions the officers must check whether they might compromise the beauty of the place and if these reasons are not enough to stop the project, they must at least impose strict conditions to limit the damage.[103]

As Luigi Piccioni and James Sievert have shown, Parpagliolo was one of the key figures in the Italian protectionist movement;[104] his positions against the hydroelectric companies were rooted in the vision of landscape as a common heritage which needed to be protected from the preponderance of private

---

101. Caprin 1925, p. 303.
102. Parpagliolo 1926, p. 144.
103. Parpagliolo 1927, p. 547–48.
104. Sievert 2000, pp. 157–60; Piccioni 2010, pp. 255–262.

economic interests. Nevertheless, the defence of mountain landscapes did not imply any recognition of the social costs or, using a contemporary category, of the environmental injustice embodied in the hydroelectric monoculture. Beyond the everyday loss in terms of land and access to common resources, mountaineers paid the price for the electrification of mountains with their own lives. In the epilogue I will narrate the story of the 1963 Vajont genocide in which 2,000 people were killed by hydroelectric interests. But the Vajont was just the last and most tragic episode in a long series that tells the hidden story of the nationalisation of mountain landscapes. The Gleno case was probably the most remarkable of these events before Vajont.[105] On 1 December 1923 a dam collapsed and 6 million cubic metres of water and mud submerged Bueggio and Dezzo villages in the Lombard Alps, killing at least 356 people, the exact number of victims never determined, and causing damage amounting to 130–150 million *lire*; this was the epilogue of the hydroelectric transformation of the Gleno Valley, started in 1916 with the concession of water rights to the Viganò company.

In 1923 the gigantic Gleno dam, able to contain 6 million cubic metres of water, was brand new, completed in three years at the cost of about 5 million *lire* invested by the Viganò family. The dam, however, was not built according to its architectural plan; in fact, the Viganò family changed the project during construction, from a gravity dam to an arched one, thereby altering the design approved by the Public Works Office. In October 1923, after persistent seasonal rains, the dam showed its construction faults, losing such a large quantity of water that the owners decided to dig a canal to collect and reuse it; they also ordered new waterproofing for a part of the dam. These points were used in the ensuing trial to demonstrate both the intrinsic defects of the dam and the owners' knowledge of these. Technical reports and workers' statements reinforced the prosecution's basic argument: the dam had been built inadequately, with poor materials, meagre engineering supervision and strict attention to economising; after all, the Viganòs themselves took pride in the fact that they were able to build their dam for half the cost estimated by engineers.[106] Several workers testified that the Viganòs did not follow, at least not completely, the directions of engineers; and discharge had been the punishment for anyone who had tried to protest against the quality of materials or practices employed. Having protested against the use of unsuitable cement, the worker Antonio

105. All the information about the Gleno disaster is from Barbisan 2007; Pedersoli 2006; and from the website http://www.scalve.it/gleno/

106. Pedersoli 2006, p. 61.

Merli, for instance, was fired for allegedly being a subversive.[107] Evidently in the 'electric' mountains it was revolutionary indeed to put safety before profit. Actually the theory that a subversive plot could provide an explanation for the collapse became a temporary main argument for the defence: based on the report of a military officer, the defence argued that the dam had been attacked by subversives, a theory supported also by the testimony of a convict, who professed having heard about this from two prisoners.[108] This argument was never taken too seriously by the public prosecutors since no concrete proof supported it; rather, after a four year trial, in 1927 the tribunal held the Viganòs and the engineer accountable for the disaster, accepting the basic allegation that the dam had been built defectively. Nevertheless, compared to the crime, the punishment of three years detention for Virginio Viganò and his engineer Giovanni Battista Santangelo and a fine of 7,500 *lire* seems outrageous; but it was condoned.[109] None of the public officials who were supposed to supervise the construction of the dam suffered any penalty; the fascist regime kept the profile of the Gleno case lower, punishing only a few of those responsible and avoiding revising the procedures for permission to use water and to construct dams.

To avoid any politicisation of the case, local people were excluded from the trial, except for workers who had participated in the construction. Nevertheless, a number of interviews collected in 1970s, long after the event, confirmed that distrust for the dam was prevalent among the mountaineers. One woman recalled the phrasing using among the people of the valley: 'our cemetery will be the Iseo Lake because the dam is badly built and will fall down'.[110] Another two women corroborated the fact that according to everyone the dam was bound to collapse due to the persistent infiltration of water.[111] Experts' opinions were rather contradictory; in fact, while after the event several technicians denounced the defects of the dam, it was also true that no one made any claim about them during the construction, not even the public officials monitoring the implementation of the project. As the royal inspector for public schools in Lombardy prescribed immediately after the disaster, every teacher should

---

107. *Ibid.* p. 100.

108. *Ibid.* pp. 29–34.

109. *Ibid.* pp. 136–37.

110. *Ibid.* p. 125.

111. Interview with Luigia Minini and with Caterina (last name unknown) from Dezzo, at http://www.scalve.it/gleno/Testimonianze/testimonianze.htm

talk with pupils about it without blaming science or technology;[112] progress could not be stopped and electrifying the mountains was the Italian path to it. And neither did it stop; on 13 August 1935, in Val Orba, between Liguria and Piemonte, another dam collapsed, killing about a hundred people and flooding the villages of Molare, Ovada, Silvano d'Orba, Capriata d'Orba, Predosa and Castellazzo d'Orba.[113] According to the Italian geologist Vittorio Bonaria, in this case an alteration of the original project, aiming to stretch out the dam, as well as a lack of geological inquiries were the origins of this disaster too. Nevertheless, in 1938 the Turin Court of Justice absolved all the defendants, asserting natural causes for the disasters; this time the hydroelectric corporation was much larger than the one in Gleno and evidently the fascist regime decided to support it against the determination of the judicial truth.[114]

The arrival of hydroelectric engineers in the mountains represented the full appropriation of their wildness. An eloquent 1939 documentary entitled *Oro Bianco* [The White Gold] clearly expressed this narrative; centred on water resources, it presented the Italian landscape, and particularly the mountain landscape, as a progressive tale describing a trajectory from the natural beauty of the bucolic idyll to the dangers of unbounded wild forces, culminating in images of the productive and modern landscape of hydroelectric machinery, the perfect synthesis of nature and modernity.[115] The 'electric' mountain did not kill the beautiful and wild mountain; rather the former completed the latter, ordering what had been chaotic and giving value to what had been without it. As a matter of fact, the same people who wanted dams and reservoirs were also the main supporters of the tourist exploitation of mountains.

Consuming Mountains

There is an underground link connecting Romanticism, hydro-electrification and the typical week's skiing holiday; the tourist conquest of mountains could have never happened without artists and engineers climbing throughout the Alps. Strange as it might seem, in Italy Romantic appreciation and modernisation of nature were two sides of the same coin; the organised practice of mountain vacationing in particular employed both narratives, alternating between natural preservation and economic development. Even Antonio Stoppani in

---

112. Pedersoli 2006, p. 155.

113. Bonaria and Tosatti, n.d. p. 1.

114. Raiteri 1977, p. 20.

115. Istituto Luce, Oro Bianco, 1939, without reference number.

his canonical celebration of the Italian landscape, which became the bible for generations of mountain climbers and excursionists, remained trapped in this contradiction. At the end of a long critique of the commodification of the Swiss Alps, he stated: 'if there comes a time when our Alps are packed with tourists as the Swiss Alps are now, then I will say: Hurray for progress!'[116] Stoppani was comparing the tamed Swiss Alps with the still genuinely rural Italian ones; he was not stressing the wildness of those mountains but rather their simplicity, the fact that they were still 'authentic', while lamenting that the Swiss Alps had became a mountain version of the ordinary urban environment.[117] Evidently, this discourse on authenticity vs. artifice was part of the Romantic turn that had expanded the wild narrative from the natural to the social; preserving mountains meant not only saving magnificent landscapes and wildlife but also traditions and customs that were quickly disappearing from the civilised world of the plains. If Stoppani's *Il Bel Paese* was the gospel of the Italian landscape, the CAI and the Touring Club were the churches in which the landscape of nation was worshipped. In fact, these two associations did more than just promote tourism and mountain climbing; as the founder of the TCI stated in 1901:

> We must make our youth understand our country's soul. Because, you know this, the country does have a soul. It may be transient, fluid, hidden, surely omnipresent. Tourist science is to discover this soul ... Sometimes it speaks from our women's eyes, other times from the cold collection of a museum; you may listen to it from the austere ruins as well as from the merriment of a fair or the tumult of an industrial city. This soul wafts on the uncultivated fields, in the mountains, on the fertile plains ... Give me the support of feelings, give me the soul and through it Italy itself will make the Italians.[118]

Making the Italians – this was the main aim of the nationalistic elites in the aftermath of the political unification of the country. The TCI and the CAI participated in this effort, using space as an agent of nationalisation. The exploration of the Italian landscape was a two-way road: on one hand, the landscape shaped its observers, making them national citizens and on the other, in the process of nationalising people, the landscape was also transformed, incorporating the national meanings for which observers were looking. In the

---

116. Stoppani 1915 [1876], p. 126.

117. 'When I see the alpine villages transformed into loose and rich bazaars, or meetings of corrupted and fatuous people, I would like to say that there are enough shop windows with laces and wigs, trains and crinolines on Via Vittorio Emanuele without any need to look for them on the tops of the Alps'; in *Ibid*.

118. Bertarelli 1926, p. 243.

third chapter I will examine in detail the politicisation of the Alps as the sacred place where the Great War was fought, specifically stressing the TCI's agency in this process of reinventing a 'national' nature. Nevertheless, this process did not concern only places and times of high nationalistic confrontation, such as the Alps during and after World War One; in peacetime the TCI and the CAI also functioned as machines for the making of Italians and Italian landscapes. At the core of their nationalistic effort lay their faith in the generative power of education; knowing Italy implied the appropriation of the nation's geographic and symbolic space, thereby internalising the external landscape as part of a collective identity. Both the CAI and the TCI employed three key tools in the edification of Italians' about their country: the distribution of periodical publications and guides, the organisation of leisure time and the promotion of logistic infrastructures such as mountain huts and roads. In 1895 the Touring Club published the first issue of *Rivista Mensile*, its monthly magazine, which was distributed to all members. 1909 was the birth year of the TCI guides and in the following years the association started several other periodical publications: in 1917 *Le Vie d'Italia* [Roads of Italy] and in 1924 *Le Vie del Mondo* [Roads of the World]. It is less easy to track the multiplicity of the Alpine Club's periodical publications, many of them produced by local branches but a quarterly bulletin was established in 1865, while in 1882 a monthly magazine began to be distributed to the CAI's members. In the 1930s the number of magazines dedicated to mountain climbing grew and new titles were added to the old ones, including *Lo Scarpone* [The Climbing Boot], which was to become the expression of fascist alpinism. How much these publications were actually read is another question, of course. We know that the subscriber-base of *Le Vie d'Italia* expanded from 75,000 to 180,000 in six years (1921–1927); in 1937 there were about half a million members of the association, all receiving the magazine. The other group of potential readers was the CAI's affiliates whose numbers grew from 200 in 1863 to 9,036 in 1913. The TCI and the CAI often cooperated in the field of publications: in 1934 they started the series *Guides to the Italian Mountains*, offering the most comprehensive handbooks for mountain climbers on the peninsula. Although the CAI remained more elitist and specialised than the TCI, requiring skills not common among ordinary tourists, it also contributed to the popularisation of the Italian mountains. Furthermore, the CAI was also the model for less elitist associations dedicated to the exploration of mountains: in 1884 came the Association of Milanese Excursionists; in 1898 the Pre-Alpine Federation; in 1906 the University Students CAI branch; in 1911 the Union of Italian Excursionist Workers; and in 1920 the catholic alpinist association FALC *Ferant alpes laetitiam cordibus*, chaired by Achille Ratti, who later became Pope Pius XI.[119]

Of course, mountain climbing opened the remote Alpine peaks to those who were able to ascend – and actually also descend – them but even at the time of the largest expansion of the association these skilled people were still a small minority. Hence, in terms of popularisation of the mountains, we have to look beyond expert alpinists or at least understand the wider effects that these new practices had on the general public. Scrambling over the Alps was not for everyone; even the apostle of the Italian Alpine Club, the Abbot Stoppani made this clear in his book. According to Stoppani, the CAI's aim was not to force people towards difficult ascents but rather to develop a diffuse knowledge of the mountains through some kind of soft alpinism:

> It is enough for me to suggest mountain trips to children, parents and educa-tors because I believe that among all the instructive tools these are the best. According to me, the boy who explores the hills around his native village is already a mountain climber.[120]

This vision of mountain climbing did not inform only Stoppani's writings; within the CAI two different practices of alpinism coexisted: a heroic one made for and by exceptional people and a domesticated version for everyone else. Of course, the two versions were not in opposition; the extraordinary acts of expert climbers popularised the general interest in mountains while the construction of tourist infrastructures made it easier to be acquainted with mountains even in the absence of any special skill. The Luce documentary films are extraordinary sources for exploring this double approach towards mountains. Some of them presented highly difficult ascents, showing the exceptional skills of mountain climbers, but others testified to the popular passion for mountains, describing camps and excursions accessible to everyone.[121] This 'alpinism for everybody' was, for instance, strongly supported by one of the most popular writers in nineteenth century Italy, Edmondo De Amicis. Few people know that the

---

119. Ferrazza 2006, pp. 42–68.

120. Stoppani, pp. 48–49.

121. Archivio Istituto Luce, 'Ascensione sulle Alpi dolomitiche' October 1931-A0866; 'Scalatori CAI alla prese con le Dolomiti', 1930s- no reference number; 'Ascensione ai ghiacciai del Monte Rosa', 1932- no reference number; 'L'aspra meta', 1937- no refer-ence number; 'Santa Cristina, Val Gardena', 19 August 1936-B0938; 'Raduno Cervino' 19 July 1939-B1548; 'Campeggio internazionale SUCAI' sulle Dolomiti', 1932-B0050; 'Dopolavoro Vicentino', 1934-B0516; 'Dolomiti', 12 February 1936-B0831; 'Alpi di Siusi' 20 January 1937-B1027.

author of *Cuore* [Heart], a novel that formed in generations of Italians an appreciation of humanitarian nationalism transcending class divisions, became a passionate admirer of mountains.[122] An admirer but not a mountain climber, De Amicis supported the CAI's efforts to popularise mountains beyond the limited group of alpinists. Although recognising the significance of spectacular ascents in sparking the public imagination, De Amicis celebrated the expansion of mountain climbing to women and children as a shift towards a popular alpinism.[123] De Amicis was at the same time an apostle of and a witness to the tourist appropriation of mountains; his writings not only contributed to the discovery of mountains but documented a phenomenon already in place. His ironic descriptions of the Alpine hotel micro-cosmos opened a window on the social practices with which urban people were negotiating new relationships with mountains. De Amicis employed the classical rhetoric about city people dealing with 'wild' nature; although there were few real mountain climbers, his tales are full of braggarts who never made any climbs, rich bourgeois for whom the real mountain was never as beautiful as they had thought, bored city dwellers unable to survive in the absence of the distractions of urban life and inappropriately garbed ladies, mistaking the simple lunchroom of an alpine hotel for a fancy metropolitan restaurant. In De Amicis's stories, as in every such tale, mountains could sometimes work their miracles and redeem these city people, connecting them with the authenticity of both nature and humans; after all, this was the true meaning of going to the mountains. Although employing the usual dual rhetoric about urban/rural people, De Amicis witnessed the conquest of mountains and their transformation into popular vacation sites:

> In some days of the last August, its [Cervino's] monstrous sides were swarming with attacking insects and the mountain hut was as crowed as an inn on fair day.[124]

As I said, the writer himself was not an alpinist at all; he preferred to admire Mount Cervino from the chairs that had been installed just outside the Giomein Hotel to enjoy the theatrical spectacle of the mountain.[125] De Amicis, like the CAI and the TCI, needed to find the difficult equilibrium between the popularisation of mountains and the fear that such popularisation would bring desecration and coarseness, killing the very otherness of mountain places.

---

122. For my understanding of *Cuore* I acknowledge special debt to the fruitful discussions I had with Duccio Scotto di Luzio.

123. De Amicis 1999 [1903], pp. 85–86.

124. *Ibid.* p. 130.

125. *Ibid.* p. 56.

48

Wild Mountains

An elevator rising from the interior of Cervino was the sacrilegious dream of profane alpinists, but De Amicis did not disguise the fact that, as the father of a mountain climber, he would indeed prefer to see his son ascending the peak in this prosaic but much safer way.[126]

In reality, mountains were not threatened by elevators drilled into their bowels but, nevertheless, other machinery was undermining their sacredness: whether roads, railways and cableways were actually besieging mountains instead of freeing them was a matter of discussion within the CAI and the TCI. As we might expect, they did not take a firm stand, preferring to mediate between different, even divergent, positions. This was extremely clear in the case of Mount Cervino in the 1930s, when the CAI found itself in a very difficult situation, caught between fascist modernisation, which did not allow any dissent, and the cry for preservation raised by one of the most venerable Italian mountain climbers, Guido Rey. In his last book *Il Cervino è nudo* [Mount Cervino Is Naked] Enrico Camanni told the story of the tourist occupation of that area, starting from the opening of the Valtournanche–Breuil new road, which Guido Rey had strongly opposed.[127] Even Angelo Manaresi, the CAI's fascist president, had to find a way around Rey's intransigent position and some kind of compromise with modernity.[128]

> Just to be clear: I am a supporter of mountain roads because if we want people to stay there we have to serve them with roads, which are schools of civilisation; and also because a road ascending towards mountains will bring urban people there and with them new economic opportunities for mountaineers. But I understand also the bitter feeling of sacrilege of those who love Cervino for its sharp and proud isolation, its divine silences and its difficulty of being conquered.[129]

Among those malcontents Angelo Manaresi included Guido Rey, the apostle of Cervino, who had strongly denounced the huge transformation caused to the entire valley by the new Breuil road.[130] The road had covered the sounds of nature with the noise of the city with its cars and crowds.

126. *Ibid.* p. 149.
127. Camanni 2008.
128. Manaresi 1934, p. 12.
129. *Ibid.* p. 637.
130. In 1904 Guido Rey had published *Il Monte Cervino*, with an introduction by Edmondo De Amicis, which became a classic of Italian mountain climbing (Milano, Ulrico Hoepli, 1904).

[Poetry] cannot stop either the road or the car, I agree on this, but there must be some respect imposed, otherwise even the tourism will be damaged. Someone told me that everything, lands, roads, cableways have to be sold off to an anonymous society, the *casiere* [cheese producing huts] and huts have to disappear … But we need to be careful with these things.[131]

Manaresi asked for what we today call environmental planning, aiming to protect nature from intensive tourist exploitation; although he did tolerate roads and hotels, his emphasis was undoubtedly on the preservation side, urging lower impact infrastructures. Of course, Manaresi's position was not without contradictions but, considering the context, he made a strong statement on behalf of mountain preservation:

Who could ever think of the Breuil Valley packed with cars, yellow, green, and red gas stations and sparkling garages, and roaring with clubs and simian dancing?[132]

Guido Rey's presence in the Breuil Valley seemed to have a remarkable effect on the CAI position regarding this specific issue; Rey was an icon in Italian mountain climbing, incorporated by the fascist regime for his patriotic efforts in both peace and war. His irrevocable opposition to the transformation of the valley forced Manaresi and the CAI to abandon their generally pragmatic positions on those issues and move towards a more protectionist approach.

The TCI also had to deal with the uncomfortable coexistence of modernisation and preservation in its promotion of tourism. The society's magazine offers an inexhaustible source of examples of this dialectic between protection and tourist development; after all, the TCI's commitment to tourist promotion was stronger than that of the CAI. It was inscribed in its very name and became even stronger in 1920 when the association signed an agreement with the Italian National Tourist Board (ENIT) making *Le Vie d'Italia* the official magazine of the agency for fifteen years. Obviously the basic way to promote tourism has always been the same: transforming places into goods and persuading potential consumers of their beauty. 'It was necessary, and still is, to introduce Italy to all Italians, to reveal to everybody the magnificence of our Fatherland in its thousand faces', someone wrote in *Le Vie d'Italia*, celebrating the association's thirty-year anniversary. While revealing the beauty of the Fatherland was the mission of the association, how to appreciate this beauty without spoiling it was less obvious. The TCI often used the expression 'valorizzare' which is still quite common in Italian discourse on cultural and natural resources; it may

---

131. Manaresi 1934, p. 637.
132. *Ibid.* p. 638.

be translated as 'to develop', meaning employing all measures to increase the value and help the fruition of something which has been underestimated. In 1909 the TCI president Luigi Vittorio Bertarelli wrote an article about better tools to develop (valorizzare) a mountain; according to him, proximity to a huge city, furnishing consumers for tourist services; a significant investment in transportation, mainly of the vertical sort; and finally the building of hotels and vacation houses were the essential ingredients to transform a out-of-the-way mountain into a tourist destination. Celebrating the tourist conquest of Mount Tre Croci in Lombardy, Bertarelli approved the appropriation of most of the land through a corporation to build hotels and vacation houses:

> It will be necessary to clear the soil from the coppice ... delineate comfortable paths and even to start planting ornamental trees, mainly conifers as those are preferred in the private villas.[133]

Hence, according to the TCI, developing a mountain, in the sense of giving it the right value, meant converting its desert slopes into gardens full of hotels and villas. Writing in 1911 about Mount Mottarone, situated between Lakes Maggiore and Orta, Bertarelli celebrated the electric train connecting Stresa to the peak. In his words, this providential rail track broke the isolation of the mountain maximising the natural beauty of the place, made by 'lovely trails' and 'various panoramas'. Bertarelli did not deny the fact that such beauty was, at least partially, the product of the isolation which had left those places wild; however, blending modernisation and democratisation, he argued that, without trains and hotels, that beauty would have remained an exclusive privilege for a few athlete-tourists.[134]

It is hard to blame the TCI for these opinions. Driving people to every corner of the country was the TCI's main mission; roads, maps, trains, omnibus, cableways and cars were the TCI's allies rather than enemies. Actually, the TCI had among its statutory duties the improvement of the national roads network. Therefore, this association could not possibly have been the champion of a strict preservationist approach; its focus remained on opening-up pieces of the nation's landscape to the largest number of citizens. Guides, magazines and later the images of the Luce documentaries brought Italian beauty to a public who could enjoy it without any effort. These documentaries often celebrated new modes of transportation, proposing a narrative of conquest rather than one of wilderness protection. Cableways were especially popular in the propagandistic

---

133. Bertarelli 1909, p. 289.
134. Bertarelli 1911, p. 462.

movies, probably because through them it was possible to jointly celebrate the spectacle of modernity and nature.[135] Cableways spoke of bold engineers and wild landscapes, connecting not just places but concepts by steel wires and narratives. In these movies the spectacle of mountains included the natural and the artificial, overcoming any dichotomy between them. Additionally, the cableways provided a reassuring image; the times of heroic explorers were over because modernity had finally won the last strongholds of wildness. Hence, going to the mountains was no longer an extraordinary adventure. These documentaries, together with other propagandistic tools, not only brought the mountains to the general public but also encouraged people to explore them directly, jumping from the seat of the theatre to that of the cableway. Regimented by the TCI and the CAI, and later by other recreational organisations, thousands of Italians discovered their country through excursions organised by these associations. It is impossible to survey all the organised trips that transformed mountains into places for weekends and Italians into tourist consumers. Just to quote a few examples, the TCI Turin branch organised a sledding trip to Moncenisio (in 1901) and to Monginevro (in 1907); in 1911 they went to Spluga and Cenisio again.[136] For obvious reasons, the Alps occupied most interest during these first excursions: the TCI and the CAI, as well as several other recreational associations, had a strong base in northern urban Italy, geographically close to the Alps; moreover, political motivations – namely Austrian domination and later the memory of the Great War – made those mountains central in any discourse and practice surrounding national appropriation of nature.[137] Apart from these patriotic reasons, more prosaic motivations put the Alps at the core of the excursionists' agenda. The rise of winter sports, for instance, strongly supported by these associations, contributed to focusing attention on the Alps, which offered better conditions for such activities; in fact, even in 1927 the ENIT did not include any southern Italian places on its list of ski locations. In

---

135. See for instance, from the Archivio Istituto Luce: 'Belvedere in Cortina d'Ampezzo' 02/1929-A0272; 'Nuova funivia a Chamonix' A0/60-04/1931; 'Chamonix, La più alta teleferica del mondo. Come si sale senza fatica sul Monte Bianco a 3480 metri' B0144-30/09/1932; 'La funivia del Gran Sasso' B0475-05/1934; 'Varallo. Inaugurazione della funevia per il santuario del Sacro Monte' B0737-28/08/1935; 'Sestriere. Inaugurazione della funivia del Fraiteve' B1241-26/1/1938; 'Terminillo, Inaugurazione della moderna funivia' B1242-26/01/1938; 'Cortina d'Ampezzo. Il panorama delle Dolomiti alla nuova funivia del Monte Faloria' B1445-18/01/1939; 'Sul Cervino. La funivia più alta del mondo' C0105-31/12/1940.

136. Anon. 1911, 'Il touring pel turismo invernale'.

137. I will discuss this aspect in the third chapter.

1911 the TCI published the first yearbook dedicated to winter sports, but the Italian story of skiing had started earlier. In 1901 the first ski club was born in Turin, followed by those in Milan, Genoa, Rome and Cuneo.[138] Ten years later Roccaraso, a small village at the top of the Abruzzo Apennines, hosted the first winter ski camp in central–southern Italy, thus becoming one of the most popular destinations for skiing in that part of the country;[139] and, as Luigi Piccioni has shown, this 'fortune' did not contribute positively to the protection of the environment in Roccaraso, rather contributing to its intensive exploitation.[140] Winter sports were boosted in the 1930s as a consequence of the inclusion of skiing in the 1936 Olympic Games and the imposition of a ski monoculture radically affected the landscape via the spread of logistic infrastructures needed to transform mountains into goods for mass consumption.[141]

The popularity of skiing and, generally speaking, of winter sports in fascist Italy was undoubtedly connected to the 'martialisation' of mountain climbing; as we will see in chapter four, the regime heavily employed mountains in its project to shape the new Italian, both in body and mind. Actually, this vision of alpinism and winter sports in terms of military training was not a fascist invention: since the beginning of alpinism it had been a major tenet in the promotion of a nationalistic path to mountain climbing. Introducing alpinism to the general public, someone wrote in 1881:

> Civilisation says 'I do not have tournaments, attacks against castles, continuous wars, therefore the race of my men is depleting into laziness. It needs to be restored, we need to invent something.' Hence, in the bloodless fencing halls and in the gyms mountain climbing was invented.[142]

As we will see in the following chapters the nationalisation of both mountains and mountain climbing passed through this martialisation, which transformed alpinists into soldiers and mountains into the sacred borders of the Fatherland.

138. Anon. 1909, 'Gli sports della montagna'.
139. Anon. 1911, 'Il Touring pel turismo invernale'.
140. Piccioni 2000, p. 371.
141. Patrizia Battilani has provided a list of the mountain villages that built ski lifts a an early date: Pocol in 1925, Col Druscè and Tofana in 1926, Cortina in 1926, Sestriere in 1932, Alpe di Siusi in 1935, Breuil in 1936 – in Battilani 2001, p. 225.
142. This paragraph was included in a publication produced for the 1881 Industrial Exhibition in Milan, cited in Ferrazza 2006, p. 42.

~ 2 ~

Rebel Mountains

I would like to become a rebel, my little one
I would like to become a rebel, my little one
He who lives alone in the dark mountain
To scare you until he dies

Southern Italian Folksong

Wild Landscapes

As we have seen, the mountain was without a doubt the obvious place to go in search of that little bit of wilderness left in Old Europe. Mountain climbers, engineers and day-trippers all left town for the mountains in search of that wild nature that would save – or at least improve them – but that at the same time asked to be saved – or at least improved. Therefore, in the very process of being discovered, mountains were also being reinvented. At the core of this reinvention was the contradictory notion of *wildness* as both the main appeal and the repulsion of mountain nature. In the previous chapter I analysed how the narrative of the wild mountain was instrumental in interpreting the 'natural' landscape and imposing on it the order of modernisation: dams and cableways, reforestation and hotels were to be the new face of the Italian mountains.

Nevertheless, rivers, trees and wolves were not the only subjects of this discourse on the wild. In a crowded Italy, these wild landscapes were full of people. Therefore, taming the mountains meant taming their inhabitants, because mountain-folk were part of the wild landscape and of its narrative. The rugged nature of the mountains was reflected in the character of its inhabitants; to mould the former one had to tame the latter. After all, prior to the arrival of climbers and tourists, mountains had been the realm of smugglers and rebels, outlaws and heretics, charcoal-burners and poachers – in other words, those living at the margins, able to move in a wild world. Viewed from the cities on the plains, the mountain-dwellers were perhaps colourful but, first and foremost, they could be dangerous folk, always difficult to fathom. The laws of the plains arrived somewhat blunted in the mountains. The State, the Church, even the market found it hard to become established above a certain contour.

This chapter narrates the transition from the rhetorical invention of the wild mountain to its decidedly material taming. When the discourse about wilderness shifted from places to people, it was time for the army to bring the nation into the deep mountains.

Sister Mountain

It has been some time since the last ghost roamed through Europe. However, of late, two virtual ghosts have emerged in the interstices of the great web, from times and places far-removed. I am referring to Dolcino and Margherita, two heretics burnt at the stake on 1 June 1307, accused by an absolutist Church of being the heads of a sect which, like so many others in those years, proposed a type of communist pathway to Christianity.[1] But how do two medieval heretics cope in the virtual reality of our times? They write e-mails, obviously.[2] 'Dear Mountain rebels…': thus Dolcino and Margherita address the activists of the self-organised groups that for some years have been fighting against the construction in *their* valleys of the high-speed rail system, better known in Italy as the TAV.

The idea of linking ancient heretical struggles with the new environmental resistance has much to do with a certain view of the landscape and its relation to local communities. According to this narrative, the mountain produces communities tied especially to their environment, capable of withstanding outside forces thanks to their diverse social and cultural systems.[3] In particular, common property seems to embody this mountain diversity, weaving shapes of landscape and culture. However, for the moment I would like to focus not so much on the claimed aptitude of mountain-folk for community living but rather on one of their other 'virtues' – being *natural* rebels. The construct of a rebel mountain landscape and the political use of the discourse come from far away, even if we only stay within the specific case that was our starting-point. The ghost of Dolcino (only recently has a new sensitivity to gender freed the memory of Margherita) has appeared many times in the mountains of Valsesia

---

1. Mornese 2006.
2. These letters are available at various websites. Here I refer to http://eresiaerivolta. noblogs.org/post/2007/08/05/dolcino-lettera/
3. On this point, see Burat 2006.

Wild Landscapes

since his cruel death. The mountains where Dolcino and his followers held out for many years against the crusade launched by Pope Clement V have become a symbol of revolution. Therefore we can say that this story was literally written in the landscape. Thanks to the studies of Corrado Mornese[4] and the tireless efforts of the Centro Studi Dolciniani,[5] the history of the construction and (re) invention of Dolcino's memory in Valsesia and beyond is now known.

Giving places a name is always the first way to possess them and or-ganise the landscape. The mountain where the heretics fought until they were definitively defeated changed its name from Mont Rubello (Rebel) to Mount St. Bernard because the Church wanted to mark its victory, going so far as to normalise the place names in the area.[6] The construction of a sanctuary dedi-cated to the saint completed the project of landscape appropriation. However, despite all efforts, the landscape was never completely normalised but remained a battlefield for contrasting memories and symbols. Centuries after the revolt, when the area in question was profoundly marked by the factory system and by workers' organisations,[7] Mount Rubello and its significance re-emerged in discourse and political practices on several occasions.

Gustavo Buratti has reconstructed the links between the Valsesian work-ers' movement and the memory of Dolcino as it was embodied in the landscape of the valley. In 1877, during a strike, the textile workers decided to hold their assembly on Mount Rubello and in 1898, once again, the mountain was used as a refuge for rebels, sheltering those fleeing the brutal repression of protesters against a tax on the grinding of flour in the streets of Milan.[8] Significantly, it was Antonio Labriola, one of the fathers of Italian Marxism, who noted a continuity between the Dolcinian and the Socialist movements, referring to the former as a primitive form of Communism.[9] Labriola's cultural appropriation became the material appropriation of spaces on the part of Valsesian workers who, mindful of Dolcinian resistance, sought to politicise the landscape of their valleys. In

---

4.   Mornese 2002.

5.   Materials from the Centro Studi Dolciniani are available at http://fradolcino.interfree. it/csd.htm

6.   I must thank Corrado Mornese for this information on the toponymy of Mount Ru-bello and for everything he and the Centre have done, and continue to do, to preserve the memory of this event. I am pleased to acknowledge my debt of gratitude to them.

7.   The valleys of Valsesia were home to numerous textile mills.

8.   Buratti 1987.

9.   Labriola 1906, quoted here from the 1897 Italian edition, chapter IX, available online at http://www.marxists.org/archive/labriola/works/al05.htm

1907, the workers' organisations in the area marked out their territory, erecting an obelisk on Mount Massaro because the symbolic geographical space of the former Mount Rubello was already too crowded with Catholic symbols.

Monument to Dolcino.

However, in cases like these it is always somewhat difficult to set forever the landscape of memory. Thus, while the Catholics of Biella long limited themselves to expressing in local newspapers their indignation at the sacrilegious monument,[10] the fascists later preferred other methods of showing their disapproval: in 1927 the obelisk was destroyed by dynamite.[11] In the new *Italia* made by the man of Providence, as Pius XI called Mussolini, there was no longer room for Mount Rubello and its memories. However, not even fascist dynamite, violent as it may have been, remains in the landscape forever. Conflicting memories compete for space in the nation's geography and history. As we shall see later, the mountains became rebel strongholds once again during the partisan war, and the mountains of Valsesia offered an incredibly favourable landscape for the Resistance due to both their geography and historical significance.[12] It thus comes as no surprise that in 1974, during a new Catholic crusade, this time against divorce, opponents of the Church's campaign returned to Mount Massaro and its history of rebellion, relocating a new monument to Dolcino on the site of that destroyed by the Fascists.[13]

Undoubtedly we may think that these are stories of a bygone era, not only the age-old tales of Dolcinians being burnt at the stake but also the more recent ones of socialist obelisks, fascist dynamite and a 1970s referendum. Yet landscapes and their histories die hard. They survive through changes, taking part in the transformation of places and their identities. They may therefore surface in the present, like something old from the attic being re-used to invent fashionable new objects. In the year 2000 things transpired just like that: as narrated by the writer Paolo Rumiz, the discovery in a museum's vaults of an old memorial stone dedicated to Dolcino divided the town of Vercelli between those who wanted to use it to mark the landscape again with the memory of the rebellion and others who thought it inappropriate to exhibit the stone.[14] After all, even the two letters of Dolcino and Margherita, circulated on the internet

---

10. Buratti refers in his essay 'L'altra religione' essentially to the 'Gazzetta della Valsesia' and to 'Il Biellese'.

11. *Ibid.*

12. Later on, in the Epilogue, I will return to Resistance and mountains, especially to the relationship between Dolcino's memory, Resistance and the mountain; see Secchia and Moscatelli 1958, p. 173.

13. The whole episode is reconstructed on the website of the Centro Studi Dolciniani: http://fradolcino.interfree.it/

14. The town was profoundly split over the decision of the local government to place this memorial stone to Dolcino in the historic centre of Vercelli. This issue has been extensively covered by Rumiz 2007.

between 2006 and 2007, are no more than the re-emergence from the past of a narrative linking landscape, memory and the present.

All these things, albeit with very different degrees of 'virtual' and 'real', remind us that we live in a landscape made of nature and history. The TAV rail system, due to cut its way through the valleys of Piedmont and Lombardy, is destined to cross a landscape made of time and space. Once again the rebels defending their territory can hearken back to the ancient struggles of mountain heretics and the more recent resistance of the partisans. As reconstructed by Donatella Della Porta and Gianni Piazza, the link with the memory of the Resistance to Nazi-Fascism is particularly strong in the case of the NO TAV movement. This is a construct conscious of identity, as shown by the 2003 Valsusa Filmfest dedicated to the partisans, by the presence of committees to commemorate the Col del Lys massacre[15] and, quite clearly, by the archive of resistance in Valsusa promoted by the Spinta dal Bass committee.[16] With the march on Venàus on 8 December 2003 the link between memory, landscape and rebellion becomes clear. On that occasion protesters managed to bypass the checkpoints of the police who had militarised the entire valley, using mountain paths once used by the partisans.[17] It is, indeed, just as the Italian writers Wu Ming[18] and Vitaliano Ravagli wrote: 'stories are axes of war to be unearthed'.

However, Dolcino and Margherita were certainly not the only heretics to inhabit the mountains of Italy. Perhaps if we were shared the proclivities of a nineteenth-century positivist scientist, we might be able to trace an altitudinal line separating the land of religious conformity in the lowlands from that of religious obsession up in the mountains. Perhaps I could hazard a guess and propose a nexus of causality connecting mountain environment, economic and social structures and religious cultures. However, unfortunately for the reader, I am not a positivist scientist nor do I have any simple explanation to account for the concentration of religious rebels in the mountains, apart from the obvious consideration that repression there was always more difficult. In other words, it is not easy to state whether and to what extent heresy was a typical product of the mountains or whether mountains were simply a destination for those

---

15. On 2 July 1942, at the end of a massive roundup, the Nazi-Fascists captured, tortured and finally killed 26 partisans. Information about the massacre from Pollano 2006–07, pp. 106–07.

16. Della Porta and Piazza 2008, pp. 86–88.

17. *Ibid.* p. 138.

18. On their website Wu Ming is defined as a 'mysterious collective of guerrilla novelists'; among their publications, *Q, Manituana, Altai*. See www.wumingfoundation.com/english/biography.html

in search of isolated places in which to survive. What is striking, nevertheless, is that it was not only a medieval phenomenon.

In the mid-nineteenth century, various messiahs roamed the Italian mountains. In the 1840s a priest in a small village in the Piedmontese mountains, Francesco Antonio Grignaschi, announced to his parishioners that he was the incarnation of Christ. For Grignaschi, though, there was no supreme sacrifice waiting for him, but only seven years in prison and abjuration.[19] However, putting a stop to Grignaschi's followers once and for all would have required sending the army into the valleys around Asti.[20] At about the same time, another 'Christ' was travelling across the mountains of Italy, in this case the southern Apennines; he was a certain Oreste De Amicis, like Grignaschi a parish priest in a small village and, like Grignaschi, the self-proclaimed incarnation of Christ. The only miracle of that Messiah from Abruzzo was the stopping of a train in the middle of the countryside, rather too little to arrest the modernity the train in question carried with it but enough to land him in prison.[21] Even in the South, modernity could not encounter obstacles along its course, though clearly trains would continue to stop in the open countryside, serving the needs of government officials and local dignitaries.[22] But stopping trains to serve their needs was not in contradiction to southern Italian modernisation but rather its incarnation – the lay miracle of 'secular saints' for which no one ever went to prison.

Although neither Francesco nor Oreste have left visible traces, I feel that both may help us to see that rebellious mountain that is part of our landscape's DNA. In their preaching there was no strong social dimension capable of to mobilising the masses or especially disquieting the elite. But this would occur in the case of another Christ, also active in the Apennines at roughly the same time.

On 18 August 1878, in the era of factories, science and technology, while elsewhere the telephone was being used to communicate, a bizarre procession entered a small Tuscan town, Arcidosso.[23] The people were dressed in strange

19. The story of Grignaschi is narrated in Mondo 2000.

20. Information on the intervention of the authorities may be found in the dictionary of alternative Christian thought published online at http://www.eresie.it/ under the entry 'Francesco Antonio Grignaschi'.

21. On Oreste De Amicis, see De Nino 1890; Flaiano 1982.

22. At a conference in memory of Oreste De Amicis, the historian Raffaele Colapietra recalled that the MP for Abruzzo, Giuseppe Devincenzi, used to stop trains in the middle of nowhere if he needed to, thereby performing the same miracle as the Messiah; in Associazione Culturale Flaiano 1986, p. 20.

23. This account is from Barzellotti 1885.

David Lazzaretti.

costumes and bore flags and vessels praising the advent of a rather improbable 'Republic of God's Kingdom'. But this was not the usual religious event of the Italian countryside. Indeed, the procession had been forbidden and, to enforce this prohibition, the army did not hesitate to shoot at the crowd, first killing the leader, David Lazzaretti, and then at least ten other people.[24] This was the end not only of David Lazzaretti, the Messiah of Mount Amiata, but also, by and large, of his religious movement, which barely managed to survive his death. In his influential essay on primitive rebels, Eric J. Hobsbawm spoke about Lazzarretti's experience as 'a laboratory specimen of a medieval millenarian heresy surviving in a backward corner of peasant Italy'.[25]

However, Lazzaretti's movement was not at all isolated from his *milieu* or ahistorical, despite his eschatological visions. I am not only referring to the attempts of conservative and clerical groups to manipulate Lazzaretti's movement to combat the secularism of the new united Italy. Rather, I am concerned with stressing that the religious movement in question is to be seen as part of the crisis of Italian society, and especially of mountain communities, hit by

24. The sources disagree, speaking of 10–30 victims.
25. Hobsbawm 1959, p. 65.

liberalism, by the market economy and by the drive towards the privatisation of resources. In Hobsbawm's words, 'the irruption of modern capitalism into peasant society ... has always had cataclysmic effects on that society'.[26] Viewed from the slopes of Mount Labbro or Mount Amiata, modernisation had the face of privatisation of public goods, of scientific forest management and limitation of civic uses.[27] As expressed by the sociologist Enrica Tedeschi:

> The alienability of public land and the consequent radical downsizing of civic uses – which constituted the fundamental support of this unstable subsistence economy, both as a harvest of woodland public goods (wood collection, chestnuts, small animals) and as pasture – entailed an intolerable disequilibrium of the economic structure and a threat to the cultural and symbolic system, whose keystones lay in a mentality based on the sacredness and inalienability of land.[28]

Lazzaretti's experience was a community response to the challenges of modernity; division of labour, property and profits and free welfare and education among members of the sect,[29] much more than confused prophecies about a strange coming republic, were what really frightened the lowland authorities. Viewed from the lowlands, Lazzaretti's sermons seemed to have literally set Mount Labbro on fire; the massive fires that his followers lit on the peak of the mountain were visible from all surrounding villages and risked starting the most dangerous fire that the authorities had ever had to cope with. The condemnation of the Vatican and the bloody repression of the State managed to prevail over this modern heresy, leaving only faint traces of its existence: the ruins of a strange tower on Mount Labbro, some papers left in local archives and various books written by and on the Messiah of Mount Amiata are all that remain. Some might point to other lingering effects in the landscape, such as the strong influence of the Italian Communist Party (PCI) in the area.[30] In 1948, immediately after the assassination attempt on Togliatti, the secretary of the party, Mount Amiata was shaken by a revolt put down with extreme violence by police forces who once again occupied the entire district. A year later, speaking to the militants to celebrate the victory of the left-wing coalition in local

---

26. *Ibid.* p. 67.
27. On these points, see Vecchio 1981; Moscato 1978, p. 120.
28. Tedeschi 1989, p. 25.
29. These were the aims of the Society of Christian Families, founded by Lazzaretti in 1872; in Bardelli, 1977, p. 35. On this point see also Tedeschi 1989, p. 26.
30. In the years after World War Two, by and large all the remaining followers of Lazzaretti became members of the Communist Party; in Moscato 1978, p. 144.

Monte Labbro with ruins.

elections, Palmiro Togliatti proposed an explicit comparison between the two events, the uprising of 1948 and the massacre of Lazzaretti's followers in 1878:

> In the first few decades after national unification, one man, considered a saint by the working classes, became the leader of their struggles; then, as now, the dominant classes thought they had suppressed the struggle for justice by killing him [Lazzaretti] … On 14 July history repeated itself. They thought once again that they had broken our resistance forever … but you showed they had assumed wrongly.[31]

The Wild South Show

Some presences have been stronger or at least more persistent than others, infusing the landscape with their significance and their narration. This applies to southern Italian brigands who took possession of the Apennines, occupying the mountains with their bands but also with their stories.

---

31. Speech by Palmiro Togliatti to inaugurate the PCI's new local office, Abbadia San Salvatore 26 June 1949, reported in Serafini 1981, p. 127.

Wild Landscapes

Some 120,000 men were roaming the southern Apennines; they were not mountain climbers, however, nor Touring Club members (in truth the Club had not even been founded at that time), or at least this was not why they were walking along footpaths and wooded slopes in the mountains of the former Kingdom of the Two Sicilies. Instead, those 120,000 men belonged to the military expedition sent by the Italian government to suppress the uprising in southern Italy in the aftermath of Italian unification. The facts are well known: in 1860 Giuseppe Garibaldi landed in Sicily with his thousand volunteers (and the cover of the British navy), managing to conquer the Bourbon kingdom in the space of a few months.[32] At the beginning, it was precisely the irregular nature of Garibaldi's expedition and the opportunity for a revolutionary change that fuelled the hopes of the lower classes in southern Italy for an agrarian reform which never arrived. After all, it was Garibaldi himself who fanned the flames and encouraged such hopes in an attempt to mobilise the peasant masses in the national war. The combination of failed agrarian reform, loyalty to the former king, rejection of conscription and common criminality constituted the rootstock on which southern Italian brigandage was grafted. Much has been written on the *guerra cafona* [peasant war] in the South and various interpretations have been advanced: class struggle,[33] religious and national insurgency,[34] faction fighting[35] or simple criminality.[36] However, though the historiographical interpretations may be diverse and contradictory, the result is unambiguous: between 1860 and 1870 a regular army, formed chiefly of Piedmontese troops, or at least those from central and northern Italy, found itself fighting a bitter civil war, with a staggering number of fatalities.[37] This was a war that would change the landscape of the South and its place in the national narrative.

---

32. It is impossible to refer to the whole extraordinarily extensive bibliography on Garibaldi and the Italian Risorgimento. A key and recent starting point is Riall 1994.

33. Marxist historiography interpreted the southern rebellion in terms of class struggle and failed agrarian reform. See, for example, Gramsci 1949; Molfese 1964.

34. Aside from the southern Italian historians of the time, linked to the Bourbon dynasty, interpretation of brigandage as a national/religious insurrection has recently found new supporters in neo-Bourbon scholars, generally amateur historians with an anti-north political agenda: see, for example, Izzo 2002; D'Amore 2004.

35. Colapietra 1983; Lupo 1988; Riall 1994.

36. Croce 1928; Nitti 1946.

37. The very nature of brigandage and the strong politicisation of its memory make it impossible to obtain reliable data on the death toll.

Rebel Mountains

This is what 120,000 men were doing rambling in the southern Apennines: they were taming the mountains on behalf of the newly unified State, for the war on brigandage met the State's need to extend its control over the southern interior. We could say that it was a matter of nationalising the mountains in the South in the sense of subjecting them to central control and reclaiming them from the rebels. The mountains have always played a decisive role in guerrilla tactics; from medieval heretics to partisans, the peaks were ever a haven for all types of objectors, unable to face up to regular forces in town or on the plains. However, rather than focus on military questions, I would prefer to explore the extraordinary mix of landscape and memory – Simon Schama's words – that crystallised around the question of brigandage.

The mountains in southern Italy were not only the theatre of conflict, the geographical area where rebels took refuge; in fact, rather than the proscenium, they were an integral part of that history of rebellion. Even today, for those who visit, observe or describe those mountains, it is hard to escape the memory that pervades those places. 'Brigands' mountains' – these are the words of writer and journalist Paolo Rumiz concerning the Apennines between Basilicata and Campania in his 2006 reports on the Italian mountains;[38] and things do not change if one looks at guidebooks to Basilicata, Calabria and Campania or the confused patchwork of municipalities, associations and nature preserves in the *Mezzogiorno*, often replete with references to the period of brigandage, resuscitated by a local revival that grinds out new identities and reinvents traditions. And that is not to mention neo-Bourbon or religious-traditionalist movements for which brigandage is much more than a trace in the landscape to be reactivated for tourist purposes.

Like in a game of mirrors, landscape and memory reflect one another. Travellers saw the memory of brigandage written large in the southern Apennines where the war against the rebels seemed to have left wounds as deep as those inflicted by deforestation and landscapes. For those able to hear, everything in the Apennines seems to tell of brigands: place names, like *l'erta dei Birri Morti* [the ascent of Dead Policemen] on Mount Taburno in Campania, the countless ruins of buildings destroyed by soldiers, the legends tied to places, trees, rocks. Tradition has it that the forests of the South are full of mysterious symbols, camouflaged in nature, signs from another world and another time, impossible to decipher, which, according to legend, would lead to secret hideaways

---

38.   Paolo Rumiz, 'La strada che sbuca dal passato', in *La Repubblica*, 20 August 2006; this is one of the articles in his complete report *Appennino il cuore segreto* [The Apennines: the Secret Heart] published in summer 2006 by *La Repubblica*.

and, for the more fortunate, to inestimable hidden treasure. From the hills of Basilicata where the fascist regime had sent him as an internal exile (and not to a cheerful holiday camp[39]), Carlo Levi described the process of hybridisation between brigands and the landscape. In his words, the brigands had made the popular legends about forests and mountains with their mysterious treasures and dangers come true. Never before had imaginary landscapes and material landscapes seemed so akin.

> These clay mountains are studded with holes and natural caves. Here the brigands lay low, hiding in the trunks of hollow trees the money obtained from robbery and ransom. When the brigand bands were at last dispersed, their loot remained in the woods. At this point the history of the brigands passes into legend and is bound up with age-old superstitions. For the brigands hid their spoils in the places where the peasants had always imagined there was hidden treasure. In this way the brigands came to be looked upon as beings with the dark powers of the nether regions.[40]

'He who digs, finds' – with these words the famous brigand leader Caruso responded to the crowd of peasants who wanted to know where he had hidden his treasure. Although taken in chains to the scaffold, he never revealed the secret of his gold but instead left everywhere in the landscape the chimera of finding it.[41] In the popular imagination, brigandage occupied the mountains of men and symbols; in every forest, in every cavern, a band of armed men or perhaps their treasure could be hiding; there were no mountains that were too steep or remote to run into rebels, charcoal-burners, policemen or their magical transfigurations.[42] In reality, up in the mountains it was difficult to distinguish between rebels and *others*: identities became blurred and there was a fine line between 'goodies and baddies'. Anyone could be a spy for the brigands or the soldiers; besides, as in any peasant war, blending in with civilians was part of the rebel strategy,[43] making it difficult to distinguish between accomplices and

---

39. I am referring here to an astonishing interview with the Italian Prime Minister, Silvio Berlusconi, who claimed that 'Mussolini did not murder anyone' but 'sent people [his opponents] on holiday to confine them' (in *The Spectator*, 6 September 2003, at http://www.spectator.co.uk/essays/all/11437/forza-berlusconi.html)

40. Levi 1947, p. 144.

41. Sangiuolo 1975, p. 202. Paolo Macry 1997 also speaks of the spasmodic search for hidden treasure, pp. 80–81.

42. Caprettini 2000.

43. 'Frequently, when the brigands saw the soldiers coming, they hid their arms in a furrow behind a hedge, taking the pickaxe in their hand and, by a sudden metamorphosis, became peaceful countrymen engaged in the labours of the field'; in Maffei 1865, p. 55.

victims, peasants and outlaws. Yet the brigands mixed not only with other mountain-folk but also with nature itself, managing to vanish in the woods or blend in with the trees and the rocks, disguising their voices as the calls of animals.[44]

The fact that it was not just a matter of metaphors or legends was confirmed by the repressive strategy of the Italian army, which came to consider whoever ventured into the southern Apennines as accomplices to the brigands. In an attempt to force local people to cooperate, the military authorities sought to separate rebels from peasants, forests from cultivated fields and mountains from villages; but it was a difficult objective to achieve since in the Apennines identities were ambiguous, especially in the event of revolt, and the boundaries between domestic and wild were unclear. In the everyday life of the rural South, the plains and their agriculture were intimately connected with mountains and forests. The military needed to sever those ties, limiting peasant access to the wooded mountains, preventing them from bearing food and arms and often destroying the isolated shelters of shepherds.[45] As a result, shepherds, peasants, woodcutters and charcoal-burners found themselves trapped between the mistrust of soldiers and the blackmail of brigands.

Encountering brigands, or traces of their presence, was not only the stuff of legend or mental suggestion. Rather, it was part and parcel of the experience of mountain communities in the years after unification. Meeting a brigand could have an unpredictable outcome: in his *Cronache del brigantaggio* [Chronicles of Brigandage] Vincenzo Padula recounted how brigands acting as improvised forest wardens prevented charcoal-burners from gathering firewood in the Sila.[46] Yet things could take a much more dangerous turn. According to Maffei the brigand Caruso killed a charcoal-burner in the forest of Riccia simply to distract his pursuers and gain precious time.[47] In the flesh or in spirit, the brigands were the true lords of the mountains. On Mount San Vittorino, in the province of L'Aquila, there are numerous caves where the brigands had dug small tunnels for ventilation and in which to light fires during the long

44. The ability of brigands to mimic the calls of animals made a deep impression on Swiss entrepreneurs kidnapped by the Manzo band in 1865. Their memoirs of that period of captivity are an invaluable source on the image of brigands; Friedly 1984; Lichtensteiger 1984.
45. de' Sivo 1863–64, pp. 161, 204; Sangiuolo 1975, p. 41.
46. Padula 1974, pp. 62–64.
47. Maffei 1865, p. 243.

winters.[48] On the *Scrima Cavallo*, at an altitude of 2,000 metres, one can still read an inscription engraved by brigands in the rock: 'Oh traveller, you who are passing through these places, remember that 1820 was the year Vittorio Emanuele was born, King of Italy, who transformed this kingdom of flowers into a kingdom of misery.'[49]

Caves, signs, encounters and boundaries – brigandage and repression redrew the spaces of the mountains in southern Italy in a very material way. The war against the rebels became a war against the forest, their ally. Maffei wrote in 1865,

> One cannot enter these dark and gloomy woods without perceiving at once how well adapted they are for the concealment of bandits, who, in their impenetrable recesses, may safely defy the troops sent in pursuit of them.[50]

The Apennine forest became home to bands of brigands. According to an informer of General Pallavicini, each band of rebels had one or more woods which they used for shelter.[51] The forest of brigands was a truly strange hybrid. Obviously it appeared as an archetype of wildness, completely different from the barracks of regular soldiers. Yet it was also true that the rebels had tamed it after their fashion, equipping it with various comforts. The *Selva delle Grotte* [Forest of Caves], Caruso's HQ, was equipped with a field hospital for the wounded; in the Monticchio forest Crocco had stored wine and victuals; and at Lagopesole the soldiers hunting down Ninco Nanco found army overcoats and clean linen in large quantities. To further heighten the contrast, sometimes even musical instruments, clearly destined to add cheer to the parties of brigands, were found in the middle of woods.[52]

If the forest was a friend to the brigand,[53] the army could only be his sworn enemy; controlling the mountains meant imposing the nation's authority over

---

48.   D'Amore 1994, p. 192.

49.   *Ibid.* p. 250.

50.   Maffei, 1865, p. 27–28.

51.   According to reports by Mario Monti, Crocco controlled Lagopesole, Cerro Venosa, the forests of Montemilone and Monticchio; Tortora's band the forests of San Fele, San Cataldo, Monte Sirico, Toppo De Cillis, Buccito; the thieves of Melfi and the coopers controlled the forests of Frasca alla Cisterna, Galliano and Cerro Venosa; in Monti 2005 [1959], p. 421.

52.   Maffei 1865, p. 60.

53.   'The brigand does not say goodbye to fields that he has never cultivated; his last salute when he is captured or is about to die, is addressed to the woods by which he was received and protected'; in Piromalli and Scafoglio 1977, p. 37.

Postcard depicting 'Lancers of Montebello'.

the woods or, in other words, overcoming the wild disorder. Besides, targeting the forest to eliminate guerrillas was and would have been a classic tactic of so many peasant wars.[54] In southern Italy, as early as during the French occupa-

---

54.   On south-east Asia, see High 2007; Armiero and Peluso 2008.

Wild Landscapes

Carmine Crocco, brigand.

tion (1806–1815) the army had decided to adopt this type of strategy.[55] The question of military control over the forest was also raised in the report of the Parliamentary Commission of Inquiry into Brigandage in 1863, which stated:

> It is also necessary to take some decision on the destiny of the very forests themselves. We cannot suggest cutting them or burning them. This hypothesis seems too desperate. Undoubtedly, they must be thinned out. We will have to eliminate the shrubs ... without cutting down mature trees. In this way the terrifying forests of Mount Fortore [in Basilicata] will lose all their natural hiding places now used by rebels.[56]

It is difficult to say how far the army managed to follow the sound recommendations of the Commission in its concrete practice of repression; in some cases it would seem that the forests severely suffered the consequences of the conflict. Carmine Crocco, perhaps one of the best known brigand captains, recounted in his autobiography:

> I came back to the *maquis* in Toppacivita, field of my victory. But oh how strange, it had vanished! All that was left was disturbed soil ... The general [Della Chiesa] had recognised that that position in the hands of large numbers of die-hard brigands was a serious threat to Rionero and towns nearby and decreed

---

55. This phenomenon is mentioned in Armiero 1999.
56. Relazione Commissione di Inchiesta sul Brigantaggio 1983 [1863], p. 191.

its destruction. With this public notice he gave the peasants *carte blanche* to freely go and collect firewood in the *maquis* and before you could say 'Wood of Signor Filippo Decillo from San Fele' it became a barren field.[57]

Several sources reported the burning of many forests by the military; testimony to forests going up in flames came from the provinces of Naples, Caserta and Basilicata, precisely the areas where brigand resistance was deeply rooted.[58] That the southern Apennines were an environment, if not hostile, at the very least unknown to regular soldiers can be taken as a given; in forested areas of the interior, the *Italians* moved like the blind. The landscape seemed unknown to them, different, in a word, wild. Writing to his father from the Lucanian mountains, a young officer admitted:

> Just imagine immense virgin forests which the army cannot penetrate without risking getting lost and with the certainty of no happy result whatsoever, since paths are continuously blocked by natural barriers of thorns and wasps and because the brigand knows every little passageway, every exit, every hiding-place.[59]

The war was clearly against the rebels and their accomplices – yet in some way it was even more than this. The soldiers were taming their provincial wilderness, changing it from 'nature' into nation. To undertake this twofold mission – that is, to crush the rebels and nationalise the mountains where they operated – they first had to become acquainted with these places, to move through them without getting lost. Without topographic maps and local informers, the State could never have arrived in the rebellious mountains of the *Mezzogiorno*.[60] The 'scientific' signs marked out by the military on their maps and those magic signs left by brigands in the landscape and in its narration changed perceptions of the Italian mountains. It was brigandage that put the southern Apennines, and more generally the South, on the map of the nation. Yet, before then, Italians from the other end of the peninsula had had the opportunity to see it close up.

This was clearly the experience of many soldiers sent to the South to suppress the insurgency. After months of vainly besieging the forests of Cerreto and Telese, General Pallavicini discovered from a local official that what seemed to him a perfect trap to catch brigands actually offered five easy open routes through which they could get supplies, reach a safe haven or simply

---

57. Crocco n.d. p. 86.
58. Naples State Archives, Police Papers, 13 October 1861, vol. 179; vol. 1682/131-9.
59. Negri 1905, p. 52 (letter dated Bisaccia 8 February 1862).
60. *Mezzogiorno* is synonymous with southern Italy

continue the usual activities of brigandage.[61] There is no doubt that the rebels knew the terrain better. However, the Italian soldiers' sense of being lost and of foreignness was not merely due to their poor knowledge of the areas concerned: the wildness of the mountains seemed to shift from nature to its inhabitants, giving rise to a war that was cruel beyond all imagination. The rebels' tie to the mountains was viewed as something more than just the capacity to tactically exploit the lie of the land. The harshness and wildness of mountains seemed to be reflected in the nature and especially in the cultural and genetic inbreeding of its inhabitants. Reflecting upon brigandage in the province of Salerno, one of the officials at the prefecture wrote that the harsh environment of the southern Italian mountains had produced a 'race of savages from time immemorial'.[62] Nature had honed their senses and toughened their spirits. In his inquiry into brigandage published in 1862, the Swiss intellectual Marc Monnier maintained that the pastoral system, keeping men on their own for months in the mountains, had forged a race of savages without humanity.[63] Creatures of the forest, like wild animals they were able to survive in very difficult conditions; in such terms many biographers described the best-known brigands of the South. The comparison with animals was a recurrent one: the rebel could be as wild as a boar, as fierce as a wolf and as strong as a bear.[64] Certainly, life in the forest turned the brigands into animals. It is not surprising that some army officers compared the rebels to Native Americans.[65] It could be said that the mountains of the South were, at least to some extent, the Italian Wild West. The southern Apennines represented an unexplored wild world, the frontier between civilisation and barbarism, culture and nature. These were places where war was even more terrible and where much blood was shed.

Human body parts hanging from the branches of trees like the fruits of a cruel season of war was the blood-chilling spectacle met by Major D'Ambrosio on reconnaissance in the village of Pozzillo on Mount Taburno in October 1861. The La Gala band had executed a traitor, enacting a bloody ritual en-

---

61.   Sangiuolo 1975, p. 222.

62.   Salerno State Archive, Prefecture – Cabinet, b. 18, cited in D'Urso 1977, p. 11.

63.   Monnier 1862, p. 9.

64.   Scarpino 1985, p. 59.

65.   Bourelly 1986 [1865], p. 66. General Pallavicini recalled that both among southern Italian brigands and the 'Indians' it was widely held that their chiefs were immortal; in Report of General P. Pallavicini, Spinazzola Headquarters, April 1864, in Maffei 1865, p. 252. The same kind of discourses were used about French peasants: see Weber 1989, pp. 19, 895.

tailing dismemberment and cannibalism, and the soldiers found the embers of a fire and human bones with their flesh removed.[66] Cannibalism was used as clear proof of the inhumane barbarism of the rebels, a conscious *leitmotiv* in the official narrative. 'They drink blood, they eat human flesh': with these words the Parliamentary Commission on Brigandage described the ferocity of the rebels.[67] There is considerable evidence for the brigands' cannibalism as an expression of their separateness from civilisation. In the journal of one officer, examined in depth by legal sociologist Dario Altobelli, we read:

> Our brigands did not disdain cutting flesh from their prisoners, sprinkling it with salt and pepper and, after lightly browning it over a fire, eating it dripping with blood in front of the victims themselves, with great gusto as if it were a tasty dish.[68]

Further on in the same journal, the officer recounted the tortures inflicted on a soldier falling into the hands of the brigands:

> Deputy Sergeant Nicola Scardaoni was wounded and captured by brigands. He was literally cut into pieces like butchered meat and the brigand Cellini, not yet twenty years of age, extracted the smoking liver and spleen from the stomach of the victim, cooked it as if it were calf's liver, and ate it calmly amidst his applauding companions!![69]

Cannibalism was the ultimate proof of the *otherness* of those rebels, of their savagery. But it was not the only bloody crime they were accused of. Brigands were said, for example, to enjoy torturing their victims,[70] whose body parts they often kept as trophies. It seems that genitalia and bearded chins were highly prized. Mention is also made of their predilection for rape and lack of mercy

---

66. Calzone 2001, p. 86. The same episode is also narrated in Sangiuolo 1975, p. 156, available online at http://www.brigantaggio.net/brigantaggio/Storia/Local/Airola6.htm

67. Relazione Commissione di Inchiesta sul Brigantaggio 1983 [1863], p. 185. The same expression was then reported by Maffei 1865, p. 112.

68. Bartolini 1979 [1897], p. 23. This quotation and the others from Bartolini's journal are taken from Altobelli 2006.

69. Bartolini, p. 24 (cited by Altobelli).

70. Bartolini recounted the murder of the young son of the general practitioner in Pastena thus: 'The poor martyr was roped to a grindstone, his genitals were mutilated and he was forced at knifepoint to swallow them. Then they opened up his belly and extracted his intestines, wrapping them around his neck like a tie, adding insult to agony...' (Bartolini, p. 53, cited by Altobelli). In contrast, Maffei reported the bloody murder of a shepherd suspected of collaborating with the military; after having had his arms and legs cut off, he was thrown into boiling water – in Maffei, 1865, p. 236.

Wild Landscapes

Nico Nanco immediately after his murder.

for minors, as noted in the memoir of General Pallavicini on the events in Castelvetere. There, according to the officer, Caruso's band had raped women and young girls and killed 240 men after making them witness these acts of violence.[71]

Indeed, miles from anywhere in the southern Apennines, the Italian soldiers felt a long way from home and it was not only a question of geography. For all of civilised' Italy, these mountains were the other place, still dominated by wildness. There were continuous comparisons between the regions of the South, and especially their inhabitants, and Africa. Typical of these was Farini's classic exclamation, when sent to Naples as a new lieutenant:

> These lands! … Such barbarism! Certainly not Italy! This is Africa. Compared with these peasants even the Bedouins are civilised people… Their king gives them *carte blanche* and they raze to the ground the houses of landowners and cut off their heads and ears.[72]

For 'civilised' Italy, the nature of the South was also this – wild landscapes reflected in equally wild people, forging their passions and behaviour. These were the years in which the new Positivist School of Lombroso, Niceforo and Sergi proposed racialisation of the Italian population, labelling southerners as an inferior part of the Italian race and thus explaining, on 'natural' grounds,

---

71. Report of General Pallavicini, Spinazzola Headquarters, April 1864, in Maffei 1865, p. 240.

72. This expression has been quoted by several scholars; here I am using Astarita 2005, p. 286.

the very origin of brigandage and the problems of the South.[73] The insurgency gave flesh and blood to the idea of the wild southerner and constituted a very powerful case to support his taming. After all, like every tale of frontiers and wilderness, this one had its anti-heroes too, savage and cruel, just as the film script envisaged. The whole of Italy was shocked by the tales of the brigands' ferocity because, if the insurgency was changing problems in the South into a nationwide political problem (the Southern Question),[74] in the meantime popular culture was also constructing its own version of history, simple and effective. The narrative about brigands and their actions became part of the landscape. It was in practice impossible to separate one from the other. Obviously, the official version of the 1860s southern rebellion omitted the national army's atrocities. The military also used violence to break rebel resistance and villagers' solidarity by displaying rebels' severed heads and dead bodies. Photographs taken by the military during the campaign of repression offer proof of their political use of dead bodies and violence. Through the placement of bodies in these pictures the official iconography depicted all the stereotypes of rebels and soldiers. Rebels' bodies were 'wild': naked, unshaven, dirty, often lying on the ground; soldiers' bodies were 'civilised', hence uniformed, clean and standing at the scene.[75]

The mountains of the brigands were not only tangible through the eyes; through the mouth and ears they became a narrated space, reinvented by the power of the word. It would be difficult to distinguish what Giustino Fortunato and other members of the Italian Alpine Club (CAI) saw during their climb up Mount Terminio from its renowned tales of 'brigands and murderers, betrayals and vendettas' with which they kept themselves warm throughout the night.[76] These were not just old tales being told around a fire; organising the excursion up Terminio[77] had required a massive effort precisely because the presence of brigands remained strong, if not in the real mountains, at least in the imaginary landscapes they narrated; it would take more than just soldiers sent from Turin or the passing of special laws to dislodge them. One might think that 1878, the year of Fortunato's trip up Terminio, simply came too soon after the season of

---

73.   Petraccone 2005, p. 79; D'Agostino 2002.

74.   On the construction of the Questione Meridionale see Petrusewicz 1998.

75.   Bollati 1983, pp. 142–43.

76.   Fortunato 1884, p. 36.

77.   On the difficulties of organising this trip, Giustino Fortunato wrote, 'though one no longer heard of any band of brigands, almost every proposal failed because of the poor security of the places …' – *Ibid.* p. 17.

brigandage. But the slow pace of change is all too apparent from Carlo Levi's account of fascist Lucania fifty years later:

> When I talked to the peasants I could be sure that, whatever was the subject of our conversation, we would in one way or another slip into mention of the brigands. Their traces are everywhere: there is not a mountain, gully, wood, fountain, cave, or stone that is not linked with one of their adventures or that did not serve them as a refuge or hideout; not a dark corner that was not their meeting-place; not a country chapel where they did not leave threatening letters or wait for ransom money.[78]

Mountains and stories are inseparable. The oral tradition has great weight in the memory of brigandage but often these accounts became texts, written words, even more powerful filters through which to view the southern mountains. Although literature and, more generally, high culture have been accused of being essentially reticent on brigandage, this view does not mean that there is a scarcity of narrations and/or reinventions of such events. Beyond the historical studies of brigandage, there are numerous biographies, novels and accounts, often written by less prominent authors. Such works had a considerable impact in constructing the landscape of brigandage.

One such lesser-known author was Nicola Marini who included various tales of brigands in his collection of accounts of the forest of Monticchio in Basilicata.[79] All the stories collected by Tommaso Claps, a magistrate and writer from Basilicata, dealt with brigandage.[80] The most significant exponent of the genre was probably the Calabrian writer Nicola Misasi (1850–1923), author of fifty novels and more than 200 short stories about his region. According to him, nature was not only the background framing the brigand but seemed to generate him and share some basic features with him. This was not the geographic explanation of brigandage proposed by the Massari Parliamentary Commission, which stressed that the ruggedness of the area, the dense woods, and the poor communications network were ideal terrain for the type of guerrilla warfare waged by southern bands. This was a deeper, intimate tie binding nature and the brigands. From the Samnites to the Bruttians to the rebellion of Spartacus,[81] the southern Apennines seemed to be identified as a place of proud resistance, of clashes between cultures and of untamed peoples. These

---

78. Levi 1947, p. 137.
79. Marini 1888.
80. Claps 1906. On Marini and Claps, see Nigro n.d.
81. John McNeill recalls that the last battle against the rebels guided by Spartacus was fought precisely in the mountains of Lucania; in McNeill 1992, p. 82.

mountains were wild terrain, as were their people; viewing both with admiration did not mean espousing hostile political intentions towards the emerging nation but more simply meant acknowledging the appeal of a world destined to disappear. It is no accident that Misasi, for example, maintained that it was not the agrarian question that underlay brigandage in the South but rather 'a physiological or topographical question' or, in other words, nature herself, 'strong and luxuriant'.[82]

Sharing: Common Uses and Collective Property

Contrary to Misasi's assertion, the distribution of lands and access to common resources were basic issues in the southern revolt. This was, for instance, the case with the famous riot in Bronte, Sicily in August 1860, which was the starting point of the southern peasants' disillusion with Garibaldi's revolution. 'We want the public lands; these owners have sucked our blood, now we want it back!'[83] These words synthesise what was at stake in that village on the slopes of Mount Etna, as well as elsewhere in the southern Apennines. According to the Sicilian writer Giovanni Verga, who published a short story on the Bronte riot and its bloody repression, a major misunderstanding lay behind the clash between southern peasants and the new State: for the former, freedom meant access to the land but, for the latter, the unification of the country and the end of the Bourbon kingdom.[84]

Bronte stands out as an example by which to understand the narrative connecting landscape and people; the peasants' violence clearly expressed the wildness passing from nature to humans,[85] while the very causes of the riot linked that violence with the socio-environmental framework organising humans, nature and the metabolic relationships between them. Property rights and access to and use of natural resources were major forces in shaping these socio-environmental connections. And, obviously, like everything else in the

---

82.   Misasi 1881, quoted in Piromalli 1996, p. 430.

83.   Radice 1963, p. 69.

84.   Verga 1984 [1883]; on Verga and the South see Moe 2002, chapter 8.

85.   Commentators emphasised the cruelty of the crowd, describing horrendous murders, peasant ferocity, stories of children axed to death and victims burned alive. One author wrote that the military arrived in the village to find a rebel using his teeth to tear off the breast of a dead young woman (Abba 1981 [1880], p. 267). The peasants' power lasted only a few days because the army came immediately to Bronte and punished the entire village, imprisoning rebels and condemning to death five accused leaders of the insurgency, including the 'village idiot'.

mountains, these connections were also wild, needing to be domesticated. The measure of their wildness was in the widespread existence of common property and/or access, which challenged the supremacy of private property and use. To tame the wild mountains, dams, trees and soldiers were not enough; private property needed to conquer their slopes.

The bond between the commons and mountains is manifest. If we were to draw a map of common property in Italy, we would see that it clustered especially in upland areas. Besides, it was the very multiplicity of environmental resources and their uses that required a variety of property regimes. The ecological characteristics of the mountain led to collective forms of risk minimisation but maximisation of labour efficiency. In other words, the variety of the mountain's environmental resources demanded different levels of their appropriation. The question concerned not only the legal forms of land ownership but, more generally, the access to environmental resources, thereby making distinctions between legal property rights, land use rights and rules governing resource management. The mountains were undoubtedly the space where collective forms of property/access were strong, persistent and extensive. In his work on the history of the Alps, Jon Mathieu maintained that at high altitudes an economy based on woodland and pasture is *naturally* oriented towards collective forms of resource ownership and/or use.[86] For this reason, as Carlo Cattaneo wrote in the nineteenth century, on climbing from the plains of Lombardy towards the Alps, one could note the link between the change in the physical landscape and the transformation of social structures that marked it with a progressive increase of commons, i.e. common property managed by its original inhabitants – in other words, there was 'another way of owning', in the mountain from in the lowlands.[87] There in the Alps, an overall system of rules established times and modes for using primary and secondary woodland products[88] and pasture.

It is hard to quantify the size of the commons, especially due to its uncertain definition. Often it was not land owned in common, but rather land over which groups of heterogeneous users could wield exclusive use rights. However, even if we restrict the analysis to the proper commons – that is, the land owned collectively – the data would still be uncertain; sometimes they refer to the area of the land itself and at other times to the number of *municipalities*

---

86.   On the connections between commons and the Alps see Mathieu 2000, p. 184.

87.   Cattaneo 1925 [1844], pp. 91–93.

88.   Coppola 1989, pp. 496, 505.

in which it fell.[89] For southern Italy an enquiry in 1904 offers a striking amount of information and data, not only about the area of commons but also on its altitudinal distribution, confirming, if ever this were necessary, the mountain concentration of this ownership type. (Table 2.1)

Table 2.1. Tables from the Proceedings of the Royal Commission for Commons *1902, pp. 69–72.**

Province	A. Commons controlled by the municipalities (in hectares)	B. Commons controlled by usurpers (in hectares)	Total of columns A and B (in hectares)	*Municipalities* with commons/ total number of municipalities
Aquila	65,933.46.68	10,497.70.51	76,431.17.19	115/127
Chieti	17,755.94.17	4,284.45.93	22,040.40.10	53/120
Teramo	18,777.46.41	3,101.45.01	21,878.91.42	31/74
Foggia	39,006.10.72	36,012.82.03	75,018.92.75	29/53
Bari	7,076.79.43	3,556.85.21	10,633.64.64	12/53
Lecce	5,053.09.79	45,927.65.38	50,980.75.17	29/130
Potenza	57,508.11.09	4,609.03.02	62,117.14.11	105/124
Benevento	7,401.75.29	4,222.94.37	11,624.69.66	52/73
Caserta	44,616.93.55	9,598.41.78	54,215.35.33	115/186
Campobasso	16,380.59	10,235.06	26,615.65	96/133
Avellino	10,443.23.70	675.00	11,118.23.70	63/128
Salerno	37,251.11	9,307.77	46,558.88	118/158
Cosenza	28,700.11.35	12,160.49	40,860.60.35	113/151
Catanzaro	27,512.24.90	6,990.62.88	34,502.87.78	121/152
Reggio Calabria	28,795.03	17,115.65	45,910.68	82/106
Total	412,212.00.08	178,295.93.12	590,507.93.20	1134/1768

* The figures above are composed of hectares, ares and centiares. So, for instance, 65,933.46.68 is 65,933 hectares, 46 ares and 68 centiares.

---

89. At the beginning of the twentieth century it is estimated that in the provinces of Brescia, Bergamo, Como and Sondrio there were 75,000 hectares of commons, divided into 235 municipalities; 7 municipalities had commons in the province of Verona, 220 municipalities in the provinces of Novara and Torino and 50 in Liguria. At the end of the nineteenth century in the Emilian Apennines there were over 39,000 hectares of land variously described as commons; in Marche and in Umbria there were 360 *comunanze* [commons] divided into 37 municipalities with an area of 22,359 hectares; in 1888 in the former provinces of the Papal State, the law on land use rights affected 595,293 hectares; in 1874 in Sardinia commons amounted to 186,294 hectares. Data in Corona 2004, p. 361. Information on the Emilian Apennines in Cazzola 1997, p. 71.

Out of a total of 658,000 hectares of common land, 418,000 were in the mountains (63.5 per cent), 163,000 in hill areas (24.7 per cent), and 77,000 on the plains (11.7 per cent); in Sicily of 60,000 hectares, 33,000 were in the mountains (55 per cent), 21,550 in hill areas (35.9 per cent), and 6,000 on the plains (ten per cent).[90]

The most extensive commons were, and are, largely among the valleys of the Apennines, on less fertile steeply sloping land further from urban centres, the land that ancient and present-day occupiers found least attractive.[91]

Although public property was widespread throughout Italy, it had different characteristics depending upon its location. Using an invaluable map created by Gabriella Corona,[92] we can identify three large mountain areas with three different commons systems:

- Alpine commons, in the North. Here commons were called *vicinie* or *regole*;

- Apennine commons, in the Centre and especially on the Adriatic side. Here commons were called *partecipanze* and *comunanze* (on the Ligurian Alps, *comunaglie* and *bandite*);

- Southern Apennine commons. Here commons were known as *usi civici* and *demanio*.

The system of Alpine commons was governed by a set of fairly rigid, largely written regulations, in which access to common resources was strictly related to the notion of residency - that is, to belonging to the community holding exclusive property and/or use rights. In that ecological context, dominated by the extensive presence of forests replete with upland pastures, that type of collective property fell within a strongly balanced economy based on woodland and grazing areas, with crops being less widespread. This was one of the differences between the Alpine system of regulations (or *vicinanze*) and those of the central Apennines: there, the greater demographic weight, combined with milder climatic conditions, opened the way for more crop farming compared with forestry and grazing. In contrast, the existence of written regulations, territoriality (i.e. inclusion/exclusion on the basis of belonging to the community) and the assembly of family heads, were substantial points shared by commons

90. Corona 2004, p. 373.

91. Proceedings of the Royal Commission for Commons 1902, p. 131.

92. Corona 2010, p. 91.

in central and northern Italy. The situation changed in southern Italy: there, common property largely coincided with the exercise of civic uses and with public property of the municipality[93] on which these uses were traditionally exercised. Unlike the Alpine and central Apennine commons, in the South there were generally no specific written regulations for managing public goods.[94] Perhaps it was precisely for that reason that the demands of local and national (municipalities and State) institutions were more greatly felt, in the face of the weakness of other social actors. Lastly, it is evident that in the South there was greater emphasis on land use and access rights than on property rights in the strict sense.

Despite all the cultural and ecological differences I have listed, both the Alps and the Apennines preserved singular sets of property and access rights. Their landscape was a wild one, not just in terms of the 'quality' of people and nature but also in the legal structures governing their relationships. Commons were simply another of the many singularities of the mountains; after the taming of the natural and spiritual landscape, it was time for the legal landscape also to conform to the rules of the plains. The legal historian Paolo Grossi has analysed the emergence of a discourse that criminalised common property while sustaining privatisation as the modernisation of property rights and, I would add, of socio-ecological relations. Following the main thread of this chapter, common property was to rebellion and wild as privatisation was to taming and domestication. As Stefania Barca has recently argued, at least from the Napoleonic invasion of Italy, private individual property had become the new religion. The same abolition of feudalism, driven by the French Army into the peninsula, had meant the end of any form of comingled rights of possession and access which, according to this progressive narrative, had inhibited land improvement.[95] Only with individual, free and exclusive property rights would legitimate owners make the investments required to enhance their land.

Yet the story of the application of the Napoleonic Code also shows the extreme relevance of common uses; in southern Italy, for instance, the Code implemented a special committee dedicated to solving controversies between

---

93. By contrast, as Gabriella Corona wrote, in northern and central Italy collective property rarely coincided with ownership by the municipality: Corona 2004, p. 358.

94. In over 100 municipal regulations examined by Alessandro Trotter in 1923, civic uses were cited only for tax questions, with no reference to by-laws on the preservation of woodland or other common resources; in Trotter 1923, p. 2. The absence of written regulations for civic uses in the South is also underscored by Corona 2004, p. 370.

95. Barca 2010, pp. 36–58.

feudal owners and communities whose documentation was an extraordinary monument to the importance of commons.[96] In a sample survey I carried out in one of Italy's most mountainous regions, Molise, the importance of forests clearly emerges in the commons system; resistance to privatisation and enclosures was based on a different appreciation of the ecological qualities of forests demanding multiple ownership.[97] If the forest was not only soil and timber but also a complex ecosystem comprising soil, trees, levees, woodland, livestock, pastures, water and wild fruits, that ecological diversity inevitably required pluralism in property regimes. According to the data of the Feudal Committee for Molise, about 72 per cent of common uses claimed by the communities was related to forests:

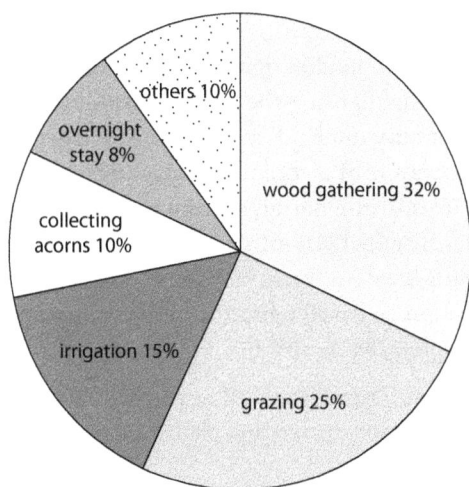

Common uses in Molise. Source: my adaptation from the Bollettino delle Sentenze della Commissione Feudale *[Bulletin of the Sentences of the Feudal Commission].*

Hence, in the implementation of the Napoleonic Code the conflicts between feudal owners and communities exposed the network of uses and rights of access which constituted another way of thinking about nature. The Feudal Committee recognised the existence of these rights but proposed a compensatory

96.   On the general relevance of the Napoleonic rule over the South and, in particular, on the abolition of feudalism see Davis 2006, pp.161–86.

97.   Armiero 2006.

approach: the users who were able to demonstrate the legitimacy of their claims could be compensated for the loss of their traditional means of subsistence. Nevertheless, property had to be private and individual. While feudal owners acquired complete control over their lands with no further obligations in terms of common uses, the so-called *demani* – that is, commonly owned lands – were divided into individual plots, theoretically distributed among poor peasants but in practice concentrated in the hands of a few buyers.[98] In a political economy narrative, improvement and progress were the main values behind that process; common property/common uses were leftovers from another time, incompatible with modernity and development. But in the mountains the discourse about commons also concerned the ecology of human–nature relationships; to reinforce the argument for their annihilation, commons were generally depicted as the main causes of any kind of environmental destruction, with a special focus on deforestation. The nineteenth-century sources from the Agency for Forest Conservation, created during the French occupation, agree on the ineffectiveness of common woodland management, highlighting the effective conditions of private forest reserves. They could not have done otherwise, due to the general process of land privatisation and the erasure of common uses occurring during these years. Of course, this was the mainstream narrative; minority voices tried to demonstrate the socio-ecological sustainability of commons, especially in mountain environments. In his path-breaking book on the hydrogeological instability of the Apennines, Carlo Afan de Rivera, director of the Bridges and Roads Corps in the Kingdom of Naples, clearly stated:

> The end of common uses in the estates, even if it aimed at positive effects, actually produced terrible damage in the mountains and plains, and for the economy of water.[99]

The ecological specificity of the mountain environment was often claimed to support commons; what worked well in the plains did not necessarily have the same successful results in the mountains.[100] That was the main argument in the 1877 Parliamentary Inquiry on Agriculture, the so-called Jacini Inquiry, used by the few researchers who opposed the abolition of common uses. In particular, Agostino Bertani for Liguria and Ghino Valenti for Central Italy were the most vocal supporters of commons in the otherwise rather pro-privatisation

---

98. On the sale of State assets see Villani 1964.

99. Afan de Rivera 1833, p. 35, but cited in Bevilacqua 1996, p. 97.

100. As Pier Paolo Viazzo states, 'different sets of tenure rights should be expected to prevail in different production zones': Viazzo 1989, p. 24.

narrative. According to Valenti, in an economy based on forest and pasture, commons were the only way to optimise and rationalise the problems of time and scale inherent in the ecology of the Apennines.[101] Support for commons was also expressed in other official inquiries. Some researchers for the 1907 survey on the conditions of the southern peasants connected the extinction of common property with hydrogeological instability and emigration.[102] The 1920s investigation on mountain depopulation (INEA Inquiry) included positive appraisals of common property like those for the Camonica Valley:

> Common property has undoubtedly worked to balance the livelihood of the mountain folk, especially supporting the poorest. When the municipalities get rid of them, they commit a crime. Obviously, the use of commons implies order, discipline and a high sense of civic awareness, because every abuse and violence against common land affects everybody … In the mountains, and especially in the Alps, forests and pastures have to stay as commons because they are indivisible and they maintain an equilibrium with the private property which goes beyond today's individual profit.[103]

Nevertheless, these were still isolated voices; the mainstream vision dictated a massive injection of privatisation into the sick body of the mountains. In relation to the Lombard Alps, for instance, the Jacini Inquiry prescribed shifting from common to private property as the only way both to preserve and to use forests.[104] Fifty years later the INEA Inquiry was able to celebrate the positive results of privatisation in the Lombard Alps[105] and to support the expansion of such policies in other areas where the commons were still resisting this process.[106]

While for the Alps there were contrasting opinions as to the ecological efficiency and the social sustainability of commons, the farther south one went, the less difference of opinion one heard. Criticism against southern Italian public lands was widespread. An inquiry into commons in southern Italy at the start of the twentieth century expressed unreserved condemnation, even if in truth it was not so much about the functioning of commons but rather the continuous usurpation they experienced. The impossibility of maintaining the integrity of collective ownership represented, however, a radical criticism of the

---

101. Grossi 1977, pp. 292–307.
102. Corona, 2010, p. 97.
103. Sala 1935, p. 312.
104. Jacini 1883, p. 124.
105. Medici 1935, p. 80.
106. Brocca 1934, p. 72.

system, also reinforced by certain remarks on how common uses functioned. In particular, the members of the commission were concerned with the health of State woodlands since neither forestry laws nor community self-regulation seemed sufficient to ensure their survival:

> The prime enemies of the woods are the populations concerned with their maintenance. The inhabitants go to cut woodland at the points closest to where they live so as to save on travel time and distance; they cut young plants and destroy the woods without leaving plants for reproduction.[107]

Grazing would complete their destruction.[108] The same opinion was to be confirmed twenty years later by a well-known expert on forestry, Alessandro Trotter, who in 1923 wrote:

> We can indeed establish the greatest disorder and maximum degradation in commons pastures or in those belonging to the municipality, while conditions are far better (with some exceptions) on privately owned pastures.[109]

That negative view of the commons was largely echoed in public opinion. The TCI committee for the protection of forests, discussed in the previous chapter, argued that all the common uses, and especially those related to grazing, were harmful for the environmental equilibrium of mountain lands.[110]

While the law of 1888 and even more that of 1927 provided the legal framework for the elimination of common use, in the mountains commons were eroded day by day and progressively enclosed within individual estates. The usurpation of common lands by private owners and the legal attack upon common use did not occur without conflict. After all, the commons were just another expression of the rebel mountain. The protesters' repertoire was varied: it involved pickets and blockages of public tenders for selling common lands, petitions to the authorities, retaliation against buyers/usurpers, squatting and arson of public archives.[111] Like a microcosm of the world at large, all these strategies are found in the case of the Ragno Forest in the southern Apennines;

---

107. Proceedings of the Royal Commission for Commons 1902, p. 162.

108. *Ibid.*

109. Trotter 1923, p. 2.

110. Serpieri *et al.* 1911, p. 95.

111. A complete inventory appears in Brunello 1981. Similar strategies of resistance and confrontation have been illustrated for the case of France case by Whited 2000 p. 40 and Weber 1989, p. 115. This without considering, of course, E.P. Thompson's classic 1975 work on *Whigs and Hunters.*

in 1860, the collective users of that forest violently confronted the owner who had prohibited the exercise of their customary rights in the name of a more rational and profitable use of the forest. Once a feudal possession of the D'Avalos family and consequently subjected to a complex web of communal uses, the Bosco Ragno was partially destined to be ploughed and divided into sections in which the rights to clear the land were sold to contractors, intentionally chosen from villages other than the ones closest to the forest. That system of logging in sections was substantially a form of privatisation of the resource and implied forbidding access to the forest for pasture, for gathering wood and wild fruits. The users did not passively accept the end of their customary rights, resorting to the classic repertoire of mobilisation to resist the enclosure: letters to the authorities, riots, occupation of the land and picketing, just to name a few tactics. The Apennines were indeed a rebel environment. That said, rebellion was ultimately tamed in Bosco Ragno as elsewhere.[112]

In the aftermath of the civil war, in 1877 the government promulgated the first national law on forest management, which, while giving private landowners the right to manage their forests however they saw fit, imposed limits on common uses [*usi civici*]. In 1888 and 1891 new laws reinforced the hegemony of private property against common rights[113] and meanwhile, as part of its struggle against common uses, the new State sold extensive areas of public and Church lands. John McNeill has estimated that between 1877 and 1910 half of the Italian forests were privatised; on examining the effects of privatisation in Lucania, one of the southern provinces most affected by brigandage, McNeill revealed that sixty per cent of its forests disappeared between 1877 and 1900.[114] What happened in the Monticchio Forest in Lucania provides an excellent example of the taming of the rebel mountain. The forest had been the headquarters of the largest rebel band. Hence, redeeming Monticchio Forest was symbolically and materially critical to the national State. After defeating the rebels, the new State also wanted to tame the legal landscape of Monticchio. Therefore the forest, previously owned by a convent, was expropriated by the State and turned over to a private company. Along with use of the land, divided into plots and given to trustworthy and loyal colonists from central Italy, local inhabitants' rights to forest access were terminated.[115] According to an old proverb that said poor

---

112. Armiero 2009, pp. 61–63.

113. Rabbeno 1883; Valenti 1911, p. 119; Corona 2010, pp. 98–102.

114. McNeill 2002, pp. 225–27.

115. Labollita 1863; Ciccotti 1904, p. 253–54.

peasants had to be 'rebels or emigrants', at that time only one option remained for them; according to Donna Gabaccia, between 1870 and 1910 about 13 million Italians left the country.[116]

116. Gabaccia 1997, p. 3.

~ 3 ~

Heroic Mountains[1]

Mount Grappa you're my homeland.

The Mount Grappa Song

At the Borders of the Fatherland

As we have seen, the nationalisation of Italian mountains was not accomplished merely by excursionists and mountain climbers: engineers and politicians concurred in drawing the new modernised landscape dominated by 'national interests', in which private property and reservoirs took the place of pastures and common lands. In no way was this a peaceful process; mountains were lands of frontiers in both the European and the Turnerian sense. As in the case of the southern Apennines, they were the space of internal 'otherness' but, as in the Alps, they also marked the traditional geographical borders separating Italians from the foreigners, remarkable borders indeed, especially in the early twentieth century when the Alps ceased to be the playground of Europe and became a theatre of World War One.[2]

In this chapter, I will argue that the war changed the Alpine landscape both with words and with bombs, creating a hybrid environment in which the nationalisation of nature was particularly strong. The politicisation of the Alpine landscape coming from the Great War included nature and humans; the Alps were celebrated as the natural bastion of the nation, the ultimate borders of the Italian community and, at the same time, their inhabitants became the prototypical true patriots standing guard over the nation. It was then that the myth of the Alpini (Italian Alpine Corps) was born and it persisted for a long

---

1. A previous version of this chapter appeared in M. Armiero and M. Hall (eds.) *Nature and History in Modern Italy* (Athens: Ohio University Press, 2010). Many thanks to Ohio University Press (http://www.ohioswallow.com) for allowing me to publish it here.

2. Leslie Stephen, *The Playground of Europe* (1871) is the Bible of this vision.

time in the collective memory. War memorials, monuments, journals, together with powerful explosions, trenches and military roads changed the landscape of the Alps, blending stories and ecologies once again.

Landscape with Bodies

> Visitor, the mountain that you ... are on the verge of piously ascending was ravaged and mutilated by the war. Some of its forests burned down in terrifying fires sparked by exploding grenades, while others were sacrificed to provide wood for trenches and soldiers' shelters. Its beautiful and verdant fields were devastated, scarred by trenches, earthworks and exploding shells ... but like the face of a mutilated brother, the ravaged face of the mountain is even more beautiful.[3]

This description, taken from a Touring Club Italiano (TCI) guidebook, contains all the main ingredients of the post-war rhetoric about mountains: nationalism, the merging of natural and internal landscapes, signs of destruction and memories of a lost serenity. But what is even more interesting is that these considerations are voiced in the first of TCI's six volumes dedicated to battlefields. The publication of that series was clearly a deliberate effort on the part of the TCI to recast Italy's mountains in a nationalistic and patriotic tone, namely as a great natural sanctuary of Italian heroism. Those books, published in the late 1920s and early 1930s, were hardly unique in the European culture of the time. One has only to think of the *Guides illustrés Michelin des champs de bataille*, published in Paris in 1919,[4] or Thomas Cook and Sons' patriotic war-site itineraries.[5] According to the historian George Mosse, Europe's modern rediscovery of its nature is directly connected with the experience of the Great War. Placing war and death within the natural space was a way to attenuate their emotional impact.[6] Naturalise death, nationalise mourning – this was the policy of European governments during the war and especially the post-war period. What has often escaped notice, though, is that this strategy did not focus on just the perception of death and the management of collective mourning but also on the perception and 'management' of nature itself. War, as I shall later show, had indeed imposed itself on nature, leaving deep traces on the land; but the effects of the political organisation of mourning and memory on nature turned out to be as durable as those of explosions and fires.

---

3.   Touring Club Italiano (TCI) 1928, p. 1.

4.   On Michelin guides, see Troyansky 1987, pp. 131–33.

5.   Mosse 1979, p.12.

6.   Mosse 1990.

The decade following the Great War has been called an age of memorials. More than 30,000 war memorials were built in France alone.[7] Great Britain set up a special commission to honour fallen soldiers, the Imperial War Graves Commission, which in 1923 sent out 4,000 headstones a week to supply 500 war cemeteries in France and Great Britain.[8] In Germany, 'heroes' groves' were planted across the countryside, a tradition dating back to the Franco-Prussian wars of the 1870s.[9] In Italy, the memory of soldiers killed in battle was entrusted to Alpine memorials and, in a small part, to *Parchi della Rimembranza* [Memorial Parks] patterned after their German counterparts. In the Italian organisation of the cult of fallen soldiers, it was not just mourning that was nationalised, but also the places where the war had been fought. A network of war cemeteries, funerary monuments and pilgrimages to battlefields turned national sanctuaries redesigned what James M. Mayo defined as the 'political landscape'.[10] It was the war cemeteries especially that impregnated the landscape with meaning, transforming it into a new hybrid of nature and memory. The visible and unseen, words and silence, artificial and natural combined to give rise to a rhetorical landscape of war and its national memory. As Kathy E. Ferguson and Phyllis Turnbull have put it, war memorials are 'national narratives ... written directly onto material soil'.[11] The organisation of space became the organisation of memory through the politicisation of absence.[12] It is what one does not see – namely the remains of the fallen as well as the meanings and events these evoke – that informs the landscape, causing reality to merge with its representation. Yet I do not think we should see this phenomenon as dematerialising the landscape, as reducing it to mere discourse. It would be very hard indeed to dematerialise the vast network of war memorials, cemeteries, monuments, gardens and parks which, as Jay Winter notes, dot European countries, from big cities to rural villages, from the mountains to public buildings, giving visual testimony to the collective memory of war.[13] And it would be absurd to think of battlefields, such as the Alps, as immaterial. How could we regard as inconsequential the imposing war memorial of Redipuglia on the

7.   Gouch 2000, p. 214.
8.   *Ibid.*
9.   Mosse 1979, p. 13.
10.   Mayo 1988, p. 62.
11.   Ferguson and Turnbull 1996, p. 1.
12.   *Ibid.* p. 7.
13.   Winter 1995, p. 1.

Redipuglia.

slopes of Mount Sei Busi in Friuli?[14] The architecture of the monument, the surrounding landscape, the relics on display there and, above all, the deafening absence of the 100,000 Italian soldiers buried there, are at once a tangible reality made of stones, cypresses and bones and a cultural medium that is a window onto a landscape that lies behind the observer, a landscape that refers to personal and collective pasts rather than to what is facing him. When we look out from the observatory of Redipuglia today, it is actually difficult to recognise a war landscape, although everything in sight reminds one of it. The monument preserves the memory but does not impede the agency of both nature and mountain communities that eventually led to reforestation. The contrast between the memorial, evoking a former landscape, and the newly rising forests, which tell a different story, that of a mountain depopulating, makes Redipuglia an emblematic hybrid of history and nature, of discourse and object, so closely intertwined that it can be difficult to distinguish the natural from the artificial, the ecological from the cultural.

---

14.   On Redipuglia, see Dogliani 1996.

The Alpini War Memorial at the Passo del Tonale.

As we have seen, the 'rearranging of memory', as the Italian historian Mario Isnenghi defined it, had a major impact on Italian mountains.[15] The natural spaces where the war had been fought were sanctified and vast war cemeteries were created. These artificial spaces became, in a way, vehicles for meaning, capable of transferring perceptions and discourses along a triangular

---

15.   Isnenghi and Rochat 2000, p. 498.

path linking individuals, the nation and the landscape. The mountains had modified both war and the soldiers. Mountaineers had been turned into heroic Alpini and the wearisome and robotic war in the trenches had given way to bold deeds entrusted to the skill of individual soldiers.[16]

The geographic position of the Alps along the boundaries of Italy evoked a defensive conception of war that went hand in hand with the celebration of the fallen. The Alps were the geographical sentinels of the nation, the keepers of the memory of Italians rising in arms to defend their homeland. War and politics thus redrew the map of Italy. The names of insignificant, out-of-the-way places became universally known; formerly uninhabited peaks were populated with the ghosts of the fallen, at once present and absent; and the mountains became the destination of national pilgrimage by school children, families of fallen soldiers and omnipresent authorities. Nature had transfigured warfare and the soldiers and then preserved the traces of war;[17] politics organised and put an official stamp on that memory.

Alpine tourism gave a decisive boost to the mass diffusion of this dual cult of nature and memory. Both the Club Alpino Italiano (CAI) and the Touring Club hastened to organise guided tours, hikes and pilgrimages to battlefields and war memorials. Antonio Berti's guides to the eastern Alps[18] and the TCI's above-mentioned guides to battlefields were more than a collection of itineraries through the vestiges of a recent war. They were true handbooks for the political and cultural use of the landscape, a landscape that had been reworked into an inseparable unity of memory and nature. The aim of the TCI, as well as that of several Alpine organisations, was to celebrate heroism and sacrifice, while placing a nationalistic stamp on recently acquired geographical spaces.[19]

What did these patriotic outdoorsmen, these nationalistic Alpinists, find in the mountains? First and foremost, of course, they found what they were looking for. The organised memory of war modelled the spiritual landscape of the beholders as well as the geographical landscapes they beheld. The rethink-

---

16.   Gibelli 1998, pp. 101–02.

17.   One could say that mountains have created and preserved a distinctive war landscape. Of course it is hardly surprising that the traces of the war have survived more easily in high mountains or, more generally, in less frequented places. However, politics have also had a role in preserving those traces. On this subject, see Valente and Dall'Igna 2002.

18.   On Berti's guidebooks, see Isnenghi and Rochat 2000, pp. 499–500; Cuaz 2005, pp. 91–2.

19.   After World War One, Italy obtained territory on its north-eastern borders (Trentino, Venezia Giulia and Istria) from the Austro-Hungarian Empire. On patriotic efforts to make those areas known to Italians, see Gibelli 1998, p. 345.

ing of the war experience, its consolidation in the literary canon of memorial literature, all punctuated by a procession of war memorials, served to guide those pilgrims' quest and gaze.

Broken Column in memory of the sacrifice of the Alpini.

Heroic Mountains

'Life Is Healthy and the War Gentle.'

Hence, however absurd it may seem, the Great War led to a discovery of mountains.[20] And even more absurd, although that discovery occurred in the middle of a bloody war, it essentially used an alienating narrative that spoke of a bucolic landscape. George Mosse has called our attention to German postcards from the war front showing anti-climactic images of bucolic nature in the midst of the conflict. On these postcards, the battlefield was pictured as a field in bloom with a rabbit peeking through the grass.[21] Likewise, descriptions of war in Italian mountains were also immersed in surreal, pastoral scenery that seemed to take the edge off the harsh life of the trenches. In a 1915 report from the frontlines, Mario Mariani, a journalist who was the author of several books on life in the trenches, wrote: 'Oh peaceful townsmen who are discharging your own duty to your country on the scorching sidewalks of your cities, busy with the civil and industrial mobilisation, none of our soldiers envies you. Here [in the mountains] life is healthy and the war gentle.'[22]

Such descriptions, which we might collect under the heading 'bucolic reinvention of mountain war', abound in World War One memoirs. The testimony of Ardengo Soffici, a writer and artist enlisted as a volunteer in the army, is a prime example of this kind of rhetoric. In his journal he unequivocally wrote:

> The trench is idyllic, sometimes. It seems that nature, despite all the efforts of men to make it cooperate with their plans of murder, still wants to give them tangible proof of its indifference, eternal serenity and neutrality; nature reminds them of the unchanging, triumphant beauty and freedom of the world and life. I have noticed some signs of this sublime impassivity of things and brute animals. There are, for example, some blackbirds – blackbirds from peacetime – that every morning and evening are chirping to each other in a pile of stones next to the command of the company ... Likewise a lot of nameless wild flowers, yellow, blue, and violet, continue as if nothing were popping up on the parapets of the line ...[23]

---

20. Of course, the use of the word 'discovery' is disputable here. It is not only true that alpinists from several countries had already 'discovered' the Alps, at least from the eighteenth century on, but we should also remember that smugglers, poachers, herdsmen and mountaineers in general did not need the invention of hiking or climbing to be familiar with *their* mountains. In my use of the word, I mean the encounter between the entire nation and the Alps through the war experience.

21. Mosse 1990, pp. 126–36.

22. Mariani 1915, p. 41.

23. Soffici 1928 [1919], p. 81.

Il 'Dito di Dio' sotto la Terza Tofana (Dolomites). [God's finger under the Terza Tofana].

The military surgeon Angelo Malinverni, nicked in the shoulder by a bullet during the Sleme attack, found time as he fled to notice two spots on the grass, one red, the other white: one was a drop of his own blood, the other a lily: 'picked the lily, looked at it, smelled it. How strange that flower seemed to me in that instant! ... If I had been killed then and there with the flower in my hand, wouldn't that have been an elegant death?'[24]

This bucolic narrative worked well for both novices and old hands of the Alps. For instance, the chaplain Carmine Cortese, who was a priest from the South, described his first meeting with the Alps using exactly this register:

---

24.   Malinverni 1942, reprinted Balbi and Viazzi 2000, p. 90.

Heroic Mountains

Il Corno di Cavento.

Peaks: poetry of the mountain! 1 February 1917, 2,000 and many feet up, perched on the back of a mountain, in the midst of the immaculate veil of this sea of snow, with some black shadow in the valley, produced by trees, buried waist high, black with some points still higher, towards the giant backs ... and peaks, tops, peaks, sharp, slender, lean, squat, plump, hilly; a symphony of white peaks that make you sense the divine ... peaks that seem to speak but melancholy. Peaks that have nothing to do with the land ... but which speak with the sky.[25]

But according to Pietro Jahier, an intellectual who was a volunteer in the Alpini, even for those who were perfectly familiar with the Alps, the war revealed some unexpected faces. Speaking with the conventional paternalistic tone about the privates in his division, Jahier wrote:

Today is the first time they have walked for a stroll, just to enjoy it. They usually go to the mountains for firewood, to build a sled for the hay. But this was the first useless walk, just a poetic walk ... Not even a sack, without a tool or a beast to take care of.[26]

25. Cortese 1998, p. 114.
26. Jahier 1934, p. 61. On Jahier, in English, see Roshwald and Sites 1999, pp. 320–22.

At the Borders of the Fatherland

Naturally, such memoirs were mainly written by a small elite of educated officers who were often volunteers. They were rendering their experience of the war using the only cultural tools at their disposal – that is, the classical high culture of Arcadia[27] and the 'Romantic' culture of weekend hikers and alpinists. It goes without saying that their bucolic discourse about mountain nature had very little to do with the reality of high-altitude war.

The 'elegy of the trenches', which made a violent, unnatural death banal and natural, was one of the filters through which the mountains came to be seen in the post-war period. Despite flowers, chirping birds and snow-capped peaks, death never completely vanished from battle scenes. The reverse of the 'elegy' was heroism, which war memorials transformed from image and discourse into monuments that became a permanent feature of the landscape. Heroism and elegy were closely connected since both arose from the encounter with mountain nature. There was no room for poets or heroes in the trenches down on the plains. The historian Antonio Gibelli has stressed the role of the Alpine war theatre in putting a heroic stamp on the conflict.[28] The pervasiveness of that heroic vision of war in the mountains is borne out by Achille Beltrame's illustrations for the most widely read illustrated weekly of the time, the *Domenica del Corriere* [The Sunday Courier]. As a historian of the Alpine Corps remarked, these drawings seem to show athletic feats and challenges to nature rather than war scenes.[29]

What happened was a shift from the external nature to the internal, from the nature of the Alps to that of the mountaineers. In wartime and post-war mythology, the Alps became the repository of a valuable genetic and environmental heritage which produced a particular type of Italian: the Alpine mountaineer. As I have already shown, it was not the first time that the natural landscape had been regarded as the mirror or even the very substance of the inner landscape, the character of its inhabitants. Ratzel's anthropogeography had been influential, as had been certain discourses on the presumed racial differences between the North and South of Italy.[30] Thus, the post-war nationalisation of the mountain landscape produced at once a new Nature and a new Man (the masculine is, of course, the only genre of this rhetoric) and both epitomised the virtues of a nation that war had regenerated. Rhetoric about Italy's mountain soldiers, the Alpini, played a central role in this reinvention of the landscape. It certainly

---

27.   On this subject, see Scotto di Luzio 1999, pp. 110–11.

28.   Gibelli 1998, pp. 101–02.

29.   Oliva 1985, pp. 108–110. Similar observations in Cuaz 2005, pp. 85–6.

30.   Petraccone 2005.

changed the perception of mountain people as contrasted with city dwellers. The foolish and gullible mountaineer at the mercy of astute townspeople was replaced by the symbol of the healthy simplicity of the mountains; while the unhealthy complications of the city produced neurotic and recalcitrant people, the simplicity of mountain life was seen as virtuous, especially essential in times requiring strict obedience.[31]

Basically, the mountaineers' bowing to the ecological constraints imposed by the Alps was seen as the reflection of their innate inclination to a resigned and conservative acceptance of hierarchies and power relationships. With his lyric prose imbued with religious sentiment Piero Jahier became the champion of that rhetoric; he explicitly counterposed the urban citizens' willingness to change things with the mountaineers' inclination towards adaptation, no matter whether they liked their condition or not:

> [Mountaineers are so disciplined] because the mountain is their master and absolute lord … In cities you go on strike to improve your lot. But it is up to the mountain to improve your lot, if it feels so inclined … [Mountaineers are so acquiescent] because they regard social evils in the same way they regard natural evils … You do not rebel when rocks wipe out your field in an instant or when you arrive with your sled to find that a landslide has swept away your winter stock of wood …Your task is to preserve and repair.[32]

While in the rhetoric of war, the mountains had forged the character of the mountaineers, in the concrete experience of war that perfect symbiosis of human and nature became apparent, as well as useful to the nation. In fact, the Alpini, the main heroes of the Italian martial mythology, relied for their qualities strictly on the terrain on which they fought. They were recruited from mountain villages or from among students and professionals who were CAI members and had learned to love the mountains. The purpose, of course, was to take advantage of these soldiers' knowledge of the terrain, their knowledge of mountain-climbing techniques and their familiarity with life at high altitudes.

> Mountaineers and mountains are one and the same. The land merges with its people. You can easily find a thousand plainsmen who have never paid any attention to the shape of the land or seen a foot of unpaved ground. But the mountaineer has a feeling for the mountains. He has a geographical sense of the area he lives in …. He feels and sees the geographic reality of his homeland.[33]

---

31. On the Italian cultural representation of townspeople vs. peasants, see Bollati 1983, pp. 48–63.

32. Jahier 1934, pp. 121–22, 125.

33. Battisti 1918, pp. 30–31.

The author of this passage is Cesare Battisti, one of the symbols of Italian irredentism,[34] who was hanged by the Austrians in 1916. Battisti was also a geographer and hence ideally suited for the task of politicising the natural landscape and its inhabitants. As the historian Marco Cuaz has recently showed, Battisti contributed decisively to the building of the myth of the Great War as capable of transferring the virtues of the mountains from the materiality of places to the spirit of the mountaineers.[35] The death of Cesare Battisti, who had himself fought as a volunteer in the Alpini, boosted the heroic image of the corps.

It is indubitably true that mountaineers knew the mountains and their dangers better than anyone else. Even officers did not hesitate to turn to valley dwellers for advice about landslide risk before choosing camping sites for troops.[36] But from the perspective of nationalising the mountain landscape, which included its inhabitants as well as its nature, that empirical lore was seen not so much as a social mediation between nature and culture but rather as a mediation between spiritual and material landscapes. In their nationalistic transfiguration, the multiple activities of mountain people[37] were no longer viewed merely as an economic strategy for optimising natural resources and work; they became a metaphor for rural frugality as opposed to urban consumerism. The poverty of mountaineers became a virtue as did their adaptation to ecological adversities; social power and structures disappeared from the scene, while any form of inequality was naturalised especially after the war by the regime's rhetoric. Socially pure and ecologically isolated, mountaineers embodied the virtues of the race in opposition to the vicious melting pot of the cities.

Violated Landscape

Bucolic elegies, hero-mountaineers, war memorials and battlefields – these were the founding pillars of post-war mountain geography and of what the nation's pilgrims saw, not necessarily with their eyes, in what was finally the national landscape. However, along with images and discourses, other things had been settling into the landscape. While the mountains had reconfigured war and above all the soldiers, exalting their courage and determination, the reverse

34. 'Irredentism' was a nationalistic movement aiming to incorporate into Italy the eastern provinces under Austrian control (Venetian, Trentino, Alto Adige, Friuli, Istria, Dalmatia).
35. Cuaz 2005, pp. 83–84.
36. Cognetti De Martiis 2001, p. 256.
37. On pluriactivity in the Italian mountains, see Coppola 1989; Tino 1989; Armiero 2006.

The area of the 5 Torri.

was also true. The mountains could not remain the same after the fury of the conflict had swept over them. The antithesis to bucolic elegies about war in the mountains was the description of deep scars left by the war in the Alpine landscape. In a book published in 1929 one can read:

> War has left conspicuous traces here [in Venetian Tridentina] and the Alpine landscape bears its perturbing stamp: *chevaux de fries* [entanglements], barbed wire, heaps of crushed bags arranged along the edges of trenches and the remains of former Austrian barracks.[38]

The same sort of descriptions can be found of all the Alpine battlefields. 'Everything speaks of death on the Sabotino', wrote the Italian war reporter Luigi Barzini in 1917. According to his descriptions, the Trentino mountains were devastated by trenches, dugouts and explosives, to become a huge ossuary, where even the soil had acquired the red stain of blood.[39] The Marmolada in the Dolomites was depicted as an immense ruin, still carrying the stigmas of war: 'tattered remnants of clothing, shell casings and shrapnel, battered wooden

---

38.   Virgilio 1929, p. 14.
39.   Barzini 1917, pp. 109, 147, 182.

At the Borders of the Fatherland

Ruins on the 5 Torri.

beams, rusted bayonets, stockless rifles, petards, bomb shells, crushed canteens, harpoons, loaders, cartridges'.[40] With more or less the same words, Mario Rigoni Stern, one of Italy's few mountain writers,[41] depicted the landscape that confronted refugees of Asiago upon their return at the end of the war:

> Even the most remote forests bore the signs of war: cut down or uprooted trees, sheds, artillery emplacements with their cannons still pointed towards the Val di Nos and Val d'Assa, ammunition deposits, dugouts, trenches, barbed wire … The smell of iodine tincture, rotted wood and explosives still hung in the air.[42]

The conflict had left deep scars in the Alpine landscape. Immediately after the end of the war, Meuccio Ruini, an Italian politician particularly attentive to mountains and their problems,[43] spoke of the destructive axe that had been

---

40. Virgilio 1929, p. 106.
41. On Mario Rigoni Stern see, in English, Siddel 1998.
42. Rigoni Stern 1994, pp. 553–554.
43. He was among the founders of the Parliamentary Committee 'Amici della Montagna' [Friends of the Mountain] devoted to the promotion of activities in favour of mountains and their people. On Ruini's commitment to mountains, see Gaspari, 1994.

swung against Italian forests, especially after the defeat of Caporetto.[44] The botanist Lino Vaccari estimated that war had robbed Italian forests of at least two million cubic metres of timber.[45] According to statistics from the *Istituto Nazionale di Economia Agraria* [National Institute for Agricultural Economics], the mountains of Vicenza lost 4,680 hectares of forest and over 5,700 hectares were severely damaged.[46] As is usual in such surveys, those figures are approximations; other sources speak of a nationwide loss of 15,000 hectares of forest with 25,000 hectares severely damaged.[47]

While all wars affect forests,[48] the impact of the Great War was especially dramatic, mainly because wood was one of the most essential materials used for military purposes. There would not have been trenches, barracks, telegraph poles or ammunition without the contribution of forests. One could say that the entire front had been built on the roots of trees.[49] Significantly, Colonel William B. Parsons of the US 11th Engineer Corps said that lumber must be considered war munitions.[50] In Britain,[51] France,[52] in the countries occupied by the German Army[53] and in the rest of Europe, World War One had a double impact on forest ecosystems: along the front, it was the fury of the battle that dramatically changed forests,[54] but forests situated far from the front were also deeply affected. For example, Italy's Fontana Forest in the former hunting grounds of the Gonzaga family near Mantova, witnessed intensive logging for the construction of bridges over the Piave River.[55] In the *Altipiano Dei Sette*

---

44. Ruini 1918, p. 34.

45. Vecchio, Piussi, and Armiero 2003, p. 182.

46. Pittoni 1938, p. 141.

47. Gabbrielli 1994, p. 3.

48. McNeill 2004, pp. 388–410.

49. Schubert 1978, p. 180.

50. *Ibid.* p. 181.

51. According to John McNeill, half of Britain's productive forests were felled in three years (1916–1918). See McNeill 2004, pp. 388–410.

52. In France, by the close of operations in May 1919, the American Forestry Troops had produced: 218,211,000 feet of lumber; 3,051,137 standard gauge railroad ties; 954,667 small ties; 1,926,603 miscellaneous round products; 39,065 pieces of piling; 4,669 fagots and fascines; and 534,000 cords of fuel wood. In Clary 1978, p. 184.

53. The best known example is the forest of Bialowieza in Lithuania, 5 per cent of which was cleared by the Germans after the battle of Tannenberg; in Schama 1995, p. 65.

54. The most detailed work on the ecological consequences of World War One on the forests is Corvol and Amat 1994.

55. *Ibid.* p. 162.

Comuni [Seven Towns Plateau] in the province of Vicenza, 35 per cent of the forests were destroyed and fifty per cent seriously damaged.[56]

The Italian forests suffered additional stress because they had to make up for the huge amount of lumber imported by Italy before the war; ironically, many of Italy's forest resources came from the Austro-Hungarian Empire – that is, from the other side of the battlefront. Considering both the higher demand for wood for military purposes and the decrease in imported lumber, Italian forests would have needed to have produced about four times more than they had before the war. It seems to me that looking at the war *as if nature existed* reveals how closely intertwined were ecology, economy, and politics.

The fact that the Great War, like all wars, significantly modified nature is unquestionable and possibly obvious, although it seems less obvious when we look at the ways in which historians have generally dealt with this subject. Still, one might wonder how durable those war scars were. Just how deep did they go? Speaking of battlefields in Flanders, Voltaire remarked that after only a few years nature had already obliterated all traces of the war.[57] Of course, because of the technological potential deployed, the Great War had deeper and longer-lasting effects than previous conflicts. According to Pietro Piussi, a leading Italian forestry expert, in many areas of the Alps for decades after the war, lumber was checked with metal detectors before being processed in sawmills. That precaution was necessitated by frequent accidents caused by dangerous war fragments impregnated in the wood.[58] A similar situation existed in France, where studies on the forests of Lorraine, Marne and Aisne, which French scholars appropriately called *bois mitraillés* [machine-gunned forests], revealed that wood products from those areas were riddled with huge quantities of metals and war materials.[59] In addition, there were the indirect ecological consequences of war, such as infestations of xylophagous insects attracted by the huge amounts of wood damaged in the fighting and impossible to remove. Such was the case in the forests of the Altipiano dei Sette Comuni where 14,000 hectares of forest were infested by scolytid beetles. 300,000 firs were cut down to save the remaining trees and 90,000 more were sacrificed and used as bait to eliminate the infestation.[60] Something similar occurred in the Panaveggio Forest in the Trentino region where a recent study of tree age

---

56. Battisti 1994, p. 65.
57. Quoted in Troyansky 1987, p. 121.
58. Pietro Piussi, e-mail message to the author, 8 March 2007.
59. Bach 1994; Gaudemard 1994 ; Arnould and Simon 1994.
60. Battisti 1994, p. 65.

Italian military cableway, Terza Tofana (Dolomites).

At the Borders of the Fatherland

Landscape of the Marmolada Massif with stairway cut into the rocks by the Italian Alpine Corps.

structure and variations in tree-ring growth has shown a high concentration of disturbances around the time of World War One.[61] Direct military operations were certainly responsible for a large part of those disturbances, but the invasion of the bark beetle *Ips typographus* and subsequent intensive cutting in the immediate post-war years were also a consequence of the war.[62] In these same years, an infestation of tortrix moths was the pretext for razing 300 hectares of forest in the Venetian province[63] while in the Piedmont Alps, the destruction of forests in the Toce, Sesia, Mastellone and Tessera watersheds severely compromised the hydrographical regime of the whole area.[64]

Some of the war's alterations were even more dramatic. On 11 July 1915, Italians set off the most powerful mine of World War One, shaking Mount Tofana like an earthquake tremor.[65] In the case of the south-west cliff of Mount Piccolo Lagazuoi, a series of exploding Austrian mines repositioned an entire rock face during 1916 and 1917. Perhaps the most long-lasting traces, though, were the war machine's array of technological innovations used for coping with the difficulties of the mountain environment. Cableways, mule tracks and carriage roads transported thousands of men to high altitudes and, in many cases, these tools of war are still visible.[66] And wherever soldiers went, the forests shrank further.[67]

The war remodelled the mountains indeed. Those formerly poor, cursed and peripheral areas came to epitomise the Italian identity more than did any of the other geographical features of the country. Alpine war memorials, cemeteries and places made famous by bloody battles became the destinations of pilgrimages, both material and literary. Alpine and tourist organisations such as the CAI and the TCI played a crucial role in consolidating the heritage of memory and in making it accessible.

Even if its political significance has varied, this memory has survived long after the war; it has always been there, embodied in the landscape, as those who frequent the Alps know very well. Its traces, hidden in the soil, have been

---

61.   Motta *et al.* 2006, p. 157.

62.   Motta, Nola, and Piussi 2002, pp. 495–507.

63.   Gabbrielli 1994, p. 4.

64.   *Ibid.* p. 5.

65.   Vidulich and Pasquali 2000, pp. 115, 127.

66.   For example, in his history of the Alpine Mountain Corps, Gianni Oliva mentions the cableways of Mount Adamello and Mount Cavento and the roads running through the Avio Valley; in Oliva 1985, pp. 116–117.

67.   As in the case of the 'Seven Village Plateau' analysed in Vescovi 1994, p. 580.

Lagazuoi.

Detail of the Italian barracks on the Piccolo Lagazuoi.

a danger, a source of raw materials, a treasure for collectors, a tourist attraction and a historical goldmine for researchers. It was only ten years ago that the Italian Parliament passed a new law for the conservation of the historical heritage of World War One (Law 78 – 7 March 2001). Evidently, the existence and even the conservation of memory do not imply its political exploitation but if we want to look further at this issue – that is, at the politicisation of the memory of the war and specifically of its landscape – it is time to move to the fascist era.

~ 4 ~

Dark Mountains

The mountain, taking us away from the grey uniformity of plains, is closest to the stars, in the same way in which the sturdy, wise and quiet mountaineer is closest to the heart of Italy.

Arnaldo Mussolini

Revelations

For those who travel from Rome to Abruzzo the connection between Fascism and landscape becomes suddenly obvious. Passing through the Apennines near the village of Antrodoco, a gigantic DUX materialises on the slope of Mount

Monte Giano.

Dark Mountains

Giano, taking everyone back to a time when Italian mountains and the country as a whole were under a dark shadow. Fortunately for us and for the landscape, the fascist regime did not have the resources to transform Mount Giano or any other mountain into an Italian version of Mount Rushmore, impressing the rocks with Mussolini's strong profile.[1] Nevertheless, they did leave a trace in the soil. In 1938–39 the recruits of the new fascist Forestry Corps [*Milizia Forestale*][2] planted pines on the slopes of Mount Giano, using live trees to write that impressive DUX, more or less still visible today.[3] Actually, as we will see in this chapter, the fascist regime left much more than that word inscribed into the Italian landscape: its politics, rhetoric, and economic policies shaped the nature of the country.

No one could express that concept better than Mussolini himself. Speaking in Reggio Emilia on 26 October 1926, he stated:

> It is imperative that we create; we, people from this epoch and this generation, because we have the duty to make the face of the Fatherland unknowable both spiritually and materially. In ten years, comrades, Italy will be unrecognisable! This is because we will have transformed it, we will have made it new, from the mountains, which we will have covered with a green coat, to the fields, which will be completely reclaimed…[4]

Reforestation, reclamation and also railroads and dams, urban planning and new rural towns, nature conservation and national parks – confronted with such imposing transformations, the tree composition on Mount Giano, that gigantic living DUX written with pines, looks quite a modest encroachment on the landscape. Nevertheless, the Mount Giano case can be used as a metaphor, exemplifying the power of words over nature; as is evident from that slope, rhetoric became the mould in which the landscape was forged. Indeed, on the slope of Mount Giano nature mirrored the words – that is, the narratives – of the regime.

Mount Giano was not the only manifestation of the connections between Fascism and mountains. On 3 November 1929, the inhabitants of Rome were awakened by one of the usual parades marching through the city streets; not surprisingly, it was dedicated to agriculture and the rural world but this time mountaineers were included, among the ranks of peasants. It is hard to say how

---

1. On Mount Rushmore, see Schama 1995.

2. On the creation of the new *National Forest Militia*, see Pavari 1934, pp. 72–74.

3. 'Duce', *Il bosco* 16 (1937), p. 1.

4. Benito Mussolini, *Discorso del 30 ottobre 1926*, Reggio Emilia, available online at http://www.dittatori.it/discorso30ottobre1926.htm

they were recognisable as mountaineers; nevertheless, according to the author of a report on the parade, there they were, bringing a special, unmistakable flavour to the event.[5] Mussolini's famous speech of 26 May 1927 on the rural-ising of fascist Italy was incarnated that day to the people of Rome; then, the countryside flooded into the city but at other times it was the opposite with the countryside being invaded by city people. In the late 1930s, for instance, Romans could find relief from the congestion of urban life on close-by Mount Terminillo – but it was not geography that connected that mountain to the city. According to the fascist narrative, the regime revealed the mountain to the capital, extolling its accessibility and beauty. Along the road from the capital to Mount Terminillo a stone bore the following inscription – 'Mussolini revealed its mountain to Rome'[6] – and this revelation was both discursive and material. While a new road connected the capital to Mount Terminillo, pictures of the Duce skiing on snow-covered slopes were published everywhere, making this mountain part of the fascist narrative. As the president of the Italian Alpine Club wrote in 1937, 'two days spent by Mussolini on Mount Terminillo are more valuable [to the cause of mountains] than one hundred speeches, reams of essays, and crowds of committees'.[7] Actually Mussolini was only pretending to ski since, as we can see in the picture, he carried ski poles but wore no skis.

Was the 'pseudo-skier' Mussolini proof of the fraudulent exploitation of nature in narratives without any concrete basis? Were narratives only de-ceptions to hide the concrete policies of the regime? Mussolini was indeed on the slopes of Mount Terminillo, bare-chested, with ski poles but without skis; in fact, that image contributed to the touristic boom on Mount Terminillo,[8] and in the mountains in general. The appropriation of Mount Terminillo was accomplished through the construction of new roads, hotels, cableways and other infrastructure as well as through narratives that became true even when they were false, as in the case of the 'pseudo-skier' Mussolini.

5.   Pesce 1929, p. 76.
6.   Rinaldi 1937, p. 21.
7.   Manaresi 1937, p. 91.
8.   The Istituto Luce produced several documentaries on the Terminillo touristic boom; see, for instance: 'Il trofeo "Stoppani" per la gara di ski è stato vinto da Battisti dello "Sci club" reatino' 1934- B0408; 'Lo sci sul Terminillo'2/1935-B0622; 'Una gita sul Terminillo' 25/03/1936- B0856; 'Il vice segretario del PNF Morigi e il vice presidente della Società Sportiva Parioli di Roma Vittorio Mussolini inaugurano il rifugio realiz-zato dalla Società Parioli in meno di un mese' 13/01/1937- B1025; 'I campi di neve della montagna di Roma' 10/02/1937- B1041; 'L'inaugurazione di una nuova moderna funivia' 26/01/1938- B1242.

Dark Mountains

Mussolini, the 'pseudo-skier'.

In this chapter I will analyse how fascists appropriated Italian mountains through both rhetorical discourses and concrete policies. Obviously, the relationship between Fascism and mountains was part of a wider narrative on ruralism and nature and there is no doubt that the rhetoric of ruralism and the practices of fascist policies were strikingly contradictory. While the rural narrative praised the racial qualities of rural people, proposing a general return to the land, fascist policies aimed to restrict and control people's activities and movements in the mountains, assuming that they were always harmful to the environment and the nation. As regarded the mountains, fascist policies focused on forest protection, choosing to sacrifice the interests of mountaineers to the 'superior interests' of the nation. Up in the mountains the planting of forests to protect artificial reservoirs, the imposition of taxes to lower the number of goats and of laws to restrict common uses and the militarisation of the strongly repressive forestry corps were the actual face of fascist rural policy.[9]

---

9.   Several of these issues have been addressed in Gaspari 1994.

Revelations

Nevertheless, stressing the gap between rural narratives and concrete policies is insufficient to understand both. Obviously, this interpretation would reinforce the dichotomy between narratives and the environment, while my argument blends them. The fascist discourse on race and the making of the new Italian was steeped in nature, in which mountains played a significant role. From this point of view, narratives and dams, rangers and mountain climbers, goats and discourses about them all left concrete traces in the mountains; mountains for their part left their traces in the fascist narrative. In fascist discourse the centrality of reclamation and improvement exemplifies the mutual constituency of narratives and nature. Nature, as marshes, mountains, drainage, floods and reforestation, was at the core of this narrative but it informed much more than just these features and their transformation. Reclamation was the way in which the fascist regime constructed its narrative about the remaking of the nation; through reclamation, the regime aimed to rescue Italians from a kind of corruption, including malaria[10] and urbanism. Nevertheless, the example of reclamation helps us to see both sides – that is, how much nature filled fascist narratives and how much fascist narratives shaped nature. This discourse on reclamation and improvement was visible in the Italian soil in the exhausting transformation of the Pontine Marshes, as well as in the improvement of mountain pastures and forests. The rhetoric of ruralism became roads and buildings in a network of new country towns created by the regime; the imposition of a new forestry regime manifested itself in the reforestation projects which accompanied a peculiar mix of tree planting and dam building. Nature and narratives under the fascist rule – not so much a contradiction, it was a complex blend.

Tales of Two Landscapes: Damnation and Redemption

In October 1934 the fascist regime celebrated twelve years of its forestry policy with a special exhibition in Bari, dedicated to the memory of Arnaldo Mussolini, Benito's younger brother and, as we will later learn, the guru of forest protecion. Among several objects displayed there, a two-sided model was especially persuasive in illustrating the fascist narrative of nature and its salvation. It reproduced in miniature a mountain valley before and after the intervention of the new Fascist Forestry Military Corps: degraded lands, poor forests and ruined pastures, landslides and wild watercourses on one hand, new woods and improved meadows, forest roads and mule tracks, hydro-geological installations

---

10.   On Fascism and malaria see Snowden 2006, chapter 6.

against slides and floods on the other.[11] Unfortunately that two-sided model did not survive but from descriptions it seems to have dramatically embodied the fascist narrative of landscape as a tale of damnation and redemption. Although basically dedicated to the mountain, that exhibition may be considered a prototype of the general fascist vision of nature, beauty and improvement; it proposed a binary narrative which moved from damnation to redemption through the regime's agency. The celebration of the new fascist landscape was possible only within that binary narrative and, as in every story of redemption, there was no salvation without damnation. Therefore, to understand the fascist narrative of reclamation and improvement, which was at the core of fascist attitudes towards nature, we need to examine the counter-discourse about mountains as disrupted environments in need of rescue.

The image of mountains as ruined environments was not a product of fascist rhetoric: as we have seen in the previous chapters, it emerged from a longstanding cultural tradition that excluded mountains from the realm of beauty and civilisation. During the so-called Liberal Age (1860–1922), the inclusion of mountains in the nation meant the taming of their natural forces as concerned both people and landscape; therefore, the assumption was the wildness of mountains and the need to civilise them. Although grounded in the same negative vision of mountain environment, the fascist narrative shifted from the wildness/orderliness discourse to ruined/reclaimed rhetoric. After the Great War and the celebration of the peasant and, above all, of the mountaineer as the resilient and obedient soldier, it was inopportune to insist on the supposed wild character of these people and their environment: in fascist Italy there was no room for rebellion, even that of nature.

Of People and Trees

The forestry exhibition of 1934 expressed that damnation and redemption vision of mountain landscape. At the core of the damnation narrative there was still the forest; the naked slope represented on one side of the miniature was the perfect location for the two typical plagues of mountains: landslides and floods. As in the past, during the fascist regime forests and deforestation were the major topics in the discourse on mountains and their damnation; due to chronic hydrogeological disorder, the geography and geology of the peninsula imposed the protection of slopes as the crucial issue in the narratives and policies about mountains. In the twenty years of fascist rule, the Italian mountains were

---

11.   Verger 1934, p. 408.

Revelations

Landslide on the Gallico torrent, 1928.

hit by more than 1,000 landslides, with an average of fifty such events every year. In some years, such as 1926 and 1934, the number of landslides totaled about a hundred; if we also consider the 1,200 floods that occurred during the same period, generally connected to poor forest coverage, we can understand the strength of the perception of mountains as a ruining landscape.[12] It was not by accident that in his passionate praise for the protection of forests the leading botanist and conservationist Lino Vaccari described the dramatic floods and slides occurring throughout in Italy in 1926:[13] the inundation of Bari in November had been particularly shocking, leaving twenty people dead and fifty injured, plus 200,000 cubic metres of mud throughout the city.[14]

12. Data from the Sistema Informativo sulle catastrofi idrogeologiche [Information System on hydrogeological catastrophes], available at http://sici.irpi.cnr.it/

13. Vaccari 1932, pp. 3–13.

14. Data at http://sici.irpi.cnr.it/

To common people forests are just storage for wood ... and pasture a tool to get meat and cheese. Probably they do not even suspect that the floods which are destroying their sources of profit began when they took up the axe and overgrazed the pasture.[15]

Published with an introduction by Achille Starace, then secretary of the Fascist Party, Vaccari's book aimed to create an awareness of forests among Italians; as usual, the point of departure was the hydrogeological disorder caused by human deforestation. Therefore, in the fascist narrative the salvation of mountains needed to come to pass through the salvation of trees, as always in Italian history.

There were two key figures in the forestry politics and rhetoric of the regime: Arrigo Serpieri and Arnaldo Mussolini. Serpieri was a well-recognised expert in the field of agricultural economy, rural sociology and forestry; he was both a scholar and a politician, during the regime becoming the architect of the reclamation plan.[16] Arnaldo was, first and foremost, Benito's younger brother; he ran the official party newspaper and after his premature death became the icon of the fascist love for trees and forests, a sort of guru of fascist protectionism. His sayings and speeches about the necessity to protect forests became famous in the fascist 'environmental' narrative. Urban parks, gardens, even single trees have been dedicated to his memory; even today in Italy Arnaldo's name seems to represent the green and therefore more digestible tradition of fascist culture. It was in 1996 that the municipality of Latina, the main city in the reclaimed Pontine Marsh, decided to rededicate its urban park to Arnaldo Mussolini, sparking harsh debate about the real defascistisation of the Italian right-wing party that held power in Latina and was a solid ally of Silvio Berlusconi at the national level.[17]

Although both Serpieri and Arnaldo Mussolini were deeply engaged in the politics of forests and mountains, they followed quite different paths. We can say that the former was more a technician and the latter essentially a touter but the situation was actually more complicated; and I believe their relationships with forests made these differences especially recognisable.

---

15.   Vaccari 1932, p. 16.

16.   The historiography on Arrigo Serpieri is quite extensive; among other works, see D'Antone 1979; Fumian 1979; Stampacchia 2000.

17.   In 1995 the right-wing party Movimento Sociale Italiano, which had been strongly connected to the fascist ideology, had changed its name to Alleanza Nazionale and presented itself as post-fascist. On this, see S. Z. Koff and S. P. Koff 2000, pp. 41–48. The news about the naming of the park after Arnaldo was in all the Italian newspapers; see, for instance, Mauro Maulucci, 'Latina riscopre Mussolini', in *Il Corriere della Sera* 4 December 1996.

Revelations

Arnaldo Mussolini.

Arrigo Serpieri

Serpieri attached his political engagement to scientific activity and had begun both long before fascist rule. After his early research on forests and pastures in the Swiss Alps, in 1910 Serpieri was the main author of a remarkable book on forest conservation as a defence against hydrogeological disruption; the following year he began his political involvement, working on the compilation of a new forestry law; in 1912 Serpieri was appointed director of the National Institute for Forests. Although coming from a reformist background, Serpieri joined the Fascist Party, seeking in it the opportunity to realise his plans for the modernisation of the country.

In 1933, speaking at the national conference on mountains, Serpieri stated:

> For many years I have been depicted as an enemy of forests, even if a bitter twist of fate put me in charge of an institute for forestry. Why was I considered an enemy of forests? Because I believed, and I still do, that we cannot implement in our mountains the same forest policy as France or Germany because our forest policy cannot be disconnected from the integral needs of mountain economy and life. We cannot defend and enlarge our forests, although these measures would be fundamental for their protection, against mountaineers and their lives.[18]

---

18.   Serpieri 1932, p. 5.

I could not find any reference to such an accusation in the sources; perhaps Serpieri was exaggerating and no-one had actually accused him of being an 'enemy of forests'. Nevertheless, this was the way in which he pointed out his special approach to forests. According to Serpieri, the forest problem had to be understood and solved within the larger context of Italian mountains. He rejected as impractical a general and extensive reforestation plan. Italy was not like Germany or France: extremely mountainous and overcrowded, the country needed management of agriculture and grazing on the slopes rather than a general ban on these activities. Extending trees would have jeopardised the very survival of mountaineers who needed to use the resources of mountains; simply conserving them was not their priority. In his scholarly works, Serpieri stressed the opportunity to envision mountains as an organic and coherent environment, criticising narrow approaches that fragmented that unity into fictitious segments.[19] That vision guided his political and scientific activities; in fact, whereas the protection of forests for hydrogeological purposes was a relevant part of Serpieri's legislative actions, and primarily of his forestry law of 1923, it is also true that he worked diligently in integrating mountains into reclamation and improvement plans that went well beyond a tree-based approach. The forest was an excellent defender of mountain stability but good pastures and well maintained farmlands could also offer the same results without placing all the burdens on the shoulders of the mountaineers. Arrigo Serpieri's approach was akin to that of Le Play, in the sense that he refused to separate mountains and people, always sceptical about solving environmental problems by reinforcing repression against local people.[20]

> It is not necessary to oppress the economic life of the mountaineers to protect and extend the forest, if we are able to transform the current, sometimes primitive, even barbaric, forms of agriculture and grazing into rational and more intensive activities; if we are able to discern between the rational cutting of forests and their destruction…[21]

Going beyond speaking only of reforestation, Serpieri stressed the regenerative power of reclamation and improvement; writing in 1928 he argued that the problem of the Italian forests was qualitative and not only quantitative. Yielding two cubic metres of wood per hectare, generally just good for fuel, the Italian forests showed an extremely low rate of productivity, which

---

19. This is very clear in Serpieri 1932, pp. 5–7.
20. Kalaora and Savoye 1986; on the reception of Le Play's theory about forests, see Gaspari 2000.
21. Serpieri 1928, p. 6.

Reforestation of the Taverone basin 1938..

called for improving the quality of trees and not just extending their quantity.[22] It was not by chance that Serpieri strongly supported the activities of the Secretariat for Mountains, which he chaired for sixteen years from 1919 to 1935; according to the Italian historian Oscar Gaspari, the Secretariat was often accused of obstructing the Forestry Military Corps, preferring pastures over forests, grass over trees. As a matter of fact, Serpieri was also quite critical of the repressive attitude of the Forestry Military Corps, always praising the technical side of that institution above its military character.[23] Illustrating the results of the reclamation policy, Serpieri explicitly stated that although the Military Forestry Corps did offer good results, these results were insufficient without all the other provisions necessary to improve the living conditions of the people in the mountains.[24]

---

22. *Ibid.* p. 6.
23. Gaspari 1994, pp. 32–34.
24. Serpieri 1931, p. 320.

Arnaldo Mussolini came from a different background and had a different destiny; in fact, while Sepieri encountered his political decline opposing big landowners who resisted both responsibility for reclamation and the consequent expropriation of their lands, Arnaldo enjoyed greater fame after his death, becoming an icon of rural Fascism. In fascist hagiography, Arnaldo's passion for forests and mountains was depicted as an expression of his exceptional spirituality. In the aftermath of Arnaldo's premature death, Benito wrote a short biography of his brother in which he celebrated his spiritual qualities: his piety, love for trees and nature, humility and compassion.[25] In that biography, Benito included a short poem written by Arnaldo in 1930–31 which expressed his view of nature as a path towards a spiritual dimension in the usual fascist aulic style – trees and plants, the human soul aiming to the heavens and the contemplation of nature freeing the human soul and connecting it with both Earth and people (in Arnaldo's words, 'our suffering brothers').[26] In another commemoration following his death, he was defined as a 'true rural man':

> Arnaldo loves plants, trees, forests with a sort of mystic, although material, passion; this is another proof that in him there was a perfect harmony between soul and mind.[27]

In this case, the author emphasised both sides of Arnaldo's engagement with forests, the poetic and the technical, trying to reconcile these quite different views. Arnaldo was not a scholar in the field of forestry but he had received some training in agronomy, having attended a specialised high school in his native Romagna. However, that did not become his profession; at first he was a town clerk and then began his journalistic career when, in 1922, his more famous brother handed him the reins of the fascist newspaper *Il Popolo d'Italia* [People of Italy]. His engagement with the rural politics of the regime expressed itself in work in the journalistic field, essentially in touting Benito's activities. The Forest Committee, which he was said to have founded in 1928 and chaired until his death in 1931, was basically a propaganda agency dedicated to disseminating what he called 'forest awareness' among Italians. As Arnaldo stated clearly, the Committee was meant to popularise the fascist love for forests embodied in its plans to protect and improve trees, manage watersheds and increase the production of wood.[28]

---

25. Benito Mussolini 1932.
26. *Ibid.* p. 66.
27. Guarnieri 1937, p. 1.
28. Arnaldo Mussolini 1934, p. 76.

Revelations

More than a fascist invention, the Committee represented a fascist version of previous associations and agencies working in the field of forest conservation; the regime amalgamated them into the Committee, erasing any form of freedom and independent activities. The composition of the Forest Committee was contradictory, including not only private and public entities but also agencies with opposing aims, as, for instance, the federation of hydroelectric enterpreneurs, obviously supporting dams and reforestation, and Pro Montibus, a private association dedicated to the protection of nature.[29] That contradiction existed in the Committee as well as in its leader, Arnaldo. In an article written to celebrate Arnaldo after his death, someone tried to present this contradictory approach toward forests in a positive way, as the usual fascist ability to move beyond conflicting interests; hence, the article celebrated Arnaldo's gift of looking at parks, gardens, poplar cultivation, hydroelectric works and tourism altogether, as a coherent system.[30] Several times in his speeches Arnaldo expressed his concerns about being misunderstood as a poet and a nature lover, qualities which evidently had a negative connotation in his rhetoric; during the 1928 national forest day celebration, Arnaldo stated:

> Now, the usual sophists will say: you are a poet, you love forests because you like the beauty of the landscape and you go after your romantic reveries. Lie down. The landscape is important but we will never subordinate the real interests of mountain economy to it. Never. The truth is otherwise. Fifty per cent of our holy and rugged territory is in the mountains, which we need to keep populated because the plains are already overcrowded. We want roads for mountaineers, rich pastures instead of poor grazing lands, good herds of cows instead of destructive goats. We also need to improve the small and medium production of timber, manage logging properly, protect water and soil, control the streams and avoid the ruin of hydroelectric dams ... We need to dedicate ourselves to this battle, which I wish to call the Battle for Mountains, but we are already fighting too many battles.[31]

From this point of view, Arnaldo Mussolini and Arrigo Serpieri shared the same basic assumptions: nature was worth protecting as a matter of national interest, while rhetoric about the beauty of landscape was left for occasional poetic passages in their more inspired speeches. Even on these occasions, beauty was in tamed rather than in wild nature. It was not by chance that Arnaldo Mussolini choose the Po Valley, one of the most anthropic regions of Italy, as

---

29.   Vaccari 1932, p. 377.

30.   'Per la redenzione montana', in *Il Bosco* 1936:11, p. 4.

31.   Arnaldo Mussolini 1934, p. 81.

his example of beauty, stressing the amount of human work embodied in that landscape:

> With deep fondness I have always admired Italy for its monuments, museums, and all the various manifestations of its genius … But above all the works of the land have always attracted my appreciation; in my frequent trips through the peninsula I love to observe the beauty of the Po Valley, its sorted and leveled fields, the rows of vineyards, the wisely pruned trees …[32]

Although in fascist mythology Arnaldo was celebrated as the apostle of trees, these lines testify to his connection with the rhetoric of ruralism, which went beyond discourses on forests. As he made clear, the Italian landscape was beautiful indeed but its beauty relied on the work of humans rather than on that of nature. Even his beloved trees were mentioned in the context of wise human management. The contradiction between preservation and development, ruralism and modernity was inherent in fascist ideology and not just in Arnaldo's vision. Lino Vaccari, already quoted as one of the most famous Italian biologists and environmentalists, closed his volume on forest conservation with this rather confusing paragraph:

> I can see the day when in the dark forest wheels in hundreds of factories will squeak, the whistles of locomotives will echo and beautiful roads, bringing civilisation and richness, will be opened.[33]

Closing a volume dedicated to the protection of forests with this image showed the contradiction between a modernist development religion and a narrative based on love of nature and conservation. Nevertheless, that confusing discourse was the best expression of the reclamation policy of redeeming and improving rather than simply preserving nature.

While Arnaldo Mussolini and Arrigo Serpieri shared this general vision of improvement as the key to relating to nature, they were divided on many other issues. Arnaldo seemed to be much more focused on trees than was Serpieri; obviously, as the president of the Forest Committee he had to concentrate his interest on them. Moreover, Arnaldo and the Committee were basically devoted to a cultural enterprise, aiming to popularise love for trees without being involved in technical or legistative problems, matters at the core of Serpieri's activities. However, the focus on propaganda also implied a vision of the forest question: Arnaldo wanted to protect trees against the negligence of Italians and wanted to teach the people respect for forests and so the result of his efforts had

---

32.   Arnaldo Mussolini 1934, pp. 59–60.
33.   Vaccari 1932, p. 382.

to be reflected in both changing the Italian attitude toward forests and improving the land. Arnaldo did not seem to be particularly confident in the Italian stance towards forests; for that reason, even more than Serpieri, he was always a passionate supporter of the Milizia Forestale, which represented the repressive hand of fascist forestry policy. In 1928 Arnaldo inequivocally said: 'Since we are prejudiced about the spontaneous will of people [to act properly], go ahead with the Milizia Forestale with its discipline and expertise'.[34] I will speak later about the role of the Forestry Military Corps and the search for the guilty, or the scapegoats, in the narrative and practices concerning ruined mountains; but for now it is important to remember that Serpieri had a different attitude towards both repression and mountaineers.

Arnaldo Mussolini and his Forestry Committee became the heart of fascist propaganda on forest protection; therefore, the analysis of their cultural politics is instrumental to an understanding of the environmental discourses of the regime, at least in relation to mountains.

According to Benito, Arnaldo was the creator of the Committee's official publication, *Il Bosco* [The Forest], which, in fact, was a fortnightly magazine enclosed in the Mussolini brothers' newspaper *Il popolo d'Italia* [People of Italy].[35] In its fifteen years, *Il Bosco* was the voice of the Forest Committee, pursuing the main goals of the regime in the forestry field. More than highly specialised articles that were typical of the other Italian forestry magazine, *L'Alpe* [The Alps], *Il Bosco* opted for a simple and popular tone, dedicating much of its space to propagandistic activities sponsored by the Committee and other fascist organisations. The *Festa degli Alberi* [Arbour Day] occupied a central place in the pages of *Il Bosco* as well as in the activities of the Committee. Even if it was the Serpieri Forestry Law of 1923 that established Arbour Day as an official festivity, according to fascist mythology Arnaldo was instrumental in the rebirth of that tradition, started in Italy in 1899 thanks to the Minister of Education Guido Baccelli. The Feste degli Alberi increased in number from 2,516 in 1927–28 to 4,325 in 1929–30;[36] every school was involved in the celebration, which included speeches, parades and the planting of trees. Although fond of symbols and rhetoric, the Forest Committee encouraged celebrations that also had a material content; planting a few trees for the sake of the rite was not enough.

---

34. Arnaldo Mussolini 1934, p. 81.
35. Benito Mussolini had founded *Il Popolo d'Italia* in 1914 to support the Italian intervention in World War One. Later the journal became the official newspaper of the Fascist Party.
36. Vaccari 1932, p. 379.

124

Dark Mountains

In 1937, for instance, *Il Bosco* criticized the Arbour Day celebration in the Venetian region, calling it 'much too symbolic and Petrarchist', expressing the Committee's preference for activities which could actually improve the conditions of mountains.[37] Images from the Istituto Luce documentaries emphasised the mobilisation of masses of people in the celebration, showing men, women and children working on the slopes, digging, tilling and planting.[38] Thousands of people for thousands of trees – the power of numbers, which Mussolini loved, also worked on these occasions. A 1936 Istituto Luce movie spoke of more than 7,000 Arbour Days with two million trees planted. Arnaldo stressed the connections between forest propaganda and schools:

I strongly believe in the effectiveness of school propaganda. The future generations must clearly understand the importance of trees and forests, water and gardens in the national economy. Respecting trees must become a norm...[39]

The fascist organisation of free time was instrumental in the celebration of Arbour Day. Not only school students but also members of fascist youth organisations and workers in leisure associations were involved in the celebrations. In 1936 in Milan, the Railroad Workers Organisation gathered 2,500 people for the screening of three movies produced by the Luce Institute for the Foresty Committee; the three movies worked together as a triptych, illustrating the typical binary narrative of the damnation and redemption of Italian mountains.[40] The first depicted the appalling conditions of mountains, deforested and ruined by streams; the second attempted an explanation of the causes of that situation, presenting a massive forest fire caused by a cigarette butt; in the third the time of redemption came with the celebration of Arbour Day and the planting of trees on the slopes.[41] The message of the Forest Committee was plain and simple: the mountains were in dreadful condition due to the negligence of the Italian people and Fascism was repairing them, regenerating nature and culture together.

Arbour Day offered the perfect example of the fascist narrative blending the remaking of nature and people; in planting trees the regime was also

37. 'Festa nazionale degli alberi', in *Il Bosco* 1937: 9, p. 2.
38. Archivio Istituto Luce: 'La festa degli alberi a Montemorello presso Firenze' 04/1931- A0768; 'Capranica Prenestina. La festa degli alberi'03/1932- A0943; '2500 dopolavoristi milanesi partecipano alla Festa degli Alberi' 23/11/1942- C0299.
39. Arnaldo Mussolini 1934, p. 4.
40. This event is in 'Per la redenzione montana', in *Il Bosco* 1936:11, p. 4.
41. *Ibid.*

sowing the seeds of the new Italian because the act of planting a tree went far beyond a shrewd policy to contol floods, protect slopes and ensure a fuel and wood supply. Fascists loved trees and, as usual in the fascist narrative, Benito embodied the general vision and transformed it into words and images. Along with Mussolini 'the harvester' and 'the pseudo-skier', there was also another image, albeit less popular than the others; it was Mussolini 'the tree seed sower' in a nursery of the Forest Military Corps in the middle of the reclaimed Pontine Marsh.[42] Someone, apparently present at the scene, described that icon, saying, 'His ample, peaceful, and lilting gesture was both simple and solemn; everybody there, perceiving the highest meaning, admired him in religious silence'.[43] The photograph was depicted as a painting, probably to lend it a solemn and hieratic character; in it Mussolini appeared as a secular priest officiating at some kind of religious ceremony. Hence, Benito 'the tree sower' became an icon of fascist love of forests; as Benito scattered those seeds in the land, so was Fascism reforesting Italian mountains. But that icon of Mussolini 'the tree sower' spoke also of the spiritual content of the forestry policies. The tree was an accumulator of meanings that Benito used to celebrate private and public memory. He planted an oak for the birth of his son Romano[44] and launched the idea of celebrating the refoundation of the Empire with what he called Imperial Forests.[45] *Il Bosco* announced that 'following Mussolini's orders, the Minister of Agriculture had asked the Forest Military Corps to implement an extraordinary plan of forestation to celebrate the foundation of the Empire, planting ten million trees on 2,500 hectares of land.'[46] A few months later, the magazine published the results of that campaign: the Milizia Forestale and the Balilla Youth Organisation[47] had already planted Imperial Forests in 532 municipalities, covering about 2,000 hectares. Again Fascism stressed the combination of both the symbolic and material aspects of that rite; the periodical of the Veterans Organisation, which was in charge of the reclamation plan, clearly stated:

---

42. Milizia Forestale 1938, p. 41.
43. Merendi 1935, p. 5.
44. Divisi 1929, p. 129.
45. Cremonesi 1937, p. 17–19.
46. 'Il verde manto di boschi completerà la bellezza imperiale della patria' in *Il Bosco* 1937: 5, p. 1
47. The Opera Nazionale Balilla, founded in 1926, was specifically dedicated to the pre-military training of children; it was named after a boy-hero who threw stones at Austrian soliders. About the Balilla organisation, see Dunnage 2002, pp. 82, 91–92.

Dark Mountains

Mussolini 'the tree seed sower'.

Through pure and meaningful celebrations, from big cities to remote villages, people have been present at the planting of thousands of trees which will remind future generations of our glorious imperial conquests. [Beyond the symbolic value] this celebration shows that our people understand the relevance and necessity of covering mountains and plains with pines, firs, ash trees and chestnuts.[48]

The Forests of Empire followed another patriotic use of trees in the construction of nationalised memory; as we have seen in chapter three, the celebration of fallen soldiers was often embodied in the planting of Memorial Parks, where nature became the monument and medium of remembrance and celebration. In December 1922, immediately after taking power, the fascist government issued an ordinance to regulate the construction of Memorial Parks:

The Ministry [of Education] has ordered that all Italian pupils will realise this noble and merciful idea: create in every city, village and neighbourhood a Me-

---

48. 'I boschi dell'Impero' in *La conquista della terra. Rassegna dell'Opera Nazionale per i Combattenti* Maggio 1937 –xv, n. 5, p. 17.

morial Avenue or Park. For every fallen soldier of the Great War a tree should be planted; the trees will vary on the basis of region, climate and altitude.[49]

Trees for the Empire, trees for the heroes of the war – with forests fascists developed not only policies but politics, using them in their narrative of the nation's redemption. Under the regime, reforesting mountains and protecting existing forests were the duties of the new fascist Milizia Forestale, diffusing the love for trees was the task of the Forest Committee and celebrating the glory of the Fatherland through trees became part of the routine mobilisation of everyday Italians. Everywhere, slogans on walls and in newspapers and other media reminded the population that Mussolini loved trees and would expend every effort to protect them. The sayings of Mussolini declared the fascist love for forests but they also implied that forests had enemies and must be protected.

As the redemption narrative needed its heroes, including Arnaldo and, partially, Serpieri, so the damnation of mountains required villains. The debate about who or what should be blamed for the deforestation and the consequent disruption of Italian mountains became the main issue in scientific and political discourse.

Was the mountaineer the enemy of trees, the villain in the damnation tale? Was the fascist regime forced to choose between trees and people, at least in the mountains? In official discourse Fascism refused to choose between them and stressed the positive role of mountaineers in the new, redeemed environment. In 1929 one of the leading Italian forestry scientists, Giovanni Friedmann, published a defence of the mountaineer, which included a critique of the high bureaucrats in the party, too easily inclined to blame mountaineers for the destruction of the mountains.

> Some days ago I was on a trip with a friend of mine, who is now a big cheese, and who loves mountains ... While we were hiking, my friend discovered the usual truth about deforestation. As long as he confused pines with firs or larches, it was not a big deal – after all, it is just an issue of names; as long as he believed that farmed land gives more profits than forests and pasture, nothing was questionable; as long as he blamed the old destroyers of the mountain who sold the forests for profits to sordid speculators, thank goodness, they are all dead. But when he started judging the mountaineer too severely, then someone needed to say something, because the mountaineer in the same way as, and even more than, his forests is sacred. Once he has left we will not be able to replant him and he will not put down his roots in the mountains again.[50]

---

49. This document is quoted in Agnoloni *et al.* 2008, p. 335.

50. Friedmann 1929, p. 568.

Dark Mountains

Mocking the incompetence of the 'big cheese' from the city, Friedmann defended the mountaineers, who were not, in his view, guilty of the destruction of forests. In the article he juxtaposed the normally opposing elements of forests and people into a new unity; mountaineers became exactly like trees – they could be transplanted, they held to the soil with their roots and they were even more sacred than forests. Advocacy for mountaineers was largely diffused in the fascist discourse about the disruption of Italian mountains. Experts and politicians argued that mountains and mountaineers had to be rescued together without pursuing any kind of forced separation between people and their environment. In 1929 someone wrote in the Italian official forestry journal: 'Save the mountain! This is the cry we must repeat ... But first and foremost we must take care of mountaineers because there is no substitute for them and without them no mountain can be rescued.'[51] In the proceedings of the 1930 Piedmontese conference on mountains a speaker expressed the same idea: the mountaineer was the 'natural keeper' of mountains rather than its enemy.[52] Even in the South, where deforestation and tillage were extremely dramatic, the parable of the good mountaineer endured; according to the chair of the Institute for Agricultural Development in Campobasso, the degradation of the Appenines was the by-product of the large-scale emigration that had abandoned the farmed lands of the slopes without any kind of maintenance.[53]

These were not opinions of isolated scholars; the belief that mountains and mountaineers had to be saved together, overcoming the dichotomy between people and forests, became a mantra in fascist discourse. That was, for instance, the postion of Arrigo Serpieri who always stressed the necessity to mediate between the protection of forests for the hydrogeological equilibrium in the mountains and the needs of mountaineers.[54] In 1928 he wrote:

> For the forest, of course, which is one of the fundamental agents of an organic adjustment of the mountain. A thousand times yes, for the forest but more importantly and realistically for the mountain, whose reclamation is essential for the improvement of physical, economic and moral conditions of our country. For the forest, yes, but also for the mountaineers, in whom all rural virtues are sublime. We must not push them away from their village but should offer them better standards of living so they can continue to love it.[55]

---

51. Mattei 1928, p. 177.
52. Cibrario and Rondelli 1930.
53. Pallotta 1930, pp. 309–10.
54. Serpieri 1932.
55. Serpieri 1928, p. 5.

Serpieri expressed the official orientation of the regime on the subject; as a matter of fact, the Minister of Agriculture declared in 1930 that Fascism solved the mountain problem, substituting the struggle between mountaineer and forest with collaboration and harmony.[56] Obviously, the rhetoric of the regime failed to explain how that shift from struggle to harmony could ever occur.

The problem was that Fascism needed to balance its rural rhetoric with its inclination towards a harsher control over mountaineers' activities. Punishing and praising was the contradictory policy that the regime imposed on the Italian mountains; in public discourses the mountaineer was the hero of ruralism but in the forests and on the slopes he became the villain to control and punish.

Of People and Goats

Let us consider goats, for instance. Among other more famous battles, the fascist regime embraced one against goats. Apparently fascists did not get along with these animals; in fact, other fascist regimes in Mediterranean Europe also shared this Italian idiosyncrasy. In the 1930s, for instance, the Greek dictator Metaxas proclaimed that goats and forests could not coexist, implementing a series of laws and regulations to limit the number of those animals.[57] Mussolini's crusade against goats was extraordinarily powerful though; according to Thirgood, no Mediterranean country experienced a campaign of such intensity.[58] In Italy, goats became the key figures in the damnation narrative about the mountains. They were largely blamed for the destruction of Italian forests and, although there was a debate between defenders and enemies of goats, it is indisputable that the regime conducted a determined campaign against them. First, goats were banned from the so-called protective forests; in other words, if forests were considered crucial for the mountain's hydrogeological equilibrium, no goats were allowed, even to the extent of limiting the free exercise of private property rights. It did not matter whether the forest was public or private – goats had to be driven out of it. Later, the regime intensified its battle against goats, shifting from controlling the allowable space for pasture to cutting the number of animals through a new tax on goats (Royal Decree 16 January 1927). It is difficult to evaluate the real impact of those laws; according to a researcher of the National Insitute of Agricultural Economics, the official statistics underestimated the number of goats generally by fifty per cent, thereby making it

56. Acerbo 1930, p. 5.
57. Petrakis 2006, p. 111.
58. Thirgood 1981, p. 79.

difficult to evaluate the impact of these fascist policies.[59] Italian historian Anna Treves has estimated that the total number of goats decreased from 2.5 million in 1926 to 1.8 million in 1930.[60] The scale of that contraction is even more striking when we analyse it on a micro level. In the Lombardian Val Camonica, for instance, the decrease was from more than 13,000 animals in 1908 to about 5,000 in 1933;[61] in the province of Aquila in the Apennine the number decreased from 350,000 in 1881 to 200,000 in 1930;[62] in the Gran Sasso area the number of goats fell from 30,000 to 10,000;[63] in the Venetian province of Vicenza in 1868 there were 25.8 goats and sheep per square kilometre, in 1930 there were only 6.3.[64]

Although the data are unreliable, the law must have been rather effective because even the fascist union of animal husbandry protested against it, demanding its revision. The union was not alone in the struggle to safeguard the goat. In the 1920s and 1930s national inquiry on mountain depopulation, several researchers criticised the fascist rule against goats, depicting it as one of the main causes of mountaineers' disappearance. Unequivocally, one of the researchers wrote: 'For our mountains the goat is what the camel is for the desert, or what the reindeer is for the arctic regions'.[65] Those who advocated the necessity of finding a compromise between goats and trees stressed the rationality of goats grazing in the Italian mountains, illustrating the economic advantages of that activity: goats were more efficient converters than cows, transforming marginal land into profitable pasture and producing the same amount of milk as a cow but consuming half the forage.[66] Nevertheless, the inquiry on depopulation offered a variety of opinions about goats. Whereas some stressed the positive results of goat grazing, the majority defended the fascist regulation, urging the complete eradication of those animals. According to Guido Ghilardi, a researcher working on the Piedmont Valleys, any precaution adopted for private pastures was obliterated on the commons, therefore generating profitable goats whose profits were net of expenses.[67] Although recognising the high productivity of

59.   Brocca 1934, p. 33.
60.   Treves 1976, p. 122.
61.   Sala 1935, p. 348.
62.   Almagià 1937, p. xiv.
63.   Ortolani 1942, p. 52.
64.   Pittoni 1938, p. 117.
65.   Brocca 1934, p. 44.
66.   Brocca 1934, p. 45.
67.   Ghilardi , p. 459.

Goats. Cover of La Conquista della Terra *September 1937.*

goats, another researcher pointed out that this was possible only because goats were fed from others' lands, making profits without investing anything in the maintenance and improvement of pastures.[68]

Some echo of that battle around goats even reached the fascist press. *Il Bosco* published a series of articles obviously defending the government policy on the subject. The protection of forests, which was the basic mission of the

---

68.   Sala 1935, p. 346.

Committee, came before any other consideration; after the 'chitchat' of liberal governments, Fascism took action, chosing trees instead of goats. The Secretary of the Committee Enrico Brenna wrote in 1937:

> Goat grazing, as it was at the time of the dead and gone regime, has destroyed forests, spoiled mountains, impoverished their inhabitants ... Authorities and demagogues said that they wanted to reconcile the needs of poor people with regulations and the requirements of selviculture. And they have been so successful in this mediation between opposite interests that we all know where they have driven us. The parts were inverted: those who should have obeyed instead ruled and the authority of the government disappeared. Only the fascist regime has the strength to enforce the discipline on goat grazing thanks to its strong will and to the virtues of the Milizia Forestale.[69]

Articles like this did not leave any room for mediation; reforestation was the only way to save the mountains and it was an open alternative to goats.[70] To sustain the fascist policies on goats, *Il Bosco* published letters from owners of forests describing the damage caused by these animals and the results accomplished by the Milizia Forestale.[71] In its campaign against goats, *Il Bosco* used the authority of Arnaldo Mussolini: highlighted in little boxes the journal repeatedly published one of Arnaldo's sayings – 'Goats and reforestation are irreconcilable; the authority of some tribunal must intervene to pass judgement not only of legal separation but of irrevocable divorce.' The debate over goats and their removal was more problematic in the other Italian journal dedicated to forests, *L'Alpe*, which hosted some voices critical of the fascist policies on the subject. In 1929 the journal published a special inquiry on a small southern village, Africo;[72] according to this investigation, fascist policies against goats were worsening local living conditions. In that local environment, largely occupied by mountains and deteriorated forests, goats constituted the most rational use of land; until 1927 more than 2,000 goats were raised in Africo, producing 100–120,000 *lire* yearly from wasteland covered by shrubs.[73] The inflexibility of the facist legislation on goats, which applied the same principles to different local environments, and the Milizia Forestale's extreme severity in its enforcement were the main reasons for the concern of the authors of that inquiry as

---

69. Brenna 1937, p. 1.

70. *Ibid.*

71. 'Le capre', in *Il Bosco* 1937: 6, p. 2.

72. 'Associazione nazionale per gli interessi del Mezzogiorno d'Italia', in *Alpe* 1929: 5.

73. *Ibid.* p. 205.

well as of other opponents in the battle over goats.[74] Several sources stressed the harshness of the Forestry Military Corps on the subject: in Africo during the first nine months of enforcement of the new rules the rangers fined the shepherds 4,000 *lire*.[75] In his famous account of peasant life in a small village in the southern Apennines, the Italian antifascist Carlo Levi wrote:

> The government, it seems, had just discovered that goats were harmful to crops because they had a way of nibbling at growing things and a law had been made covering every town and village in the nation which set a tax on goats equivalent almost to their market value … The goat tax, then, was a catastrophe and because the peasants had no money to pay it there was nothing they could do about it. They could only kill off the goats and that left them without milk and cheese.[76]

Levi was an antifascist exiled by the regime to a remote village in Lucania and therefore not particularly sympathetic to fascist policies; however, on this matter he found extraordinary allies. Arrigo Serpieri, for instance, although directly involved in the making of the fascist forest policy, denounced excessive fervour in the application of anti-goat measures. As the forest fines increased from 30,000 in 1925 to 48,000 in 1928, bearing some relationship to the 1927 law, Serpieri had no doubt that,

> Tragic voices came from the mountains. Entire areas are depopulating, life is dissolving … In these conditions, even the sacred protections of forests, even the war against goats is becoming cruel.[77]

Serpieri linked the battle against goats to the depopulation of the Italian mountains and thus to national security; he was not alone in that observation. The issue of depopulation in mountain regions became crucial in fascist discourse on ruralism. That rural narrative could be used to advocate for goats: the eradication of these animals could result in the technical and economic improvement of the Italian livestock industry but the price would be extremely high in terms of the cultural and racial strength of the nation. It was not the survival of goats but that of mountaineers that was at stake in the Italian mountains. Giovanni Broca wrote:

> To save the forests they take goats away from us, they narrow the pasture, they

---

74. This was also lamented in the INEA report on the Cannobina Valley; in Brocca 1934, pp. 69–70.

75. 'Associazione nazionale per gli interessi del Mezzogiorno d'Italia', in *Alpe* 1929: 5, p. 206.

76. Levi 1947, p. 47.

77. Serpieri 1929, p. 347.

limit the amount of animals, they measure our forests: in other words, they put all the burdens on the mountaineers' back.[78]

Hence, the battle was not really over goats but over people; speaking of animals was just another way to return to the never-ending question of the agency of mountaineers in the making of the ruined mountain landscape. Should the regime have rescued mountains from mountaineers or rather saved mountains through mountaineers? The goats were a pretext by which to address that basic and extremely controversial issue.

Of Fascists and Mountaineers (A Love Story?)

A few months after the enactment of the new tax on goats, in May 1927, Mussolini delivered a speech that can be considered the guiding tenet of the fascist rural narrative. While up in the mountains the new Military Forestry Corps was engaged in widespread repression of mountaineers' activities, including goat grazing, in Parliament Mussolini celebrated the virtues of rural people, calling for a general return to the countryside. He argued that ruralising Italy was the only way to rescue it from what he called a 'demographic decay' caused first and foremost by industrial cities, which, in his words, made 'people infertile'.[79] Italians had to return to the countryside to find the 'power of numbers', becoming a large population ready to conquer its own empire. Mussolini's countryside was first and foremost the reclaimed lands that the regime was conquering plot by plot, fighting with marshes, mosquitoes and floods. Nevertheless, mountains also played a significant role in the discourse about ruralism as the foundation of the nation; actually, they were the only 'natural' place in the fascist rural world, which was, for the most part, anything but natural. If mountains were the Italian wilderness, the discourse on ruralism was the fascist way to appropriate this, making nation out of rocks and soil. In the fascist narrative about mountains, nature and people mirrored each other; mountaineers were strong and reliable due to their direct contact with a still wild nature, or at least what was perceived as a still wild nature, and nature, in spite of its harshness, was beautiful and productive because of human work. Stubborn folk for rough environments – that was the way in which the fascist narrative explained the merging of spiritual and material landscapes in the making of the Italian moun-

---

78. Brocca 1932, p. 82.

79. Similar arguments were also found in Nazi propaganda: see, for instance, the examination of Friedrich Burgdörfer's ideas on urban infertility vs. peasants' fecundity in D'Onofrio 2007, pp. 18–19.

taineers. According to that narrative, while taming nature, Italian mountaineers absorbed its wildness; hence, the external landscape became tidy and civilised but the spiritual landscape, the 'people's soul', preserved the pristine power of the unbounded nature of mountains. As we have seen, the Great War offered incredibly rich images and discourses on the heroic mountaineer as the by-product of the Alpine environment; and, in fact, fascist rhetoric referred largely to the bellicose virtues of mountain people as a genetic/cultural heritage that had to be preserved for the sake of the nation. Speaking to the Alpine soldiers, Mussolini himself outlined the issue in these terms:

> Be proud of your mountains, love the life of our mountains, do not be seduced by the so-called big cities, where men live crammed in boxes of stone and cement, without air, light and space and often in poverty; be proud of your large and robust offspring because gloomy would be the day on which the race of the vigorous Alpine came to an end.[80]

Fear for the Alpine soldiers' possible extinction and the celebration of mountaineers' contribution to the cause of the nation were the *leitmotivs* of that rural discourse about mountains and people. The extensive 1930s inquiry on the depopulation of mountains represented the most visible expression of this anxiety and it was widespread everywhere in fascist rhetoric. A high ranking official in the Italian Army estimated that the number of mountaineers enrolled in the Alpine Corps had decreased by an average of forty to fifty per cent, as high as eighty to ninety per cent of total soldiers in some battalions.[81] In 1938, a year before the outbreak of World War Two, the president of the Italian Alpine Club lamented the disappearance of 200,000 mountaineers, dreading the possibility of a huge depletion of the Alpine Corps.[82] But what was special about mountaineers and what was the link between their unique qualities and the natural environment? Briefly, the basic idea of that bellicose version of the rural rhetoric was that, in bonding with 'nature', mountain people were physically and morally stronger than those from the city. The power of mountains in shaping the characters of their inhabitants was not a fascist invention though; we have seen, for instance, that the narrative about the southern rebels of the 1860s–70s was tied to the Apennines, proposing a direct correlation between the wildness of places and that of humans. Nevertheless, whereas a longstanding tradition from Rousseau and Romantic literature stressed the agency of mountains in

---

80. Serpieri 1932, p. 7.
81. Etna 1930, p. 36.
82. Manaresi 1938.

making people free and rebellious, the fascist rural discourse domesticated that vision: mountains, as the symbolic place of wilderness, shifted from the kingdom of freedom to that of obedience, transforming the insubordinate mountaineers into obedient rural folk, ready to become alpine soldiers.[83] The mountain became the factory of that kind of man and the masculine was the only proper gender for the narrative; in 1938, opening an exhibition dedicated to mountains, the president of the Italian Alpine Club stated:

> A strong race of mountaineers lives and works in the shadow of deep valleys, surviving with incredible effort; people made for war and children, for work and battle, people always ready for the harshest tasks the Nation asks them to perform.[84]

These arguments were quite common in the fascist narrative connecting natural landscape and the nation's soul. As a researcher for the national inquiry on depopulation wrote, the Alps transmitted fierceness, obedience and deference to authority to mountaineers, making them a 'noble progeny of shepherds, soldiers, workers and fighters'.[85] In the fascist narrative, places and people merged; as the Alps had always been the geographical defence of the nation,[86] so had their inhabitants also been the natural guardians of its borders.[87] Therefore, defending mountains and mountaineers meant defending the Fatherland along its borders; this was, using Arrigo Serpieri's words, an 'authentic fascist enterprise'.[88] Praising the necessity to protect mountains and mountaineers, a textbook produced by the Italian Alpine Club with the Ministries of Culture and War – such an eloquent cooperation – incisively stated: 'When the resistance has been defeated up in the mountains, Imperial Rome will have been carried away'.[89] Fascist discourse dramatically exploited the Great War rhetoric of Alpine soldiers as the nation's protectors; as we have seen, the regime systematised the celebration of memory and mourning, building an extensive network of war memorials in the Alpine battlefields and, above all, concentrating the political

---

83. On this rhetoric, see Armiero 2010.
84. Manaresi 1938, p. 190.
85. Pittoni 1938, p. 168.
86. The president of the Italian Alpine Club wrote: 'The mountain is first and foremost the defence of the Fatherland. It defends the Fatherland with its rocks and men'; in Manaresi 1938, p.10.
87. Cibrario and Rondelli 1930, p. 13.
88. Serpieri 1932, p. 7.
89. *Manuale della montagna* (Roma: Ulpiano, 1939), p. xiv.

decisions about that issue in the hands of government;[90] finally, the regime advanced the popularity of the *Alpini* by using them in its propaganda, as, for instance, in parades and military documentaries.[91]

Rallies and movies brought mountains and their 'keepers' into the heart of Italian cities. The rallies embodied the politicisation of mountains through the celebration of mountaineers as both alpine soldiers and genuine rural folks; the overwhelming 1929 gathering of Alpini in Rome, together with Mussolini's speech at the Colisseum, was the prototype of the appropriation and rearrangement of the Alpine myth. While in rallies mountains were present merely through the evocation of words and memories, documentaries offered viewers sitting comfortably in a city theatre an extraordinary opportunity to meet the Alps and their soldiers. These documentaries emphasised both the extremes of natural environments and the ability of soldiers to cope with them. It is difficult to say whether one was more impressed by the immense expanses of snow or by the swift skiers who, armed to the teeth, were traversing them;[92] the same could be said about the vertical walls climbed by soldiers carrying heavy pieces of artillery.[93] At the end of the 1930s the Ministry of War and the Luce Institute released a documentary entitled 'On the Fatherland's Sacred Borders'; for the first time in the history of the Italian army about 200 men were involved in a massive military exercise covering about 200 km and reaching 3,400 metres up the mountains.[94] Italians discovered the beauty of the 'sacred borders' of the nation through the military celebration of the soldiers dedicated to their protection; it was a wild beauty, possibly even frightening, for the spectator who both witnessed the spectacle of wildness and learnt that the regime knew how to tame it. The Alps were the borders of the nation in a double sense: of course they were the natural barrier protecting Italy from outsiders but they were also a frontier in a more Turnerian sense, representing the space of wild nature, where the new, strong, fascist Italian was being created by exercise and the environment.

---

90. Dogliani 2008, p. 98.
91. Archivio Istituto Luce, 'Esercitazioni Alpini sui monti coperti di neve', 1934-B0401; 'Alpini a Roma', 22/4/1937-B1080; 'Esercitazioni Cervino', 1938-B1254; 'Sondrio Pizzo Plaù. Simulazione militare', 08/09/1939-B1571; 'Scuola Militare Duca d'Abruzzo', 9/8/1939-B1560; 'Alpi Giulie, Batteria Conegliano', 9/8/1939-B1561; 'Strada per il Museo degli Alpini', 29/11/1940-C0096; 'Scuola Rocciatori', 31/4/41-Co114.
92. *Ibid*. And especially 'Esercitazioni al Cervino', 1938, B1254 and 'Esercitazioni alpini sui monti coperti di neve', 1934, B0401.
93. Archivio Istituto Luce, Alpi Giulie – Batteria Conegliano, 9 August 1939, B1561.
94. Archivio Istituto Luce, 'Ai sacri confini della Patria', n.d., no reference number.

Fascism also changed the core of the traditional Alpine corps' rhetoric. It shifted progressively from a defensive narrative, which represented armed mountaineers protecting their valleys against the enemy, to an aggressive one that celebrated brave mountaineers building the empire in far away lands. In the fascist discourse, mountaineers had the appropriate qualities to 'overcome the various difficulties offered by the colonisation of wild lands; they had the spirit of enterprise and mastery and ingenuity in realising goals and prevailing over any kind of obstacle'.[95]

Hence, in that discourse about mountaineers as raw material for Alpine soldiers there was something more than just an appreciation of their skills in coping with altitude; mountains produced excellent warriors because they preserved the pure stock of the Italian race, whatever it was. As the Italian historian Silvio Lanaro put it, the fascist rural narrative was an identity discourse that soon became a racist discourse.[96] Quoting Benito Mussolini, Giuseppe Tassinari, agronomist and Minister of Agriculture, wrote in 1940: 'Land and race are inextricably bound; it is through the land that we make the history of our race; the race rules, develops and fertilises the land.'[97] Tassinari included this quotation in his celebration of the fascist reclamation policy, which seemed the perfect manifestation of the mutual constituency of land and people. Nevertheless, the racialisation of the rural narrative also contained a contradictory relationship between wild/tamed nature and the Italian peasant; mountains, more than any other place, were the perfect spot for this relationship to become visible. If it is true that the natural environment produced the sturdy mountaineer, rising from rocks and glaciers, the necessity to master such powerful nature made that genesis possible. In other words, dealing with wild nature, either taming it or simply living within its limits, transformed mountain folks into the prototype of the pure Italian stock. Daunting farmed terraces and untamable winter storms may be considered the two sides of a mountain face, and for the fascists both represented the national landscape, embodying the soul of the people. From this point of view, fascists did not differ from the Nazis: as David Blackbourn puts it, according to the Nazis, it was the 'racial energy' of the German people that created the 'harmonious picture of farm, town and garden, settlement, field and landscape' characteristic of their homeland. That narrative racialised landscapes, counterposing the beauty of the German environment against the Eastern European landscape, described as empty, wild and abandoned, the

---

95.   Gortani and Pittoni 1938, p. 536.

96.   Lanaro 1991, p. 964.

97.   Tassinari 1940, p. 193.

Ruralism. Cover of La Conquista della Terra. *December 1937.*

result of the racial inferiority of its inhabitants.[98] Recently Thomas Lekan has recalled Ernest Rudorff's arguments about landscape as the by-product of a secular interaction between a 'people defined as a spiritual community and its natural surroundings'.[99]

In *Il Bosco* the relationship between race and nature was clearly expressed in several articles. In one of them, revealingly entitled 'Race and Mountain', we read:

> The Italic race, the most authentic Italic race [is] the race of the strong alpine people. These are the people from the mountains, the closest to the heart of Italy from which they sustain themselves. As a matter of fact it is up in the mountains that this pure race of labourers, shepherds, farmers has been able to preserve itself pure and authentic, isolated from the rest of the world ... It is up there that hybridisation has hardly ever occurred, while instead the defence of integrity has been tenacious.[100]

Stressing the connection between internal and external nature, spiritual and material landscapes, Fascism built its own 'blood and soil' narrative in which the racial quality of people was embedded in the national landscape, a result of both natural and racial/historical forces.[101] In a basic textbook on the supremacy of the Italian race, one could read: 'the natural environment is, without discussion, an extraordinary producer of men, affecting both individuals and the collective'.[102] Prof. Eduardo Zavattari, one of the most authoritative proponents of Italian racism, expressed the same argument in an article on 'Natural Environment and Racial Characteristics,' published in the fascist journal *La difesa della razza* [The Defence of the Race]. According to Zavattari, the variety of the Italian landscape impressed its vigour and strength on the Italian race, producing 'the pure Italian, steely and sturdy as mountains, obstinate and brave as peaks rising to the sky'. As he put it, biological and spiritual characteristics moved

---

98. Blackbourn 2006, p. 253.

99. Lekan 2005, p. 82.

100. 'La razza e la montagna', *Il Bosco* 1938: 14, p.1.

101. Although we are focusing on the connections linking race, nature and ruralism, nevertheless environmental determinism was just one among several schools in the racist discourse of Fascism; for a comprehensive history, see Gillette 2002.

102. Marro 1940, p. 36. On the relevance of this book and its author in the making of Italian racism, see Gillette 2002, pp. 114–5.

from the natural environment to the Italian race, forcing land and people into one narrative.[103]

Mountain landscape occupied a special place in that discourse; mountains were the repository of both genetic and cultural resources which Fascism aimed to protect and revitalise. In a basic text on fascist politics and narratives about mountains, the agronomist Carlo Remondino wrote:

> The mountain is well-known to climbers for their ascensions, to sportsmen for their exercises and competitions, to natural scientists for their studies … but it is not fully recognised as an immense repository of ethnic energies ready to be employed for the physical, economic and moral life of the country.[104]

Indeed the mountaineer was the perfect prototype of the new Italian the regime wanted to create. First, mountaineers were prolific, a quality essential in the fascist rural vision. The 'demographic battle' was launched by Mussolini with his famous speech in May 1927 and later reinforced in his preface to the Italian translation of Richard Korherr's book *Regresso delle nascite: morte dei popoli* [Decline of Birth: Death of Peoples].[105] Analysing what he defined as the demographic decline of Italy, Mussolini stressed the divergent performances of city and countryside; in his images, while the former was sick and infertile, the later still preserved the vitality of the Italian race. Bologna, for instance, cited as a negative case of urban demographic decay, was able to increase its population thanks only to the rural folks moving from the plains and the Apennines to the city.[106] According to some data furnished by *Il Bosco*, in rural villages where the large majority of people worked as farmers the birth rate was eight points higher than the national average.[107] In Piedmont, one of the more mountainous regions of Italy, the birth rate was 0.2 per cent in the urban areas and 0.6 per cent in the mountain valleys.[108] Therefore, the depopulation of mountains was not the result of a demographic decline but rather of an unbalanced relationship between mountains and cities. To save the mountains, and with them the nation, Fascism needed to deal with that relationship, changing it in both its material and discursive reality. If there was anything that fascists were really good at,

---

103. Zavattari 1938 quoted from the anthology *Eia, eia, eia alalà. La stampa italiana sotto il fascismo 1919-1943*, ed. Oreste Del Buono (Milano: Feltrinelli, 1971), pp. 347–8. On Zavattari's environmental determinism in racial matters, see pp. 84–85.

104. Remondino, p. 52.

105. Korherr 1928.

106. Mussolini 1928, p. 100.

107. 'La razza e la montagna', in *Il Bosco* 1938: 14, p. 1

108. Manaresi 1938, p. 413.

it was repressing; hence, repression was the principal tool used to change the unbalanced relationship between mountains and city. With two laws, one issued in December 1928 and the other in July 1939, the regime aimed to freeze the flow of rural people from the countryside to the city, making the movement of people towards urban areas extremely difficult.[109] Bernardo Viola, the hero of Ignazio Silone's novel *Fontamara*, an epic account of a mountain village under fascist rule, had to lie in order to travel from his rural community to Rome: 'if the soldiers stop you – the *patrone* told him – just say that you are going to Rome for a pilgrimage or to visit a relative dying in the hospital'.[110] Fascism transformed the Italian mountains into an enormous ghetto, closing all avenues to emigration; mountaineers became a reserve army of workers for both internal and external colonisation.[111]

The fascist repressive attitude towards mountaineers did not relate just to those who wished to move but also to those who remained. The Milizia Forestale was the expression of that policy. Born in May 1926, it arose from the militarisation of the former Forestry Corps by the inclusion in its ranks of a large number of Blackshirt activists. The Milizia had a strongly military character, as demonstrated by training given to its members. A 1938 Luce documentary showed the practical training of the Milizia basically as a military drill: in the film the rangers seemed to attack a forest rather than protect it, firing among the trees.[112] That bellicose character was also stressed in every meeting with Mussolini; another Luce Institute film depicted rangers singing their war songs to Mussolini,[113] while on another occasion they climbed some trees and saluted the Duce with their machine guns. The imperial adventure completed the militarisation process; the Milizia Forestale participated in the war effort, organising the exploitation of African and Albanian forests for the needs of the Italian Army[114] and even fighting on the ground, as in the Ogaden Battle which opened the way to the fascist invasion of Ethiopia. *Il Bosco* celebrated the participation of the Forest Military Corps in the imperial war:

---

109. Dogliani 1999, p. 216.

110. Silone 1967, p. 205.

111. Sori 1973, p. 286.

112. Archivio Istituto Luce, 'Le esercitazioni annuali della Milizia Forestale', 31/08/1938, B 1366.

113. Archivio Istituto Luce, 'Viaggio del Duce in Piemonte', Maggio 1939.

114. Archivio Istituto Luce, 'Milizia Forestale in Albania', n.d., n.n.

Carabinieri[115] and Forestali had met each other in their daily service in the rugged Alps or in the rocky Apennines, the former protecting the public security, the latter defending the forests, and they had fraternised immediately … Both rural people, they had received from nature the simplicity of customs and the tenacity of will which is proper only for those who were used to dealing with the harshness of nature before they learnt to deal with the hidden dangers of humans.[116]

In the 1937 forest exhibition dedicated to the memory of Arnaldo Mussolini, the Forest Military Corps occupied one pavilion to celebrate its contribution to the conquest of the Empire.[117] Just to be sure that there was no misunderstanding about the martial and warlike character of the Milizia, a volume dedicated to its activities opened with two pictures: the first portrayed rangers in the Ethiopian Valley of Death, and the second a soldier of the Milizia working at a heavy gun machine.[118] However, the Empire was not the primary location where that warlike attitude was supposed to be employed; rather it was in the Italian mountains that the Milizia Forestale flexed its muscle in dealing with the celebrated rural people. The data about the exponential increase of fines following the creation of the Milizia speaks for itself: while in 1925 the former Forestry Agency issued 30,000 fines, collecting 810,000 *lire*, in 1928 the new Forest Military Corps issued 68,000 fines, with revenues reaching about four million *lire*.[119] These figures are obviously questionable, as were most data released by the fascist agencies that aimed to demonstrate the success of the regime against previous governments; in addition, the very nature of the totalitarian state prevented any democratic control over those figures. Nevertheless, it is not central to my argument to ascertain how many fines were actually issued and paid; rather what is truly striking is that the supreme chief of the Milizia decided to emphasise this aspect, confirming the centrality of repression in the Milizia's activities. Evidently these actions satisfied the regime and were being repeated in the forests, on the slopes of mountains. The Milizia Forestale was fighting a daily war, which had its victims too. *L'Alpe* magazine reported a number of rangers killed or seriously injured while on duty; in 1931 two rangers were killed, one in the famous pine forest of Ravenna and the other in a forest

---

115. The *Carabinieri* are the national gendarmerie of Italy, policing both the military and civilian populations.
116. 'La colonna Agostini nella battaglia dell'Ogaden' in *Il Bosco* 1936: 20, p. 2.
117. Domenichelli 1937, p. 380.
118. Milizia forestale dal v al xv anno 1938, Bergamo: Officine dell'Ist. It. d'arti grafiche.
119. Data from Agostini 1928, p. 201.

close to Lauria in Lucania.[120] In a forest near Brescia a poacher attacked and seriously injured a ranger[121] while in 1935 a wood thief killed a ranger with an axe in a forest close to Udine.[122] The sequence would continue, repeating more or less the same sorts of episodes. *L'Alpe* did not give any information about the other side of the story – that is, the violence exerted by the Milizia against the local people – but it must have existed. Even a supporter of rangers could not avoid speaking about a war fought in the Italian forests:

> Ranger fighting with poacher is typical of the dull guerrilla war in which every day stewards struggle against criminals … and more than one ranger is killed while on duty, often slaughtered in an ambush.[123]

Making Mountaineers

The prohibition of movement was the fascist repressive strategy to 'save' the mountaineers: without freedom to leave they remained stuck in their environment, preserving the genetic and cultural heritage they embodied for the sake of the nation. But apart from preserving that legacy, would it have been possible to create mountaineers, or at least to hybridise the main stock of the population with the kind of qualities emanating from the mountains? Here we find another contradiction in the fascist narrative about mountains and people: the fascist regime did not aim only to preserve a kind of pure Italian stock, likely to be found in remote mountains; it also wanted to create the new Italian, blending old traditions and fresh fascist virtues. Therefore, whereas Fascism closed mountains to emigration, it opened them to a different kind of movement, exactly the opposite – immigration from cities to mountains. In the narrative this was the visionary rural plan, implying the relocation of large portions of the Italian people into the countryside. Quoting Mussolini's call to leave the cities if possible, *Il Bosco* proposed:

> Why shouldn't we start to transfer people from cities towards mountains which are full of attractions, adapted to a healthy and simple life, where the cost of living is much cheaper because the local products are available from the back yard.[124]

---

120. 'Notizie ed echi', in *L'Alpe* 1931: 4.
121. Tegani 1931.
122. 'Notize ed echi', in *L'Alpe* 1935: 1.
123. Tegani 1931, p. 464.
124. 'Sfollamenti', in *Il Bosco* 1938: 6, p. 1

Revelations

The celebration of mountains succeeded only by condemning cities. We have already considered Mussolini's accusation against industrial cities, blamed for the demographic decay of the country. In the fascist rural narrative, mountaineers were more prolific than urban people not for social or economic reasons but because their entire system of values was radically different. To put it simply, generous and thrifty mountaineers preserved a patriarchal family structure with women entirely devoted to reproduction; on the contrary, the inhabitants of cities were depicted as egoistic and neurotic, completely addicted to their commodities and comforts.[125] This dual rhetoric of rural vs. urban people was the central issue of a particular fascist movement called '*Strapaese*', which can be translated as 'Super-Village'.[126] Strapaese supporters, the savages, as they called themselves, were convinced that the secret of the Italian race was its *paesanismo*, that is, its profound rootedness in rural villages.[127] No fascist text or speech could better express the contrast between mountain and city than this short parable published by the founder of Strapaese, Mino Maccari:

The great chief: what in the hell is that white and smoky rubbish over there on the plains?

One of the *Ras* [fascist local leaders]: that is a city, O powerful chief. There are hundreds of factories, schools, universities, offices, clubs, public gardens, artificial lakes, monuments made of cement, toilets, hospitals...

The great chief: I see. Raze it immediately. Flood it with wildmen, pillage it, ravage it. I want the biggest remains of that city to be contained in one of my fists! And over there, among those dark live oaks and those soft pillows of olives, what is that little red and grey spot?

That is a godforsaken place, an old village far away from the rest of the world, without roads, railroads, schools. There is just an old, half-destroyed church with a blind priest; there is also an inn smelling of salami and prosciutto with some ramshackle benches but with a healthy, smiling young lady serving a powerful wine. In those little houses miners, shepherds, and woodsmen live. Their women have black eyes, large hips and large breasts due to maternity. Around the village, woods and wild boars proliferate ...

The great chief: Stop here. Honour to the wild village. Listen to me my fellows. Take our flags up there and build the capital city of our empire; no one should even try to civilise this sacred temple of power, health, and love![128]

---

125. Marescalchi 1938, pp. 3–4; Pavari 1930, p. 568.

126. Ben Ghiat 2001, p. 26.

127. Fottivento 1927, p. 44.

128. Maccari 1926, p. 4.

Dark Mountains

This dialogue between the great chief and the local leader is emblematic; it says that only the village, which seems to be a mountain village with forest, wild boars and woodsmen, preserves the genuine soul of the nation. And the soul is embodied in nature as well as in social memory: live oaks, wild boars, an ancient church and, of course, the bodies of women used to express the exuberant fertility of the race. Following Mussolini's thesis about the infertility of the urban environment, Strapaese supporters proposed a sort of sensual link between rural nature and rural people; in the pages of their magazine were frequent references to the lively sexual life of the Super Village folk, compared with that of urban dwellers. While in the marshes nature entered the bodies through malaria, in the wild version of the rural world sexual life was the contact point between internal and external nature: on one hand, women's voluptuous bodies symbolised the power of nature over these people; on the other, we should not confound what was seen as a natural 'function' of women – that is, reproduction – with some kind of sexual freedom. Strapaese was a place for large families and fertile mothers; the sensuality emanating from rural nature was confined to those subjects. Strapaese supporters were the fundamentalists of the rural rhetoric; they envisioned the redeeming of Italian urban people only in terms of a radical palingenesis, criticising any middle ground or shortcut to a reconnection with rural roots. Going to the countryside on holiday was not an option for them.[129]

However, Strapaese never became mainstream in the fascist narrative. In fact, apart from his drastic calls to leave the city, Mussolini's discourse was more oriented to a compromise between rural and urban environment in the making of the new Italian. Mountains were particularly suited for that middle ground narrative inasmuch as they were, of course, the homeland of 'native'

---

129. 'When we are in September, the good burghers recall that there is countryside somewhere and that they must go there, because is good for the health. After the beach, these [city people] need to escape to the countryside. Two more things to be included in the family budget between the costs for the theatre and those for the cod liver oil … and the salts of Montecatini; two essential accessories for the perfect functioning of the family. With those attitudes and intentions, in September half the world seizes the country by storm, reducing it to the usual clichés and taming it to its purposes and calculations. The countryside, this immense power of the earth … shall submit its corners and its hills and its most beautiful nests to noisy, petulant and demanding people. They are a breed of intruders and exploiters! What do they know of country life, of that world that has nothing in common with their own world? Only the peasants from the plains and the mountains understand forests, turf, trees, lawns, crops and animals'; Fottivento 1928.

mountaineers and they were also the open-air gymasium and sanctuary where generations of climbers and excursionists were moulded both in body and soul. Giovanni Marro, an Italian racist scientist, defined the Alps as the place where the 'grandeur of our people' was shaped.[130] In the fascist narrative, there were not only mountaineers by birth but also those by choice and will. While in rural discourse fascists stressed the natural strength of mountaineers as if it emerged from rocks, in their propaganda they preferred to insist on the creation of an alpine stock arising from their institutions and policies. By 1934 a new military school of mountaineering, based in Aosta, formed the elite of the Italian alpine corps; selected by military physicians, pupils were supposed to learn the theory and practice of mountain climbing and fighting.[131] Training had always been part of the military experience but in this case it acquired wider significance:[132] the regime was able to generate its mountaineers, demonstrating sufficient spiritual and material resources to create the new Italian. One might say that military training in the Alps was dedicated to the making of good soldiers rather than to the making of new Italians from a delicate relationship of nature, culture and the regime's will. But we need to remember that Fascism permeated Italian society with military forms and practices; therefore, making good soldiers and fascist Italians was basically the same. This was also true in the case of mountaineers. Fascism developed a series of programmes to drive people into the mountains as part of its general biopolitics aiming to shape the body and soul of the Italian people. The picture of the bare-chested 'pseudo-skier' Mussolini on Terminillo Mount was a clear message, regardless of his skiing ability; mountain passion had to enter into the canon of the perfect Fascist. That picture spoke of health and virility, exactly what Fascism sought to deliver to the Italian people through mountain activities. In 1934 the meeting of the Directorate of the Fascist Party was held in Sestrieres in the Susa Valley and an official comunication informed its members that they should bring complete ski equipment;[133] evidently they had to provide an example to the Italian people,

---

130. Marro 1940, p. 293. On Giovanni Marro see Gillette 2002, pp. 111–126, 136–183.

131. Archivio Istituto Luce, 'Scuola Militare Duca d'Abruzzo', 9 August 1939, B1560.

132. Among several other documentaries on military training in the Alps, see Archivio Istituto Luce, 'Fiamme Verdi', 1939, without a reference number; 'Esercitazioni sul Cervino', 1938, B1254; 'Alpi Giulie Batteria Conegliano', 9 August 1939, B1561; 'Esercitazioni alpini sui monti coperti di neve', 1934, B0401.

133. Recarli 2004, p. 137.

although not necessarily showing any particular skill – after all, the secretary of the party had broken his leg skiing in Sestrieres.[134]

Starting with the children, the regime pushed Italians to the mountains to become stronger and healthier. The fascist organisations, which regimented a large part of the population from childhood, sent thousands of young Italians to the mountains and the sea on vacation. According to the Italian historian Patrizia Dogliani, the summer camps grew from about a hundred in 1926 to 3,000 in the mid-1930s, while the number of children involved in the programmes increased from 100,000 to half a million.[135] Of course only some of these summer camps were in the mountains; precisely 280 out of the 3,000 were defined as mountain camps, although there were an additional 330 river camps, some of which may have also been in the mountains. Fresh air, exercise and good food were the main ingredients of the tonic administered in the camps, together with a massive injection of discipline, indoctrination and martial culture. The films of the Luce Institute dedicated to summer camps showed children marching through the fields, doing physical exercises on the grass or, for those in need of an extra dose of discipline, peeling potatoes.[136] Summer camps were basically focused on the physical improvement of the Italian stock, somehow implying the countryside vs. city dichotomy I have already discussed. Weak and wan upon their arrival, Italian children returned from summer camp totally regenerated; the mountain cured what the city had made sick. Describing the young guests of its Alpine village, the Italian Touristic Association stated:

> Wan faces, emaciated lips, skinny and fragile bodies: everything revealed the impairment of these children, while it was impossible to find a smile, the divine gift of childhood, on their faces. The majority of these little ones came from families living in crowded and unhealthy environments, without air, sun, breath: families where tuberculosis hovered.[137]

---

134. Serafin and Serafin 2002, p. 39.

135. Dogliani 1999, p. 159.

136. Archivio Istituto Luce: 'Colonie montane', October 1931, A0848; 'Nava Arma di Taggio', 1933, B0342; 'Cinquecento Bambini partono da Roma', 10 July 1935, B0708 ; 'Partenza da Roma', 4 October 1935, B0743; 'Santa Cristina', 19 August 1936, B0938; 'Mareson Belluno Colonia Alpina Generale Giurati', 1936, B0924; 'Campeggio Balilla Moschettieri Romani a Colalbo', 12 August 1936, B0937; 'Colonia figli Marittimi ad Aquila', 4 August 1937, B1141; 'Pianaccio, colonia montana dell'ONC' 10 August 1938, B1354.

137. Tedeschi 1928, pp. 337–38.

Revelations

The Mussolini Village in Calabria was described as a refuge for children with poor health,[138] while an inscription at the entrance of an Alpine camp reminded visitors that there 'nature was working to heal suffering youth'.[139] The connection between mountains and health in the treatment of tuberculosis is well-known;[140] here, instead, I want to stress the application of mountain therapy beyond the realm of diagnosed illness. The extensive summer camp programmes were related to the fascist project of human reclamation rather than to a specific health policy on tuberculosis or other diseases. As a matter of fact, emphasis on the healing effects of mountain sojourns progressively disappeared with the advancing age of the people involved in the activities: no one made any reference to the poor health of university students or workers engaged by the regime in numerous mountain activities from sport competitions to collective hiking. The significance of sports in Nazi and fascist culture is well documented;[141] it entails the theory and practice of social engineering in both the collective and the personal body, imposing the authority of the State in matters such as hygiene, fitness, reproduction and sexual life.[142] However, in the case of mountain sports, the making of the new Italian did not take place only in the realm of the body but also in that of nature. Natural landscapes and fascist 'cultivation of bodies' through discipline and physical training would produce the improvement of the Italian stock that Mussolini praised. As the president of the Italian Alpine Club stated, their aim was to overcome the dicothomy between mind and body, soul and blood:

> Here is the intellectual: an emaciated and suffering face, eyes dimmed by myopia, a fragile and skinny body, shortness of breath, yellow face and hands. Here is the sportsman and you will see the thick head of a strong, healthy and unexpressive nitwit on vacation, an athletic body below a chicken brain ... In this opposition between intellectuals and sportsmen, brains and muscles, ideas and actions is the entire tragic story of our nation-building... [143]

Manaresi did not explain the connections he suggested between that body/mind opposition and the history of Italian nation building; his main point was

138. Carullo 1929, p. 418.

139. Soldati 1925, p. 1110.

140. Thomas Mann's *The Magic Mountain* (1927) is the archetype of any narrative about tuberculosis and mountains; see also Guillaume 1986; Carmellini 2005; Patriarca 2001.

141. Ambrosi and Weber 2004.

142. Dickinson 2004, p. 3–4.

143. Manaresi 1932, p. 108.

to underline the dichotomy and endorse the fascist project of human reclamation. Nevertheless, his reference to intellectuals vs. sportsmen demonstrated a belief that human reclamation should not only be an improvement of bodies; mountaineering was the answer to that problem, offering a holistic approach to the advancement of the race. In fact, going up into the mountains was not the same as training onself in the stadiums and gyms scattered everywhere by the regime. Climbing was a spiritual and a material journey, probably the only physical exercise able to reconcile mind and muscle, making peace between the two characters in Manaresi's parable. It was not by chance that one of the most controversial fascist intellectuals, Julius Evola, was intrigued by mountaineering. Explicitly reinforcing Manaresi's argument, Evola stated that rock climbing was the most accessible means for achieving that desired union of body and spirit.[144] Nevertheless, Evola's concept of spirit and therefore his vision of mountaineering as a reconciliation of body and soul were rather complicated and obscure, as were all aspects of his doctrine. What I want to note here is Evola's racialisation of mountaineering as both a product and a producer of superior races. In an essay significantly entitled 'Race and Mountain', Evola maintained that the mountain environment was the only one that could invite people 'to return to their origins, to their inner realisation'.[145] According to his vision, mountain climbing could shape the deep attitudes of Italians, mending some weaknesses of the Mediterranean race which he summarised in an excessive need for communication; in the mountains Italians would learn to appreciate silence and to act without an audience.[146] Evola's reflections were part of a larger debate that involved the Italian community of mountain climbers at that time; as Fascism pushed towards a heroic and competitive type of mountaineering offering medals and recognition to climbers, a new generation of climbers increasingly stressed the technical and, in some sense, acrobatic aspects of their relationships to mountains. They formed the so-called 'Oriental style', which stressed their climbing techniques, in contrast to the 'Occidental', more attentive to the contemplative dimension of climbing, and consequently rejected any official ranking for mountaineering activities. Domenico Rudatis, an alpinist deeply influenced by Julius Evola's thinking, was the most vocal advocate of the Oriental climbing style, stressing the connection between it and the super-human. In 1934 Rudatis wrote in the Alpine Club magazine:

144. Evola 1998, p. 9.
145. *Ibid.* p. 34.
146. *Ibid.* pp. 33–34.

Revelations

We have overcome the idyllic perception of mountains through the aesthetic of peaks and the religion of action … The principle of power which lies at the base of every manifestation and through which our soul communicates with nature identifies itself with our will and therefore we are able to admire nature and the infinite aspects of mountains.[147]

In another article Rudatis plainly stated that climbing in the Dolomites produced a different kind of citizen, radically superior to those 'equalised' in western democracies, and spiritually renewed by Italian Fascism.[148]

Although this debate was rather heated in the specialised literature, it did not involve the large mass of people mobilised by the regime in the mountain experience: the children in the summer camps, the university students in the winter sport tournaments, and the *dopolavoristi* [members of the Leisure Time Fascist Organisations] on their weekend trips were not interested in choosing between technical or spiritual approaches – probably they were using both without sensing any contradiction.[149] The Italian Alpine Club was the main agent of the going-to-the-mountains fascist plan; as we have seen, the club was in no way a fascist creature but the regime was able to absorb it, as it did many other associations. The Italian historian Alessandro Pastore has analysed how Fascism occupied every aspect of the CAI, hand-selecting its leaders, moving its headquarters to Rome and, tragically, adopting racial laws to aryanise it.[150] In the meantime, Fascism stressed the club's militarisation, which became extremely clear in 1930 with the appointment of Angelo Manaresi, a former alpine official and Undersecretary at the Ministry of War, as president; to highlight further the militarisation of the club, in 1936 a general of the Alpine Corps, Celestino Bes, was proclaimed co-president of the association.[151] During Manaresi's ten-year presidency, the CAI was transformed from an elitist but free association to a mass fascist organisation; in only three years the number

---

147. Rudatis 1934, p. 62.

148. Rudatis 1938, p. 140.

149. The lack of involvement of most climbers in that debate is apparent even in the pages of the CAI magazine; see, for instance, the position of the Apennine climbers expressed in Marzio 1934, p. 426: 'we go to the mountain with our souls, but also with our feet and arms, also with the special mysticism of our Umbrian region; we have to fight with wild nature without any help from the touristic organisations, using both physical and spiritual training'.

150. Pastore 2003, in particular chapters v and vi.

151. Manaresi 1936, p. 201.

of local branches grew from 99 to 151.[152] A large part of that expansion occurred through alliances and forced agreements with other groups rather than with an increase in the direct membership of the club. In 1928 the CAI signed agreements with the major fascist organisations: the National Leisure Time Organisation [Opera Nazionale Dopolavoro], the Italian Touristic Association, the University Students Groups (GUF), and the Fascist Youth Organisations. The collaboration with the GUF was especially significant: by 1932 40,000 members of the fascist university association were automatically enrolled into the CAI, solving in perfect regime style – that is, through imposition – the chronic shortage of youth in the club's membership. Manaresi was the architect of that incorporation, which he heartily endorsed; it was not by chance that he delivered a speech on students and mountains at the 1931 International Congress of Mountaineering in Cortina.[153] The club's monthly magazine meticulously listed the results of its special attention towards students, offering a series of championship tournaments, excursions and prizes. Competition was crucial in fascist mountaineering education: starting in 1932 the regime organised the Littorio Games [I giochi del Littorio], national tournaments in which fascist youth organisations competed against each other in sports and physical challenges. Part of the Littorio Games was specifically dedicated to winter sports and mountain activities; the number of students participating in those competitions ranged from 1,215 in 1932 to 2,392 in 1937.[154] Describing the fifth annual Littoriali a journalist wrote:

> The fascist student is a model for students of all nations. Mussolini's student despises the profligate and empty life of the old generation who spent their city days in the coffe shops...[155]

Actually, mountain climbing as the antidote for the dissolute urban life was not a prerogative of fascist rhetoric:[156] Alessandro Pastore has found the same arguments used by working class associations dedicated to hiking and mountaineering.[157] Nevertheless, Fascism represented a turning point, transforming a recreational activity into an expression of national duty, managed

---

152. Bardelli 2002, pp. 40–41.
153. Pastore 2003, pp. 179–180.
154. Manaresi 1938, p. 77.
155. Gaifas 1937, p. 122.
156. Serafin and Serafin 2002, p. 35.
157. Pastore 2003, pp. 121–130.

by the Party/State, combining the practices of physical exercise with racist discourses on human reclamation. In the making of mountaineers the regime was appropriating both people and mountains; fascist climbers spread marks of the new era thoughout the landscape, whether the *fascio littorio*[158] placed on the tops of several Italian mountain peaks or the fires celebrating the anniversary of the Fascist Revolution. A *fascio littorio* was installed on the top of Moncenisio on 7 October 1935;[159] on the eleventh anniversary of the Fascist March on Rome fires were set on all the Italian mountains to celebrate the birthday of the regime.[160] A 1935 documentary about the activities of the fascist youth organisations vividly described how the making of mountaineers also implied the appropriation of landscape; the film portrayed a group of young fascists attacking the mountain to install – it was a mania – a *fascio littorio* on the top of Torre Venezia at 2,400 metres. In the film the act of climbing assumed the form of a military conquest, a charge against the mountain; this military version of climbing was very popular.[161] In August 1935, upon reaching the top of the Little Dolomites, a group of 3,000 members of the *dopolavoro* did not find anything better to do than to salute Mussolini by firing their machine guns.[162]

Through that symbolic and material appropriation of mountains, the new fascist Italian and the new fascist landscape were created.[163] While young fascists felt the imprint of the mountains, they were also leaving their imprint in the landscape, giving meaning to places, as was clear in the film: they conquered Torre Venezia by putting on its top the symbol of the Party and leaving fascist mottos on the rocks.[164] Meanwhile Fascism 'italianised' the names of the mountain villages on the Alpine borders as part of a wider program aiming to erase any trace of alien communities in Italy: Courmayeur became Cormaggiore, Pre Saint Didier was renamed San Desiderio and Pont

---

158. The *fascio littorio* was a symbol of power in ancient Rome and was adopted by the fascist regime.
159. Serafin and Serafin 2002, p. 38.
160. *Ibid.* p. 107.
161. Archivio Istituto Luce, 'Milizia Alpina, giovani fascisti di Belluno', 1935, no reference number.
162. Serafin and Serafin 2002, p. 62.
163. Archivio Istituto Luce, 'Marcia alpina. Giovani fascisti di Belluno', 1935, no reference number.
164. *Ibid.*

Saint Martin was changed to San Martino.[165] Hence, Fascism reinforced the process of nationalisation of the Alps, preventing even a minimal recovery of transnationalism after the Great War. Obviously, the fascist mountaineer, native or regime-created, spoke only Italian.

165. Serafin and Serafin 2003, p. 43.

∼ 5 ∼

Epilogue

Stories are axes of war to unearth.

Vitaliano Ravagli and Wu Ming

Stories, Again

When I first started thinking about the recent past of the Italian mountains, many things came to mind. Demographic trends, legislation, expansion of protected areas, tourism and transportation networks were the first aspects I began exploring, looking for what remains, and what is gone, in the mountains today.

An avalanche of numbers, statistics and maps occupied both my computer and the mountains I was trying to narrate. It was as if modernity had finally won, erasing the stories of which mountains, at least the mountains in this book, are made. Of course, statistics, numbers and maps also tell stories about mountains. Nevertheless, in the face of the disappearance of mountains from recent national history, I decided to look for the most meaningful tales that could represent the place of mountains in our common past. The result is prescriptive rather than descriptive; the two stories narrated in this epilogue are not at the heart of our common memory, at least no longer for one of them, while the other never was.[1] The 1943–45 Resistance against the Nazi-Fascists and the 1963 Vajont genocide[2] are the tales of these latter-day mountains. Both stories mobilised places and memories, embodying values and discourses that have been central in the history of the nation and of its projection on the landscape.

I believe these two stories are complementary; in both cases, the mountains' marginality made them central. During the Resistance, partisans found there the ideal environment in which to hide and fight; the Vajont massacre

---

1. On the memory of the Vajont, see Leoni 2003–2004.
2. The use of this word is explained in the Introduction.

Epilogue

is the epilogue to a long story of hydroelectric colonialism in the Alps, made possible by the marginality of these areas and their inhabitants.

The destinies of the two stories have been quite different: the Resistance has been a basic ingredient of the national common past until recent efforts to rehabilitate the fascist regime, levelling the differences between the conflicting parties – 'fascists and partisans both had their reasons'.[3] On the other hand, the Vajont massacre simply disappeared from the collective memory, at least until the 1997 presentation by the performer Marco Paolini for Italian Public Television. Apparently, two thousand people dead for profit with the complicity of politicians and scientists did not fit well into the progressive tale about Italian modernisation. Hence, as exemplars, both stories can be considered quite controversial. Nevertheless, I believe that they offer a persuasive view about the relationships between nation and mountains; with this I am not saying that these two stories have constituted the national narrative about mountains, but that they should.

Resisting Mountains

The end of Fascism and the birth of democratic Italy are surprisingly connected to mountains. In 1943, while the Anglo-American Armies were moving up the peninsula, the fascist regime collapsed; Mussolini was deposed, arrested and brought in chains to Mount Gran Sasso. However, his detention on the top of the highest peak of the Apennines ended shortly thereafter; the Nazis freed him and put him in charge of their puppet *Repubblica Sociale Italiana* [Italian Social Republic], which occupied the entire central and northern part of Italy. It was there that mountains became a significant part of the political and cultural geography of liberation.

In fact, the Resistance against Nazi-Fascism found its ideal refuge in the mountains. Exploiting the natural features of the Alps and the Apennines, the partisans were able to confront a much better armed and equipped enemy. The natural advantages of mountains in guerrilla warfare are well known; Giuseppe Mazzini, a passionate supporter of Italian national freedom, in his handbook for revolutionary war wrote:

The geography of Italy, surrounded by the Alps, crossed by the Apennines,

---

3. On revisionism about Fascism and anti Fascism, see Neri Serneri 1995; Kelly 2005; Mammone 2006. For sources with a larger impact on the general public see Pansa 2003 and the television drama 'Il Cuore nel pozzo' directed by Alberto Negrin, released by Italian Public Television in 2006.

intersected by rivers, streams, lakes, marshes, forests, hills is singularly favour-able to the guerrilla.[4]

We have already seen that, in the aftermath of Italian political unifica-tion, following Mazzini's strategy, the southern rebels found their hideouts up in the Apennines, ironically not for the purpose of building the nation but actually for opposing the process of unification. For poorly equipped rebels confronting a regular army the tactical reasons for going to the mountains were quite obvious: the terrain offered the opportunity to attack and hide, avoiding any direct confrontation with the superior forces of the enemy. That was the only strategic choice of the Italian partisans fighting against Nazi-Fascist soldiers. Once again war and landscape merged in the Italian history, affecting not only military events but also the perception of nature and the construction of memory and identity. In a devastated Italy, occupied by Nazis in the North and Anglo-American troops in the South, oddly the mountains became the epicentre of the nation; what had been marginal became central, what had been backward became the vanguard of the political resurrection of the nation. Therefore, it was in the mountains that the new Italy and the new Italian were moulded. The post-war republic was born as a mountaineer and a new democracy arose from the Alpine villages rather than from the modern cities on the plains.

With the Resistance, mountains became synonymous with choice. In his study on the Venetian partisans, Giovanni Sbordone quoted the expres-sion 'Either in Salò[5] or in the mountains: it was a crossroads', pointing out the symbolic opposition between the mountain and the urban/plain space.[6] After twenty years of obedience to the regime, crowding in fascist parades, leaving for imperial wars or reclaiming malarial marshes, going to the mountains was the way to manifest the free will of rebellion. Actually the act of going to the mountains became a symbol of severing links with the past and becoming a rebel; with respect to the cities of the plains, mountains embodied another space with other rules and values. The Resistance once again advanced the classical opposition of city and countryside that has been a staple in the narrative about national landscape; the mountain was the space of rebellion, moral choices and sharing, while the city was the kingdom of order, moral ambiguity and isolation. Of course, this Manichean narrative did not describe the reality of either of

---

4.   Mazzini 1862 [1832], p. 119, f.n.

5.   Salò was the city capital of the Italian Social Republic, ruled by Mussolini but under Nazi control.

6.   Giovanni Sbordone 2005, p. 56.

158

Epilogue

those environments: cities were also places of resistance, with sabotage, strikes
and even guerrilla activities; and in the same way, mountains were not only
places of clear choices but also of ambiguities, full of deserters, spies, criminals
and people simply escaping from the city.[7] Nevertheless, there was no discussion; mountains represented the choice of freedom, embodying resistance to
Nazi-Fascism. As a matter of fact, the image of mountains became a recurring
element in the Resistance's narrative, from songs to periodical publications.

Often in memoirs and fiction, genres not always easy to distinguish,
authors refer to the need to escape from the city. According to the iconoclast
Johnny, the protagonist of Beppe Fenoglio's autobiographical novel,[8] the men
felt suffocated in the streets of the city of Alba, which they had just liberated
from the Nazi-Fascists, and were therefore glad to exit the city and go monitoring the banks of a river; according to Johnny, distrust and hatred were the
key aspects 'of the conduct of the average partisan in the city'.[9] Resistance was
truly a world which had turned upside down the traditional certainties of the
canonical national landscape; partisans moved through mountains safely, while
they felt exposed and vulnerable on the plains. The partisan leader Armide Broccoli expressed this feeling well, describing his and his men's sense of liberation
on leaving Bologna after the battles of Porta Lame: 'we were in the friendly
silence of the countryside, our ally on so many occasions, which allowed us to
find refuge against the wiles of the enemy'.[10]

In his diary on the Resistance in the Piedmont Langhe, Adriano Balbo
unmistakably stated: 'Fascists are in the cities; there is no Fascist in the hills.
Just peasants awaiting the end of the war'.[11]

Don Berto, or Bartolomeo Ferrari, military chaplain of the communist
partisan band 'Mingo', summarised this special relationship of city, mountain
and partisans: 'we had broken off all relations with the world. Our life was no
longer a city or a village life. It was the fault of forest and mountain'.[12]

The idyll of the mountains vs. the dark environment of the fascist city
is one of the motifs in the Resistance's narrative that drew heavily on images
and discourses from the Great War. The perception of being in a separate world
was one of the main traits of the partisans' experience: writing their memoirs,

7.   Adelio and Fausta Fiore 1995, p. 51.
8.   On Fenoglio's Johnny see Belco 2001, pp. 25–44.
9.   Fenoglio 1994, p. 262.
10.   Quoted in Arbizzani 1981, p. 48.
11.   Balbo 2005, p. 32.
12.   Don Berto 1982, p. 28.

several partisans described their arrival in the mountains as a meeting with a new world, detached from the one they had left. According to the writer and partisan Luigi Meneghello, it was in the mountains that Italians felt free for the first time in the twenty years of the regime, forever connecting that elation with the landscape they met.[13]

Mountains were frequently depicted as idyllic. This was especially true when they were seen from afar, when they were perceived as symbols of freedom instead of places for hiding. In a 1945 booklet the partisans of a brigade offered a clear image of this distant vision of the mountains:

> Indeed it's true: St. Donnino, the gloomy prison of Como is behind us; before us the city is open, with its lake, its friendly and easily accessible mountains.[14]

Friendly mountains – even if in different words and images, this was roughly what Don Berto could see in the landscape around the small village of Tigletto, where he had hidden:

> I spent long hours, especially at sunset, watching the rocky mountains, the inaccessible peaks and the impenetrable dense forests. In my imagination I saw them inhabited and full of life, populated with familiar and smiling faces.[15]

Maybe because this image came from a priest, it seems indeed to refer to 'the archangelic realm of partisans', that Beppe Fenoglio satirised in his iconoclastic account of the Resistance. It was also a priest-partisan, Giussani who expressed another image of the idyllic mountain. Arriving in Belforte, a guerrilla stronghold in the Apennines, he wrote:

> The stronghold of the partisans came before me today with a beautiful day, smiling at me and it seemed to say: 'Here you will have a simple and hard life, but look how much peace and tranquillity surround you, simplicity shrouds everything; how charming are nature and the mountains, even if with every step you take you sweat.'[16]

Perhaps the most explicit image of idyll appears in the journal of Ada Gobetti, member of the Resistance in Val di Susa and one of the founders of the Partito d'Azione [Action Party]:

> Arriving in Meana it was like finding a forgotten paradise. Here the dissolution had not yet arrived. Wagons, loaded with hay, advance among the chestnut

13.   Quoted in de' Franceschi 2004, p. 88.

14.   Corpo volontari della libertà 1945, p. 6.

15.   Don Berto 1982, p. 17.

16.   Giussani n.d. p. 47.

trees, golden in the sunset; from every house smoke rises into the sky. You can hear games of children, cries of animals as if the whole world were at peace.[17]

Another partisan stressed the striking opposition between the natural tranquillity of the forest and the imminent attack of the Nazi-Fascists, which would have radically changed the sounds and shapes of the landscape.[18]

These bucolic narratives of the partisan mountain blended several themes. On the one hand, there was the classical representation of the national landscape, particularly strong among well-educated partisans from the city who had returned to the mountains of their holidays and mountain climbing adventures, this time with weapons slung across their shoulders. There was also an objective sense of relief at leaving the controlled cities of the plains with their patrols, spies, conscription and forced labour. On leaving the plains, everything changed: the landscape, climate, food, even names – partisans usually assumed *noms de guerre*. In many cases social hierarchies also changed in both the microcosm of the guerrilla bands and the so-called 'partisan republics' – that is, the areas freed from Nazi-Fascists where the partisans experimented with forms of democratic institutions.

In short, the separation was both a personal, almost spiritual, perception and an extremely practical experience. Partisans felt themselves separated from the life of the plains and the mountains reinforced that feeling with their kilometres of dilapidated roads, dense forests and impossible slopes. On the other hand, it was a strange separation because the mountains were separated and protected but not isolated.

After all, partisans were not hermits; they went to the mountains to change the world rather than to escape from it. Nature protected and offended with the same weapons: hiding the rebels, it also exposed them to cold and starvation. Hence, what made mountains a difficult environment for the Nazi-Fascists simultaneously challenged the very survival of the partisans.

The idyll was not the only narrative used by partisans to describe the mountains. In her journal Ada Gobetti clearly expressed the contrasting feelings with which partisans approached the mountains. Climbing towards the little village of Colombier through nature emanating a 'radiant and serene beauty', a fellow who was with her exclaimed:

I cannot stand this blue sky anymore, this sun, these flowers. What I am dreaming of now is a dirty coffee shop, full of bad smells and noise and electric lights.

---

17. Gobetti 1996, p. 24.
18. De' Franceschi 2004, pp. 209, 222.

Stories, Again

Partisan Republics.

Table 5.1. Partisan republics in 1944 from Peli, La Resistenza in Italia, *p. 97.*

Place	Duration
Valsesia	11 June–10 July
Val Ceno	10 June–11 July
Val d'Enza-Val Parma	June–July
Val Taro	15 June–24 July
Montefiorino	17 June–1 August
Val Maira	Late June–30 July
Val Varaita	Late June–21 August
Valli di Lanzo	25 June–late September
Friuli Orientale	30 June– late September
Bobbio	7 July–27 August
Torriglia	July–August, Mid October–Early December
Carnia	Mid July–15 October
Imperia	Late August–Mid October
Val d'Ossola	10 September–23 October
Langhe	September–Mid November
Alto Monferrato	September–2 December
Varzi	22 September–29 November
Alto Tortonese	September–November

Epilogue

I understood him perfectly; I was also missing the urban life, even in its less appealing forms because it was the normal life.[19]

Ada Gobetti attacked the partisan idyll at its heart, claiming the right to miss even the filth of the city; hers was a nostalgia for the lost bourgeois normality, which no mountain landscape could ever present. Her landscape was still bucolic, naturally welcoming, but dramatically distant from that of the urban partisans. Actually, the image of a 'flowers and pastures' nature was not what partisans were experiencing; for those who fought in the mountains, cold, snow and rain were the faces of the landscape, which therefore did not just surround them but permeated their bones, blending bodies and natural elements. Every 'honest' partisan, Federico Del Boca wrote, wished only to stay away from mountains, not seeing them even through postcards.[20] As a matter of fact, mountains so deeply marked the partisan Federico Del Boca that he was confined to a sanatorium for five long years at the end of the Resistance.[21] The landscape did not just surround partisans but penetrated their bodies, leaving profound marks; after all, what was the continuous search for food that plagued partisans in the mountains if not an issue about landscape and bodies?[22] It was, in fact, the food issue that changed the opinion of partisans about the suitability of hills for guerrillas: even if the hills were more accessible to the enemy's army, they could sustain rebels more easily and for longer than could the high mountains.[23] As Luigi Meneghello stated, although the Resistance had impressed its idea of freedom on the mountain landscape, it was also true that that landscape had left its imprints in the memories as well as in the faces and bodies of those who fought there. Didn't the most famous partisans' song repeat that there would never be any 'sun of the future' without dealing with the winds and the storms of the mountain?[24] Cold and snow were the

19. Gobetti 1996, p. 106.

20. Del Boca 1966, p. 89.

21. *Ibid.* p. 10.

22. Bocchio (Massimo) 1984; this article is published in the journal of the Institute for the Study of Resistance and Contemporary Society in the Provinces of Biella e Vercelli, and it is available online at http://www.storia900bivc.it/indexie.html

23. See, for instance, the debate on the opportunity to form partisan bands in the Langhe area – in Giovana 1988, p. 14; Masera 1971, p. 33.

24. I refer here to the well-known partisan song 'Fischia il vento' [The wind is whistling], written by Felice Cascione around 1943 to an existing Russian melody, *Katiuscia*. In the first verse the song says: 'The wind is whistling and the storm is raging / rotten shoes but we must march / to conquer the red spring / where the sun of the future is rising' ['Fischia il vento e infuria la bufera / scarpe rotte e pur bisogna andar / a conquistare la

Stories, Again

Partisans, Valley of Ossola, September–October 1944.

antithesis of the idyllic representation of mountains; for partisans they were the first material signs that the mountains were close.

It was not by chance that the movie *Achtung! Banditi!*, directed by Carlo Lizzani,[25] started with partisans marching into the snow; in the canonical memory of Resistance, to which Lizzani's work contributed, the natural landscape was immediately characterised as a place for extremes, depicting the difficulties rebels had to deal with. This was not confined to cinematographic narration: several partisans' memoirs stressed the same image. For instance, Nino Chiovini wrote in his diary:

> March 1944. It has been snowing for many days; it is a dense, thick, continuous snow. The strong wind is whistling and moaning among the few trees at Pian Cavallone, already framed in the ice. A metre and half of snow submerges

---

rossa primavera / dove sorge il sol dell'avvenir']. Information and the text of this song are available at http://www.archividellaresistenza.it

25. *Achtung! Banditi!* Directed by Carlo Lizzani, produced by Cooperativa Produttori Cinematografici, 1951.

everything: the little wall, the rocks. The barn is just a white pile [of snow]. This is a magnificent, Mephistophelean spectacle of nature but here the food supplies are almost gone and there is no wood.[26]

The closer and more concrete the mountains became, the less they were celebrated for their beauty and friendly isolation. Climbing from the village of Soprana to Batigiati in Biella province, a group of people who wanted to join the partisans quickly experienced the harshness of mountain life; Argante Bocchio tells us in his memoirs that a heavy snowfall stopped them, even threatening their lives.[27] 'Episodes from nineteenth century paintings of Aosta Valley' – those were the words used by Gianni Dolino to describe the march of his partisan band through storms and avalanches in the Alta Savoia.[28] The partisan leader and writer Nuto Revelli remembered that he and his twenty men risked dying while they crossed the Maira Valley, not because of the Nazis but because of mountains; as he wrote, 'we were on the verge of killing ourselves as alpinists instead of as fighters'.[29] Sometimes the cold would reach the partisan even before his arrival in the mountains. Trying to dissuade him from his plan to join the partisans in the mountains, everyone Gabriele Poci met during his trip told him 'the mountain is cold'.[30]

Up to this point I have tried to demonstrate that this rugged nature was at the same time threatening and protective for rebels: while hiding them from the enemy, it penetrated their bodies, subjecting them to every kind of deprivation. Nevertheless, nature met those bodies not only in their materiality – that is, in their physiological metabolism – but also in what we may call a spiritual metabolism which overcame the barriers between natural and interior landscapes. The mountain changed those who chose it, bestowing on them kinship with its very wild nature. Once again we can turn to the words of the protagonist of Fenoglio's novel, who, having finally reached the partisans, asked himself whether 'they had climbed the mountains with a human, civilised

---

26. Chiovini 2006 p. 27, available online at http://www.centroginocchi.it. This diary was published in Verbania in the magazine 'Monte Marona' in 36 instalments, with a few interruptions from 6 October 1945 to 10 July 1946; it was signed with the pseudonym *enneci*.

27. Bocchio 1984.

28. Dolino 1989, p. 136.

29. Revelli 2003, pp. 175–76.

30. Sbordone 2005, p. 54.

Stories, Again

Partisans, Valley of Ossola, September–October 1944.

face like his and a month [in the mountains] had been enough to change and dehumanise it'.[31]

The partisans' wildness was a recurrent and ambiguous topic. Firstly, dehumanising the enemy, especially irregular troops, has always been a standard practice in every military repression; as I have shown in the second chapter, the southern rebels had also been described as part of the natural landscape of the South, which, according to this narrative, projected its vicious and base characteristics onto them. In the same way, the fascist authority exploited the rhetoric of the wild rebel, trying to isolate the Resistance; according to the dictates of the fascist government in Salò, the outlaw easily became wild, hence developing instincts and qualities typical of primitive people or of 'felines looking for prey'.[32] It was not just the enemies who naturalised the rebels of the mountains: actually, their mimicry of the landscape was often material and spiritual at the same time. 'In the harsh mountains we made ourselves wolves', sang the partisans;[33] of course, in wartime, being perceived as wild animals was not necessarily harmful. In their memoirs, several partisans stressed their ability to fit perfectly into the landscape by blending with it. For instance, in

31. Fenoglio 1994, p. 76.

32. Quoted in de' Franceschi 2004, p. 67.

33. From the song 'Con la guerriglia', in *Canzoniere resistente, 2° raduno de ilDeposito* – Livorno 11 July 2009, available at http://www.ildeposito.org

Epilogue

Partisans, Valley of Ossola, September–October 1944.

his diary Aldo Aniasi compared the instincts and the astuteness of the partisans with those of wild animals, both hunted in the forests.[34] Two other partisans compared themselves to deer because as those animals they would have an instinctive perception of danger, exploiting every aspect of the forest for their survival.[35] Exploring the Piedmont Langhe to set up his partisan band, Adriano Balbo enjoyed the beauty of the landscape and identified himself with the hawks flying free in the sky.[36]

Therefore, partisans were like the animals of the forest with their comfortless lives and their ability to adapt to the natural environment, improving their 'animalism' – that is, their senses, strength and instinct to survive. In his study on the Resistance and habitat in the Emilia Romagna region, Luigi Arbizzani reported that the partisan commander Sesto Liverani knew his area of military operations so well that he was able to understand even the language of the animals:

34.   Aniasi 1997, p. 45.

35.   Sbordone 2005, p. 74.

36.   Balbo 2005, p. 33.

In the darkness the mountain lives an intense life that only a few among its inhabitants know ... The barking of a dog will have different meanings on the basis of its sound and of the circumstances in which it occurs.[37]

According to Liverani, one could foretell the arrival of the Nazis from the agitation of the animals in the forest.[38]

Hence, the merging between landscape and rebels was a physiological exchange between nature and bodies, a sort of spiritual hybridisation between partisans and mountains, but it was also the practical knowledge of the territory that would allow partisans to survive and even to take advantage of that exchange. In any case, it is typical of guerrilla tactics to use rebels' superior knowledge of the territory. A paper dedicated to the formation of partisan brigades recommended properly detailed knowledge of the military area of operations for at least a radius of fifty kilometres;[39] the measures employed by Nazi-Fascists to eliminate any transfer of information between local residents and rebels proved the strategic importance of that knowledge. A typical example was the order of the Reggio Emilia prefect on 7 July 1944, quoted by Arbizzani, which decreed the death penalty for those who helped to orient the partisans on the ground.[40]

Partisans' memoirs are filled with episodes testifying to the danger of getting lost while running through unfamiliar forests and mountains. Giampaolo Danesin told the story of his first trip towards the Cellino Valley, when he realised he was alone and lost in the middle of the mountains.[41] But getting lost was not a prerogative just of inexperienced partisans; veteran rebels too could lose their way, as happened to William Valesesia and his men in the aftermath of the Ressa battle. While they were lost on the top of a mountain, the Madonna d'Oropa appeared to them in a chalet; however, this was not a miracle but just a postcard hanging on the wall. Nonetheless it was a kind of geographic miracle, in that, through the address on that postcard, the partisans learnt they had reached an area familiar to one of them from his previous work as woodman there.[42] Through the postcard, the landscape spoke again to the partisans in a language that became understandable, at least to one of them.

---

37.   Quoted in Arbizzani 1981, p. 45.

38.   *Ibid.* p. 45.

39.   *Ibid.* p. 43.

40.   *Ibid.* p. 48.

41.   The testimony of Giampaolo Danesin is reported Sbordone 2005, p. 79.

42.   The story is told in Valsesia 1984.

168

Epilogue

Mountains were demanding environments; they offered crucial advantages to rebels but they asked for knowledge and abilities that were not common among urban people. Those who coped better with life in the mountains were mountaineers, partisans from the Alpine valleys where the bands were operating. In his memoirs, Alberto Cotti, known by the *nom de guerre* Dartagnan [sic], wrote:

> Forests, crests, bushes are easy places for the partisans born in the mountains, especially for the younger ones who will feel lost in the city.[43]

Some very basic skills, common among mountaineers, were crucial in the everyday life of the rebels: hunting, milking, gathering edibles, and cutting paths though the forest became precious talents. In his diary Nino Chiovini recalled the rations provided by a bird-hunting member of the band;[44] Federico Del Boca, by contrast, remembered the frustration he felt trying to milk cows, an easy task for other partisans who came from the mountains.[45] Pietro Granziera and other members of his band faced trouble hiding in the Genoese forests because they ate wild fruits that were inedible;[46] it is impossible to enumerate the times when partisans needed to turn to local people in order to be guided through forests and mountains.

While every mountaineer had some advantage in coping with the natural environment, some had special knowledge, accumulated in the exercise of particular activities such smuggling or poaching. In his journal Eduardo Sacchi told stories of bands, mixes of smugglers and partisans, where the former were sometimes scouts or fellow travellers, and at other times members of the Resistance, even if the author did not seem to completely trust their motivation to fight.[47] Orienting themselves in forests and mountains was vital for the rebels but being a poacher offered something more. As Luigi Arbizzani has noted, in the movie *Agnese va a morire* [Agnese goes to die] a group of partisans used a crashed airplane to build a handmade ice-breaker for a boat but, rather than a product of improvisation, it was the result of the skills of generations of poachers who had dealt with the freezing temperatures of the Alps.[48]

---

43. Cotti 1994.
44. Chiovini 2006, p. 4.
45. Del Boca 1966, p. 65.
46. Sbordone 2005, p. 82.
47. Sacchi 2002, pp. 10, 14, 16–21, 25.
48. Arbizzani 1981, p. 47.

Stories, Again

The mountain spoke to the rebel with its own language, its signs in the landscape, sometimes fixed as rocks, at other times mutable as the leaves of trees and the streams. If smugglers, poachers and, generally speaking, mountaineers already knew that language, all the partisans had to learn it in order to survive. It was easier for those who, even coming from urban environments, had had some experience of mountains. Several mountain climbers offered their skills to the cause of the Resistance. Aldo Aniasi recounted the case of Serafino Soressi, Piero De Micheli, Ferruccio Camona and Giuliano Gherardini, who were called chamois or eagles because they were able to manoeuvre on difficult trails to provide the bands with food, guns, and information.[49] Paolo Momigliano Levi told the story of Ettore Castiglioni, a famous alpinist who decided to serve the Resistance by helping people to expatriate to Switzerland and connecting the Italian Antifascist Committee (CLN) with the Anglo-American Armies.[50] Nino Chiovini became the charismatic leader of the *Giovane Italia* [Young Italy] band thanks to his experience of mountain excursions and climbing which gave him an extraordinary knowledge of the terrain.[51] The connection between mountain climbing and Resistance emerged symbolically in the journal of Ludwig Ratschiller when he found Antonio Berti's guide to the Oriental Alps in a refuge transformed for a while into the band's headquarters; that handbook for quiet mountain climbers became a guerrilla tool for Luddi, who, incidentally, joined the Italian Alpine Club as soon as the war ended.[52]

However, there was something else in the landscape, other signs, not always visible, telling stories and guarding memories. The landscape of Resistance was also made of stories wherein ancient legends combined with the deeds of recent partisans; the contemporary became a myth in the making. On the reworking of partisans' emotional experiences, Italo Calvino wrote:

> Those who started to write then [after the war], were treating the same material as that of the oral narrator: to the stories that we had experienced in person or viewed as direct spectators we had to add those stories which came to us as tales and therefore with their own voices, rhythms and gestures. During the guerrilla campaign, the real war stories, which had just been experienced, were transformed and transfigured into the stories told at night around the fire…[53]

---

49. Aniasi 1997, p. 56.
50. Momigliano Levi 2005, p. 31.
51. Otttolini 2006, p. 6.
52. Ratschiller 2004, p. 99.
53. Calvino 1974 [1964], pp. ii–iii.

Epilogue

Slopes, lodges, fragments of the national road, the gravel beds of rivers – each element of scenery could refer to a partisan story, to a hero killed by the fascists or even to a spy.

The legendary partisan leader Cino Moscatelli told in his memoirs about nights spent by his band around the fire eating chestnuts and telling tales in the mountaineer tradition;[54] as the mountaineers used to say, chestnuts filled stomachs but also mouths with words and stories.

Nevertheless, this narrative landscape was not confined only to the current time: mountains also told an older history of rebellion and war. It is well known that the Resistance consciously tried to adhere to the patriotic tradition which, from the *Risorgimento*[55] to World War One, had always been synonymous with mobilisation against the foreigner. While the link with the Risorgimento was felt mainly in terms of the symbolic identity that created the Partisans – just think of the partisan brigades named after Garibaldi and Mazzini – the relationship with the Great War was more directly tied to places and landscapes, inseparable from the events that occurred there. We can start with the unique link between the Alpine Corps and the Resistance. It is known that at the foundation of the partisan movement there was the material presence of officers from the Alpini, instrumental in the organisation of the bands, and the imagined presence of entire Alpini divisions up in the mountains, armed and ready to resist. In his history of the Alpini, Gianni Oliva tells one of those stories of unconditional faith in them: in the confusing moments after the armistice with the Anglo-Americans, when no Italian soldier had any clue about what he was supposed to do with his former Nazi allies, in Boves, Piedmont region, everyone believed that the entire Alpine Corps Division of La Punteria was hidden in the mountains around the village, fully equipped and ready to fight against the Nazis. Unfortunately for the Resistance, this was simply a legend and there was no well-equipped Alpine division hiding in the mountains. Nevertheless, this story testifies to both the popular image of the corps, ready to resist even amid Italian defeat, and the reality of some Alpine soldiers actually hiding in the forests.[56]

According to the partisan and journalist Giorgio Bocca, this alpine tradition was one of the main reasons for the strong presence of the partisans

54. Moscatelli 1982.

55. *Risorgimento* is the name given to the entire movement and struggles that led to the unification of the country into one nation.

56. Oliva 1985, pp. 203–4.

in the Piedmont region.[57] As I have already discussed, in the Italian military tradition the Alpini, more than any other corps, embodied the link between landscape and nation; theirs was a territorial army in which the Fatherland was embodied in the small highland homelands and whose defence became the defence of villages and families. The Alpini were the heroes of the Great War, the army that, on the national borders, had resisted the invasion of foreigners. Therefore, the return to the mountains and their history meant a reweaving of the threads of national history. The partisans, such as the Alpini, were an expression of a community that resisted the invader, always German; although identifying primarily with the little fatherlands of the alpine valleys, they nevertheless moved beyond these borders to become the symbol of the entire nation, thus, in their patriotic battles, connecting people from the city with people from the countryside. The relevance of this alpine corps tradition in the history of Resistance is evident in one of the better-known partisan biographies, the story of Nuto Revelli. An Alpino himself, Revelli not only chose the Resistance after Italy's disastrous retreat from Russia but also named his partisan band 'Company for the Vindication of the Fallen Soldiers', tying the fight in the mountains to the sacrifice of the Alpini on the eastern front.[58] It was this shared memory that reinforced the connection between another partisan, Adriano Balbo, and the peasants in the Langhe villages while he was trying to build his band; speaking with them, the conversation often turned to Adriano's father who had been an Alpino in the Great War, as had many others from the area.[59] There was no doubt about Adriano's enthusiasm when he discovered that his military leader was an official from the Alpine Corps.[60]

In the famous movie *Achtung! Banditi!* the two former enemies, the partisan Napoleon and the fascist Antonio, recognise themselves to be part of the same community when they discover that both had served in the Alpini. When the Nazis killed the partisan, Antonio 'converted' and fired against the Germans, joining the rebels with his weapons and comrades. The bond between Alpini and Resistance was particularly evident in the partisan bands of Justice and Liberty, which adopted the characteristic Alpini symbols – the colour green and the motto 'Pity is dead'.[61]

---

57. Bocca 1995, p. 92. Another historian, Gianni Perona, stresses the fact that the partisans came especially from the areas where the Alpine Corps recruited; in Perona 2005, p. 15.

58. *Ibid.* p. 98.

59. Balbo 2005, p. 37.

60. *Ibid.* p. 39.

61. *Ibid.* p. 87.

Epilogue

There are numerous examples to indicate how the long shadow of the Great War extended over the Italian Resistance; particularly effective in terms of the relationship between memory and landscape is the case of Mount Grappa, where the partisans' decision to remain and resist the Nazi-Fascist operation against them was without doubt deeply affected by the symbolic meaning of the Grappa landscape, filled with memories of the Great War. A decision that was a military disaster for the Resistance caused the death of 300 partisans, while another 171 were executed and 400 deported to Germany. The bands were made for guerrilla warfare rather than for pitched battles.[62]

If the landscape of the Resistance was romantically occupied by the memory of World War One, there were also layers of older meanings and stories. The historian Filippo Colombara has recently reported on the creation of the Dolcinian myth in the Resistance in Valsesia;[63] the partisan leaders Pietro Secchia and Cino Moscatelli had already linked the medieval heretical rebellion with the partisans,[64] as if the entire landscape was imbued with resistant spirits. This cultural connection, as Colombara argues, has found its epicentre in the Research Centre dedicated to Dolcino, where researchers have confirmed the thesis that Moscatelli chose his *nom de guerre*, Cino, after the medieval heretic.[65] Similar references to the tradition of resistance can be found in the Pellice Valley, where the partisans overlapped with the Waldensian community, the jealous guardian of its mountain freedom.[66]

The democratisation of the country came largely from the mountains; they were the homeland of those who had decided to fight against Nazi-Fascism. It was in those out-of-the-way valleys that Italians started to experiment with new forms of government after twenty years of dictatorship (the so-called partisan republics). At the time of the general insurrection in 1945, several cities were freed by these uncommon fighters, arriving from the mountains. Nevertheless, the mountains did not become the symbolic centre of the new Italy. Too far from the epicentres of modernity, mountains were massively abandoned, drained at the same time of people and meaning. When the rediscovery of mountains finally occurred, it was informed by the appreciation of nature and a kind of folklore heritage, omitting the controversial memory of the Resistance. Only in 2002 did the European Union Project 'The Memory of the Alps' start recovering

---

62.   Peli 2004, p. 106.
63.   Colombara 2006.
64.   Secchia and Moscatelli 1958, p. 36.
65.   Colombara 2006.
66.   Bocca 1995, p. 259–60; Gobetti 1996.

this sedimentation of meanings in the mountain landscape.[67] The project has provided detailed guides to the sites of partisan battles fought in Piedmont, Liguria and Valle d'Aosta; in 2007 the Italian Touring Club published a guide-book entitled *The Trails of Freedom*, dedicated to the landscapes of Resistance.[68] Forty years after its guides to the Great War battlefields, the TCI returned to the Alps; we might assume that the aim remains the same – the political use of landscape for the making of a national identity – but in 2007 the TCI was no longer a major tool for nationalisation. Today there are other instruments of nationalisation and both mountains and Resistance are far from them.

Dissolving Mountains

On 6 April 2009 the central part of Italy, and particularly the Abruzzo region, was hit by a powerful earthquake. It killed more than 300 people and caused the displacement of about 65,000. The old centre of L'Aquila, the Abruzzo capital, was severely damaged and is still inaccessible. Now, what is the connection be-tween the Italian mountains and the 2009 Abruzzo earthquake? There is indeed a hidden, literally subterranean, link between the stories of the mountains and of a geological and largely urban disaster, exposed by the earthquake. From the ruins of L'Aquila's National Archive other ruins surfaced: seven metal cabinets packed with 240 binders plus boxes full of rocks and small-scale models of a remote alpine valley were miraculously saved from the destruction of the old building. That was the archive of the Vajont disaster, which occurred 46 years earlier in the Eastern Alps, not far from Venice. The two stories may seem completely different – the Abruzzo earthquake was a natural calamity, while the Vajont disaster was a human-made event caused by a massive landslide crashing into a reservoir, creating an enormous wave that inundated the valley and killed about 2,000 people. Although some may think the meeting of these two tragic events in the ruins of a national archive was simply accidental, I believe that the connections were more profound. The same religion of profit without regard for safety or precautionary measures underlay the tragic effects of both events. Even in the Abruzzo case, where nature was undoubtedly the main agent, the investigations of public prosecutors are uncovering the crimi-nal conduct of private entrepreneurs and public servants who did not comply with the rules in the construction and control of buildings which therefore

---

67.   A detailed description of the project is at http://www.memoryofthealps.net/index.php
68.   TCI 2007.

collapsed too easily in the earthquake.[69] In the name of profit and economic growth, because construction has always been an important sector in the Italian economy, people died in Abruzzo as well as in the Vajont Valley; the disregard for natural constraints, the subjugation of nature to economy and the uneven distribution of environmental burdens and economic profits are the subterranean bonds connecting the two stories.

The story of the Vajont is little known in Italy and abroad; very few historians have explored this tragic event and, were it not for the work done by Maurizio Reberschak,[70] it would probably simply be obliterated in the academic world, at least in the fields of humanities and social sciences. The Vajont speaks of corruption, of connivances between political and economic powers, of the enslavement of science; it can be described as a metaphor of Italian modernisation, conquering the Alpine Valley for the wealth of the nation. Nonetheless, I believe that it is time to frame the Vajont tragedy through the lens of the environmental justice.[71] This category has revealed itself as a powerful discourse with which to explain the unequal distribution of the burdens and benefits originating from the exploitation of natural resources. And the story I am going to tell has all the basic ingredients of an archetypal narration of environmental injustice: the power of a big corporation, the resistance of local communities, the complicity of the authorities, the politicisation of science.

It was 9 October 1963. About 300 million cubic metres of rock fell from Mount Toc into the Vajont reservoir; the landslide caused a fifty million cubic metre wave that partially overcame the dam and, moving at about 100 km/h, destroyed everything in its way. The villages of Erto, Casso, Castellavazzo, Codissago, Pirago, Villanova, Faè, Rivalta and the town of Longarone were hit by the wave; indeed Longarone was almost completely destroyed. Experts

---

69. On the criminal investigations see the special issue of *Espresso* magazine 'Terremoto, il dolore e la rabbia', available online at http://temi.repubblica.it/espresso-terremoto-in-abruzzo/; Dossier Abruzzo L'isola felice, Libera Associazioni Nomi e Numeri contro le mafia, available online at http://www.libera.it/flex/cm/pages/ServeBLOB.php/L/IT/IDPagina/3951

70. Reberschak (ed.) 1983; Reberschak and Mattozzi (eds.) 2009.

71. It is impossible here to quote the immense literature produced in the environmental justice field. Generally speaking, it has been more developed in the US and Latin America than in the European context. For a basic introduction to the concept see Bullard 1990; Hurley 1995; Pulido 1996; Faber (ed.) 1998; Melosi 2000; Martinez Alier 2005. Among the few works about Europe, see Armiero 2009 and 2011; Barca 2010; Massard-Guilbaud and Rodger (eds.) 2011.

Stories, Again

Site of the Vajont Dam.

have calculated that the landslide freed energy comparable to the twice that of the Hiroshima atomic bomb;[72] about 2,000 people were killed.

In the aftermath of the disaster, the magazine of the Fire Department published an apocalyptic description of the area after the wave:

> A landscape soaked in a corrosive acid and erased with correction fluid from all the atlases. It was empty, under a cloudless sky and a cynically impudent and absurd sun as, in fact, were the sky and the sun of October 10th, both triumphant over the valley of death.[73]

---

72. Ascari 1973, p. 3, text available at the website http://www.vajont.info/. Thanks to Tiziano Dal Farra for his generous work in preserving and making available an enormous amount of material on the Vajont story.

73. Pais 1963.

Epilogue

Debris from the Vajont disaster.

Second only to the 1908 Messina earthquake, the Vajont disaster was the most dreadful event in the history of modern Italy and beyond; in 2008 UNESCO decided to include the Vajont case on its list of five 'precaution-ary tales' – that is, the five worst disasters caused by humans. According to UNESCO, it is 'a classic example of the consequences of the failure of engineers and geologists to understand the nature of the problem that they were trying to deal with'.[74] Indeed, the Vajont disaster is a tragic and powerful story about science, politics and modernisation in the Italian mountains.

At this point in our journey through the Italian mountains it should be plain that hydropower has played a major role in their nationalisation; moun-tains became national and modern at the same time. Engineers, politicians

74. Five Cautionary Tales and Five Good News Stories, International Year of Planet Earth – Global Launch Event 12–13 February 2008, text available at http://www.lswn.it/en/press_releases/2008/international_year_of_planet_earth_global_launch_event_12_13_february_2008

Stories, Again

The Vajont riverbed after the disaster.

and entrepreneurs viewed them through different lenses, which revealed an invisible landscape of kilowatts and turbines. This was the case of the engineer Carlo Semenza and the geologist Giorgio Dal Piaz who had been exploring the Dolomites since the 1920s, laying the foundation of the so-called 'Great Vajont'. We can imagine people like them roaming in the Alpine valleys disguised as tourists or mountain climbers; after all, like every extractive enterprise, the hydroelectric industry needed to exercise some form of discretion. Nevertheless, it was not only camouflage; often they were indeed passionate admirers of mountains. Carlo Semenza, for instance, was a member of the Italian Alpine Club, even becoming president of a local branch;[75] he contributed to the Touring Club guide of the Dolomites[76] and he published in the CAI

---

75. Carlo Semenza was the president of the Vittorio Veneto branch of the CAI and in 1963 the Club dedicated an Alpine hut to his memory; from http://it.wikipedia.org/wiki/Carlo_Semenza

76. Semenza 1950.

magazine.[77] After his death in 1961, the CAI dedicated one of its alpine huts to his memory. In his contribution to the TCI guide of the Dolomites, Semenza wrote his rationale for mountain electrification, based on his dual identity as expert and mountain climber:

> In regard to the landscape, although there are disfigurements, which by the way are not so relevant and are generally recoverable ... new elements of tourist interest rise [from the hydroelectric works] such as artificial lakes, dams, new roads etc. Engineers, in the name of the respect and love we owe to the mountain, should harmonise their construction with the environment, at least as far as possible. I believe I have deeply felt this duty because of my dual nature as technician and mountain climber.[78]

Semenza's point here is not particularly original and we should not be surprised by his arguments; as we have seen, hydropower was the material and discursive place where the merging of appreciation of nature and modernisation occurred most clearly. Of course, the difference here is the epilogue of the story, which comprised not just the destruction of beautiful scenery but the killing of 2,000 people, a demonstration that the domination of nature and that of humans in the name of profit are two sides of the same coin. Nevertheless, in the 1920s and 1930s the epilogue was still to come. These were years of dreams of modernisation and nightmares of recession with very little room for nature's concerns. According to Giorgio Dal Piaz's studies, the Vajont Valley was a perfect location for hydroelectric infrastructures: 'if there is a place whose special morphological characteristics are particularly adapted to the construction of dams, that place is the Vajont Valley'.[79]

Dal Piaz argued that the geographical structure resembling the North American canyons offered a perfect location for the ingenuity of engineers, even if he completed his description of the Vajont in a rather less reassuring way: 'the structural conditions of the Vajont Valley, although appearances can deceive, are not worse than those of the other Venetian mountains'.[80] That was enough for engineers and entrepreneurs. In 1929 the *Società Idroelettrica Veneta* [Venetian Hydroelectric Company] sought permission for the hydroelectric exploitation of the Vajont River on the basis of Carlo Semenza's plan, which included the construction of a reservoir containing 33 million cubic metres of

---

77. Semenza 1934.

78. Semenza 1950 quoted from Merlin 2001, pp. 91–92.

79. Dal Piaz 1940, report without title available at http://www.vajont.net/page. php?pageid=SEZPG008

80. Dal Piaz doc. CM 42, www.vajont.info

water, with a 130 metre high dam. The 1929 project was the starting point in a series of plans dedicated to the economic development of the Boite-Piave-Vajont basin;[81] as one of the protagonists of this story has written, 'in the context of the 1940s and 50s model of production, the Piave Valley was a sort of hydroelectric laboratory'.[82] Never has metaphor been more accurate; the Piave basin was a laboratory indeed and, as in every modernistic lab, in it there was no room for the 'real world' with its imperfections and everyday empirical knowledge – it had to be and work as the experts and their clients thought and wished. The technical evolution of the projects came hand-in-hand with financial and company conglomeration in the hydroelectric sector; with the triumph of the monopolistic power of SADE [Adriatic Electric Company] the various projects concerning the Piave basin were unified into a single vision, 'il Grande Vajont'. From the 1930s to the 1950s the height of the dam rose from 190 metres to 260 metres, tripling the size of the reservoir, and therefore increasing its capacity from fifty to 150 million cubic metres of water.[83] The final project aimed to collect the residual water from the Piave River and its tributaries into a gigantic reservoir to overcome dry seasons and continually fuel the power plants of Soverzene and Gardona; the whole system was meant to produce about 800 million kilowatts yearly.[84] The first version of the 'Great Vajont' was approved by the *Consiglio Superiore dei Lavori Pubblici* [Supreme Board of Public Works] in October 1943 – that is, at a chaotic period for the country, divided between Nazi-Fascist occupation and the Anglo-American invasion, virtually without legitimate government in Rome; as a matter of fact only thirteen of the 34 members of the Board were actually present for the approval of the Vajont Project, invalidating *de facto* the procedure.[85] Nevertheless, this rather dubious approval became more secure in 1948 with the government sanction to build the hydroelectric infrastructure. Ten years later the evolution of the Great Vajont project came to an end with the authorisation of the final modifications that led to the maximum scope of the reservoir: 722.50

81.   Actually, there was an older project for the exploitation of the Vajont water, dating back to 1900 – this was only to power a paper factory and therefore on a small site and with a limited purpose. Information from www.vajont.net

82.   Datei 2005, p. 11. Augusto Datei was professor of hydraulics at the University of Padua; he was involved in experiments commissioned by SADE to Professor Ghetti, to test the effects of a landslide on the reservoir. When Prof. Ghetti was on trial for the disaster, Detti was one of the experts working on his defence team.

83.   Merlin 2001, p. 51, f.n. 7.

84.   *Ibid.* p. 41.

85.   PCI 1965.

180

metres of height for 150 million cubic metres of water. It would have been the highest arched dam in the world. The story of the Vajont disaster starts with those first steps. In the face of the continuous expansion of the project the control agencies manifested a servile attitude towards SADE, approving every modification. Particularly astonishing, the 1957 authorisation arrived without even the submission by SADE of a proper geologic report; the project was approved while waiting for Giorgio Dal Piaz's survey.[86] Actually, the genesis and production of this survey is crucial to understanding the relationships between science and power at the core of the Vajont case. Briefly, as has emerged from the documents of the trial, Giorgio Dal Piaz had never prepared the survey; in a letter to his good friend and client Carlo Semenza he wrote:

> I have tried to draft the report about the Vajont but I must confess openly that it did not work out well; therefore, I am not satisfied with it. It would be very kind of you if you could write down what you have told me and send it to me, because it seems perfect to me. And please let me know whether I have to include the header of the agency to which it should be sent and also whether it must have the current or an earlier date.[87]

The highest arched dam in the world, destined to contain 150 million cubic metres of water, relied on the geologic report written by its own engineer on the payroll of the same corporation which was building it. As we will later come to learn, the story of Vajont can be understood in terms of science/power relationships.

While in Rome SADE was working to gather the authorisations needed, it had already started to deeply transform the Vajont Valley. Although, for the sake of imposing a hydropower monoculture, they might have been depicted as wild, the Venetian mountains were actually crowded with people whose ancestors had lived there for centuries. In the 1950s, the villages of Erto and Casso had about 1,000 inhabitants (967) and Longarone more than 4,600;[88] it was a classic mountain society based on agro-pasture-forestry activities and on

---

86. The lawyer Ascari wrote that the concession was made in the typical Italian style; in fact giving the permission, the Supreme Board for Public Works simultaneously requested a complete survey on the safety of the inhabitants living close to the reservoir, a survey that, of course, should have been a prerequisite for any concession; in Ascari 1973, pp. 6–7.

87. Giorgio Dal Piaz to Carlo Semenza 6 February 1957; this astonishing letter has been reported several times in different publications and here I am using the documentation available at www.vajont.info (SGI 82).

88. Population resident at 1861–1991 census, data from ISTAT; thanks to this institute which provided the database with all the data.

migrants' remittances. The historian Antonio Lazzarini has illustrated the long-term environmental and economic decline of the Venetian mountains, caused by extensive deforestation, a wheat monoculture and the crisis of traditional manufacturing.[89] In the late 1800s the effect had been a massive emigration from those areas, as Emilio Franzina's studies have clearly demonstrated.[90] As in every mountain environment, common property had had a relevant function for a long time; as a matter of fact, part of the land that the Erto municipality sold to SADE was actually the property of the citizens, deriving from a 1908 division of common lands. The same situation occurred in other communities in the valley, for instance in Forno di Zoldo, where the municipality once again sold off common lands to SADE without having the right to do so.[91] Hence, the Great Vajont occupied spaces crowded with other meanings and functions; to build the reservoir SADE needed to expropriate the lower, most fertile and water-rich lands in the valley.[92] Additionally, beyond the land submerged by water, the new hydroelectric geography created an off-limits area in the mountains enclosing the reservoir; access to the slopes with their forests and pastures was prohibited by the corporate organisation of space.[93] From that point of view the nation arrived in the Vajont as a colonial power, exploring, dispossessing and developing; the pre-existing social and environmental forms of space were literally submerged by modernity.

It was to defend their lands, properties and traditional uses that the Vajont mountaineers initiated their resistance against SADE. The first grassroots committee was born to confront the corporation at the time of the acquisition/expropriation of lands. SADE was not just building its own profitable business; the central government had labelled its activities as a 'public utility' and therefore villagers and local institutions had no option but to give away their lands. The expropriation process was a total defeat for local people in regard to both public and private properties. SADE took no prisoners. In the case of public property, villagers simply paid the price without receiving anything in return: they lost their rights to access common lands and even their very property rights, as in the intricate case of the roughly ninety hectares the municipality of Erto-Casso sold to SADE, even though those lands had been formally divided

---

89. Lazzarini 1991, pp. 47–68.

90. Franzina 2005.

91. Merlin 2004, pp. 19–26.

92. Merlin 1993, p. 18; Filippin Lazzeris 1983, p. 101.

93. Merlin 1993, p. 25 (article originally published in *L'Unità* on 10 March 1956).

among the village families in 1908.[94] Of course, the value of these lands was underestimated (3.94 *lire*/square metre),[95] but the situation did not improve for private owners. Many of them had sold their richer meadows for 35–40 *lire*/square metre and the poorer pastures for 18–30 *lire*; the mediation of Erto-Casso's mayor Caterina Filippin forced SADE to accept 100 *lire*/square metre for every kind of land, a good result but undervalued compared with 150–200 *lire* on the regular market.[96] Caterina Filippin was instrumental in the creation of the first committee challenging SADE on the issue of expropriation; in fact, the president of the committee was her husband Paolo Gallo, who, being the local physician, was a leading figure in the community. Nevertheless, this first committee did not last long; SADE, as always, succeeded in dividing the opposition, offering better deals to those who were willing to sell. Apparently, Filippin's family was among them and they secretly sold their land to SADE. Whatever the story, Caterina Filippin radically changed her attitude towards this issue; arguing that any resistance against SADE would be vain, she encouraged people to accept 'little but now', rather than to fight forever.[97] We should be aware that SADE had good 'arguments' on its side: the fact that the projects for the Great Vajont were officially a 'public utility' did not allow any options to private and public landowners; if they did not sell, they ran the risk of being expropriated. Furthermore, resisting SADE was an act of rebellion; from 1956, SADE also had the Carabinieri on its side. In that year a Carabinieri station was opened in Erto-Casso for the first time in the history of the village, essentially to intimidate, control and repress those organising against SADE.[98] The local committee immediately fell under the Carabinieri's watchful eye; according to them, the committee seems to be some kind of secret, seditious and conspiratorial association, worthy of surveillance[99]. The repressive character of the Carabinieri manifested itself on several occasions: for instance, the communist deputy Giorgio Bettiol, a member of the committee, was taken to the

---

94. According to Tina Merlin, all these lands were subjected to common use and had been partially divided among the families of Casso. Nevertheless, the division was not recognised as legal because it had not been properly regularly registered in the cadastre (apparently because the municipality of Erto-Casso refused to pay the surveyor who did the job, he did not register the transactions); in Merlin 2001, pp. 43–44.

95. *Ibid.* pp. 43–45.

96. *Ibid.* p. 46.

97. *Ibid.*

98. *Ibid.* p. 48.

99. *Ibid.* p. 61.

Tina Merlin

Carabinieri station and warned not to spread false and misleading rumours.[100]
Things went much worse for the communist journalist Tina Merlin, who was
accused of 'spreading false and misleading information aiming to subvert public
order' and had to stand trial. Tina Merlin is without a doubt the most relevant
figure in the Vajont story because she not only denounced SADE's abuses but
also foresaw the disaster years in advance. In the 1959 article that provoked
the prosecution against her and *L'Unità*,[101] Tina Merlin wrote:

> [The mountaineers who join the committee] glimpse in the egoism of the
> corporation and in the inertia of the institutions a serious danger for the very

100. Passi 1968, p. 33.

101. *L'Unità* was the official newspaper of the Italian Communist Party until 1991.

existence of the village which lies behind the 150 million cubic metre reservoir, in a landslide prone area...[102]

The trial against Tina Merlin was a defeat for SADE; the court in Milan acquitted her and the director of *L'Unità* with a remarkable judgement that, taken seriously, could have changed the story of Vajont. The judges wrote that the news Merlin disseminated in her article was neither false nor misleading; having heard a series of witnesses describing damaged buildings and other signs of geological instability, the judges of Milan were persuaded that 'the SADE reservoir constitute[d] and [was] considered by local citizens a serious danger for the village because they fear[ed] that, eroding the soil, by its nature already subject to landslides, the reservoir [could] provoke the collapse of the town'. Finally, the Milanese court recognized that the people of Vajont were anxious, but their anxiety was due to the dam and not to Tina Merlin's article.[103] If the aim of SADE was to intimidate Tina Merlin, they did not succeed; Tina had been a partisan during the Nazi-Fascist occupation and she was not easily frightened. During the years she wrote several articles on the Vajont but she became famous with a prophetic piece published in February 1961. Obviously, the pressure exerted by SADE had its effect; in her book Tina Merlin recalled that *L'Unità*'s editorial board, fearing a new trial, only reluctantly published her article on the coming landslide. Only the intercession of another journalist from Erto convinced the board to risk its publication.[104]

> Now what we have always feared and denounced, the irreparable, is happening. A gigantic mass of fifty million cubic metres of material, the whole mountain on the left side of the reservoir, is collapsing. Nobody knows whether the subsidence will be slow or will happen with a terrible crash. In the latter case we cannot foresee the consequences. It might be that the famous dam, which has been praised – and rightly - for its technological qualities stands firm (if the contrary happened ... a tremendous disaster would hit Longarone); nonetheless, we will face other difficult problems.[105]

Tina was optimistic about the immensity of the landslide, which was at least five times bigger than her prediction; apart from this, she was sadly correct: Mount Toc was basically falling down into the reservoir, threatening all the

---

102. Merlin 2004, p. 32 [article originally published in *L'Unità* on 5 May 1959].

103. The text of the sentence is at http://www.vajont.info/vaj-Merlin_assolta.html

104. Merlin 2004, p. 109.

105. Tina Merlin, 'Una enorme massa di 50 milioni di metri cubi minaccia la vita e gli averi degli abitanti di Erto', in *L'Unità* 21 February 1961, quoted here from Merlin 2004, p. 37.

communities in the valley up to Longarone. This 1961 article is a fundamental piece in the story because it proves beyond a doubt the predictability of the disaster and the widespread awareness of the pending risk. In effect, after the early mobilisation regarding expropriation, the conflict over the Great Vajont shifted to the issue of the hazard emanating from it. Evidently this was a local struggle, involving mainly the villages of Erto and Casso, but it was also part of a larger movement concerning the damage created by hydroelectric companies in the Alps, a movement that found its organised expression in the *Comitato per la Rinascita dell'Arco Alpino* [Committee for the Recovery of the Alps].[106] Everywhere in the Alps dams and reservoirs were displacing communities and erasing their rights but in the Vajont these communities' very survival was under attack. From the beginning of the story the people of the valley clearly knew that a huge dam at the foot of Mount Toc was not a good idea; even the local dialect attested to the landslide-prone character of the mountain –Toc can be translated as 'rotten' or 'soaked', not exactly a reassuring toponym for a place destined to contain 150 million cubic metres of water.[107] To corroborate their beliefs the villagers asked the opinion of a professional geologist, Prof. Milli. According to Tina Merlin, he clearly argued against the building of the reservoir.[108] Unfortunately, information about the grassroots opposition to the dam is confusing and sources are limited. Very likely the local committee remained informal for several years, meeting, as Tina Merlin recalled, in one of the taverns of Erto-Casso, the centre of public life.[109] It was only in 1959 that a formal association was created with the aim of defending its members in

106. Merlin 2004, p. 17 (article originally published in *L'Unità* on 26 May 1955).

107. In his performance the actor Marco Paolini ironised about the obvious sinister meaning of Toc in the local dialect; in Paolini and Vacis 2006.

108. Tina Merlin mentioned the negative report from Prof. Ervinio Milli in her interview for French Public Television, quoted here from *Mixer* 6 May 1996, Italian Public Television. The story of this interview is worth telling: first of all, only foreign media decided to interview Tina Merlin, even though she was the only Italian journalist who foresaw the disaster years in advance; furthermore, French television, pushed by the Italian government, did not transmit the interview immediately but only after the protests of the French media, which denounced the censorship against her. Information about this is at http://www.lastoriasiamonoi.rai.it/puntata.aspx?id=80 In an article published on 14 October 1963 the leftist newspaper *Paese Sera* denounced that while the *New York Herald Tribune*, *New York Times*, and *Le Monde* had referred to Merlin's articles in *L'Unità*, no Italian newspapers made any reference to the communist campaign against the dam; in Merlin 2001, p.167.

109. Merlin 2004, p. 61.

relation to the SADE's hydroelectric works.[110] Although subjected to the strict surveillance of the Carabinieri, this association remained relatively 'moderate' in its repertoire of mobilisation and protest. According to available sources, writing letters to the authorities was the key tool employed by villagers. In one of those letters, addressed to the area's Parliamentary representatives, the Prefects and the Chiefs of the Public Works Offices, the association wrote:

> Erto is built on an old landslide with a 40–70 per cent slope and it will be too close to the water of the lake (150 million cubic metres), which, moving and above all countersinking, could provoke slides and threaten people's lives.[111]

These expressions of concern could not be more clear and farsighted. According to Tina Merlin, private citizens, grassroots associations and municipalities wrote hundreds of similar letters.[112] For instance, in 1958 73 peasants sent a letter to the relevant offices, expressing their doubts and worries about the requested enlargement of the dam and reservoir.[113] Seeking political allies, the committee sent a letter to all area deputies:

> We are moved by anxiety over the SADE's new request to elevate the level of the reservoir from 677 to 722.5 m ... We ask your cooperation ... to mitigate the harsh and sometimes bullying attitude of the company and to find a solution which could satisfy the needs of both parties, the hydroelectric uses and the small landowners' interests.[114]

This request received no reply; only the PCI [Italian Communist Party] deputy Giorgio Bettiol appeared at the public assembly convened by the local committee in Casso.[115] I will return later to the special involvement of the Italian Communist Party in the Vajont story. If the grassroots organisations failed in accomplishing their goals, things did not proceed better for the public administration; the letters from the Erto-Casso municipality and other local governments were equally ineffectual. The provincial council of Belluno, after a unanimous vote, sent a document asking that 'all measures be employed to guarantee the safety of the people of the Vajont Valley'.[116] Hence, in 1961,

---

110. Deed of the notary Adolfo Soccal, Erto 3 May 1959, document published in PCI 1963, pp. 9–10.

111. PCI 1963, p. 11.

112. Merlin 2004, p. 60.

113. PCI 1963, p. 7; Merlin 2004, p. 59.

114. PCI 1963, p. 8.

115. Merlin 2004, p. 61.

116. PCI 1963, p. 13.

when that document was approved, the danger was so apparent that even the pro-government council of Belluno (the Democratic Christian Party ruled there) started to manifest its opposition to the dam. In fact, by that time it was no longer just rumours of mountaineers speaking about cracks in buildings and soil: in March 1959 a huge landslide (three million cubic meteres) crashed into the reservoir of Pontesei, close to Erto and Casso, killing one worker; and in November 1960 the danger came closer with 800,000 cubic metres of rock detaching from Mount Toc and falling into the lake. In 1959 the construction of a road to circumnavigate the reservoir revealed the geological problems of the area; even Giorgio Dal Piaz, who had signed the first optimistic survey, recognised the instability.[117] If these events somehow confirmed villagers' fears, SADE actually already had scientific proof corroborating the existence of a serious danger to the stability of the mountain. At least from 1957 SADE had conducted several geological surveys documenting Mont Toc's instability. The geologist Leopold Müller, one of the experts engaged by SADE, was the first, in 1957, to speak about the existence of a landslide threat to the reservoir;[118] in 1959 SADE commissioned a new investigation by the geologist Edoardo Semenza, Carlo's son, who has been credited as the discoverer of the Vajont landslide.[119] In 1961 Müller wrote that a mass of 200 million cubic metres of rocks was unavoidably moving towards the reservoir and in the same year another geologist, Pietro Caloi, changed his previously optimistic vision, speaking of 'crushed rocks' composing the mountain. There can be no question as to why in that year the father of the Great Vajont, Carlo Semenza, wrote an anxious letter to his university mentor, Professor Ferniani:

> I cannot hide that the issue of these landslides has been distressing me for months; probably, things are greater than us and there are no appropriate measures ...

---

117. SADE refused to build a bridge for local people to access the other side of the lake on the grounds of Mount Toc's geological instability. Hence, as Tina Merlin ironically argued, 'the bridge cannot be built because the terrain will not sustain it, while it can sustain a dam and a reservoir'; in Merlin 2004, p. 69. See Dal Piaz 1960, doc. 14 xxxvi/5048-5049.

118. Niccolini, Vajont una frana annunciata, at http://www.vajont.info/vajontNiccolini1.html. Müller 1961, in the archive of the Committee for the Vajont Disaster, xxxix/1729.

119. Giudici and Semenza 1960, in the archive of the Committee for the Vajont Disaster, #15. For an overview on the geological literature about the disaster, see De Unterrichter 1965, in the same archive, no reference number.

Epilogue

After so many remarkable works I find myself in a situation which is slipping through our fingers due its dimensions.[120]

SADE considered the possibility of a gigantic landslide into the reservoir so serious that it not only invested million of *lire* to build a bypass conduit in case the reservoir were split in two[121] but it also commissioned a series of tests by the *Centro Modelli Idraulici di Novi* [Centre for Hydro Modelling] to ascertain the likely effects of a landslide on the reservoir.[122]

The issue of predictability is central in the Vajont story.[123] Was the disaster an unpredictable natural event or the result of industrial and political choices which deliberately underestimated and ignored a well-known risk?[124] In 1971 the High Court of Appeals recognised the predictability of the disaster, establishing the culpability of the defendants with aggravating circumstances.[125] In effect, the story is full of signs and evidence proving that the hazard was well known to local people, SADE and even to the authorities, due to the continuous claims of the villagers, while, of course, the hydroelectric company continued to keep any negative reports secret.

People from the valley had an empirical knowledge of their territory; they did not need a geological education to discover the cracks in the soil, to notice the slipping of the trees and to feel the noises and shocks coming from Mount Toc.[126] Just a month before the disaster, the municipality of Erto-Casso

---

120. Carlo Semenza to Vincenzo Ferniani, 10 April 1961, quoted in Gervasoni 1969, pp. 30–31.

121. On the by-pass conduit, 'Ricordare il Vajont', *Sapere* November 1974, pp. 56–57.

122. Merlin 2001, pp. 129–30. For a detailed history of the experiment in Novi see Datei 2005.

123. On the predictability of the disaster, see Calvino 1974.

124. Immediately after the disaster someone wrote in the Fire Department magazine: 'The Vajont is not similar to other fatalities, nor does it resemble such past cataclysms as Pompeii, Messina and Agadir; it does not belong to the family of hurricanes, earthquakes, floods and eruptions. In the Vajont case nature became more evil because of humans and their pretence to gain high profits through technical knowledge'; in Pais 1963.

125. A synthesis of the sentence is available at http://www.vajont.net/page.php?pageid=SEZIO007

126. When the French journalist asked Tina Merlin about the scientific sources of her prevision of the disaster, she quoted the local mountaineers as the best informed people about the environmental problems of their valley; http://www.lastoriasiamonoi.rai.it/puntata.aspx?id=80

wrote yet another letter to the company and the responsible offices requesting a formal declaration of no danger:

> Here we want to know with absolute certainty that the dam does not, and will not, cause any damage to our village, its inhabitants and their goods. If you cannot give us such a formal statement, we warn you to remove the cause of risk before reparable and irreparable damage happens here, as it has happened elsewhere.[127]

While requesting an official declaration of 'no danger' and explicitly challenging the optimistic visions of the professional experts, the municipality clearly stated that, in its view, several slides would occur. The answer from the company was contemptuous: the worries expressed by the municipality were without any scientific foundation because the company was the custodian of safety, daily monitoring the mountain with its professional experts and sophisticated instruments. Everything else was just rumours from mountaineers.[128] It was true indeed that the hydroelectric company was monitoring the slides with piezometric boreholes, spotlights and other technical tools but they did not share this information with anybody. As a matter of fact, in the last weeks before the disaster, the municipality of Erto-Casso prepared its own handmade system to monitor the landslide (wooden sticks with notches) which the local guard Matteo Corona checked daily.[129] Wooden sticks vs. seismographers, peasants vs. geologists, the mayor of a mountain village vs. engineers of a powerful company – modernity was on one side of the barricade and it had to be right. When, a few days after the disaster, a journalist asked the survivors why they had stayed there even though everyone knew that the mountain was collapsing, they answered 'because we hoped that they [the experts, the authorities, etc.] knew more than we did'.[130] Unfortunately, they did not realise that knowing was not enough. The plaintiffs' attorney Sandro Canestrini in his address to the court said:

> The Vajont trial is above all a case about the responsibilities of science, technology and bureaucracy in the defence of the elites' social and political interests.[131]

---

127. PCI 1963, pp. 16–17.

128. PCI 1963, p. 18.

129. This story is told directly by Mauro Corona in the documentary *AZ Vajont 1971*, directed by Enzo d'Aquila and transmitted by Italian Public Television.

130. PCI 1963, p. 84.

131. Canestrini 2003, p. 28.

Epilogue

Tina Merlin used more or less the same words when she wrote that the Vajont 'will remain a monument to the eternal scorn of science and politics, a marriage which strongly connected illustrious academics and economic power, in that case the SADE'.[132] Here I cannot elaborate on all the almost incredible connivances between the company and public officers, supposedly monitoring the hydroelectric plant; in 1971 the High Court of Appeals condemned two engineers from both sides, the enterprise and the government, Alberico Biadene and Francesco Sensidoni. But the politicisation of science became even stronger in the aftermath of the catastrophe because, at that point, the agency of experts shifted from the prevention to the explanation of the event. The fact was that finding experts willing to work for the prosecutors and the survivors was extremely difficult and while the most renowned scholars in the field of geology, hydraulics and engineering crowded the defenders' benches, no one was available for the other side.[133] Only Floriano Calvino, an adjunct professor of geology at Genoa University, accepted the job; there was no one else from the Italian universities. In his deposition in court Floriano Calvino revealed a 'conspiracy of silence' and the tie connecting academia, political power and the electric companies. The trial papers are still sequestered but in his address Sandro Canestrini used the story of Floriano Calvino, who suffered a serious mobbing and was removed from his position at the university, evidence of the prostitution of science to economic and political power.[134] As Canestrini said, science was 'humble with the powerful people, hypocritical with everyone else, ferocious and inhumane with the poor'.[135] For this reason, the team working for the prosecutors was comprised entirely of foreign scientists, bar Calvino. Actually, even like this, matters were difficult for the prosecutors: for instance, the Italian Foreign Office refused to send an official invitation to William J. Turnbull, the chief of the Dams Service at the US Department of Defense, who was willing to work as an expert for the State.[136] In the end, the committee was formed by Floriano Calvino; Marcel Roubault, Director of the National

---

132. Merlin 2001, p. 21.

133. The attorney Canestrini quoted an interview with the mayor of Longarone in which he declared that no one from the Italian academy was willing to join the public prosecutors and the survivors in their quest for justice; the interview was published in *GENTE*, 11 December 1968; in Canestrini 2003, p. 86.

134. *Ibid.* p. 88.

135. *Ibid.* pp. 75–76.

136. Passi 1968, p. 82.

School of Geology, University of Nancy; Alfred Stucky, former director of the Polytechnic Institute in Lausanne; and Henry Gridel, professor of hydraulic engineering at the University of Paris.[137] Their final report left no room for doubt: because the disaster had been predictable and the circumstances unexceptional, corporate and public experts had not done what they should have to prevent the genocide. This survey subverted the results of the parliamentary committee on the Vajont which had proposed an 'all natural' explanation of the disaster, rejecting any responsibility on the part of public and private officers.[138] Obviously, this interpretation of the Vajont disaster as a 'natural' event – that is, beyond human control – was the basic argument not only of the defence but more generally of national public opinion. It is enough to quote here two masters of Italian journalism, Dino Buzzati and Giorgio Bocca, who both used this kind of naturalistic narrative describing the Vajont:

> A stone falls into a glass of water and the water is spilled on the tablecloth. That's it. But that the glass was hundreds of metres high and the stone was as big as a mountain and below, on the tablecloth, there were thousands of human beings who could not defend themselves. It is not that the glass was intrinsically broken: therefore, we cannot call monsters those who built it, as in the case of the Gleno disaster. The glass was built perfectly … Once again the fantasy of nature has been bigger and smarter than the fantasy of science. Although defeated in open battle, nature takes its revenge from behind.[139]

> Five villages, thousands of people there yesterday, today they are flattened and no one to blame, no one could predict. In these atomic times you could say that this is a clean disaster: humans did not do anything; nature did and it is neither good nor evil, just indifferent.[140]

The very idea that it was a human-made event crying out for justice was a controversial issue; only the communists joined the survivors in exposing the responsibilities and demanding justice. For this reason they were called 'jackals' and unanimously accused of manipulating the disaster for political ends; *Il Corriere della Sera* [The Evening Courier] spoke of an invasion of communists from the neighbouring red region of Emilia Romagna aiming to incite the

---

137. *Ibid.* p. 87.
138. Actually the Democratic Christian Party strongly supported the creation of a new parliamentary committee to counter the previous government committee which had included the public and private officers responsible for the disaster.
139. Dino Buzzati, 'Natura crudele', *Il Corriere della Sera*, 11 October 1963.
140. Giorgio Bocca, *Il Giorno*, 11 October 1963, quoted from Vastano 2008, p. 49

population.[141] While the mainstream media, the Democratic Christian Party and the Church insisted on 'naturalising' the event, the PCI tried to expose its political character.

> Paying tribute to the Vajont victims and working for the survivors also means above all sustaining the urgent popular demand for justice, which asks us to identify the criminal motives moving the electric monopoly and the connivances of the political powers leading to the disaster. We want to arrive at the chief culprit…[142]

The PCI had on its side a longstanding commitment to the Vajont, of which Tina Merlin's articles constituted the most powerful evidence. It is true that activists from the party ran to the Vajont in the aftermath of the disaster; former partisans who had fought in the valley felt a particular bond with these people and places, arriving there as volunteers.[143] Party members and the CGIL – that is, the trade union closer to communists – supported the survivors by offering their legal offices and serving as attorneys.[144]

The PCI was indeed politicising Vajont: the disaster, it claimed, was not the result of a miscalculation, corrupt public servants and acquiescent experts but actually the failure of a system based on private profit. Nevertheless, politics did not arrive there only through communists: the landscape was already political, shaped by economic interests, political alliances and popular resistance. Politics was what SADE needed to approve its plan for the Great Vajont; politics shaped the expertise, taming any doubt or scepticism; politics repressed the resistance of local communities; and finally, in the aftermath of the massacre, politics arrived in the Vajont not only in the figures of communist agit-props but in those of members of the government and institutions. The Vajont was, and would remain, a terrain for political confrontation and, as always, for divided memories. In 2005 a writer and artist from Erto, Mauro Corona, again inflamed the controversy in an interview with the radical right-wing newspaper *Il Giornale* [The Newspaper], owned by the Berlusconi family; in it he raised the classic accusation against the Communist Party, saying that it had exploited the 'incident' – and the choice of the word is not casual – to attack

---

141. Alberto Cavallari, 'I vivi ricominciano a vivere', *Il Corriere della Sera* 12 October 1963.

142. PCI 1963, pp. 67–68.

143. Tina Merlin, 'Difesero gli impianti SADE, ora la diga li ha uccisi', *L'Unità*, 18 October 1963, quoted from Merlin 2004, pp. 54–55.

144. Passi 1968, p. 95.

the government.[145] The answer arrived soon afterwards: a group of the PCI's former members, all deeply involved in the Vajont story, published a passionate defence in the magazine of the local institute for the study of Resistance.[146] In effect, it was not difficult to refute Corona's insinuations, since, at least from my point of view, the PCI's role in the quest for justice and in supporting the survivors cannot be questioned. Nevertheless, this recent story proves that the memory of Vajont is still divided. As always, contrasting memories and the politicisation of landscape have become embedded into the material fabric of places. The 2003 conflict over the cemetery of Fortogna, analysed by Lucia Vastano, is exemplary of this process. In 2003, using part of the money derived from legal compensation, the municipality of Longarone decided to transform the original victims' cemetery into a national monument, in response to a decree by the President of the Republic. Nationalising the memory implied erasing what had been there before, in concrete terms, razing the old cemetery of Fortogna, crowded with the familiar memories of those who had built it for their loved ones. Lucia Vastano quoted the emblematic tombstone of the Paiola family (seven deaths including three children): 'brutally and cowardly murdered by inattention and human greed, still waiting in vain for justice for this infamous fault. Premeditated massacre'.[147] Tombstones like this were no longer allowed in the newly renovated cemetery. The nationalisation of memory implied anesthetising suffering and rage and imposing a neat and antiseptic remembrance, with the substitution of every pre-existing personalised sign with geometric marble blocks, all uniform, bearing only the names of victims. Several survivors felt that the redesign of their cemetery, planned without their participation, was just another act of violence against them. In a letter to the mayor of Longarone one of the protesters wrote:

> Forty years ago the cynicism and arrogance of the owners of the dam obliterated an entire village and its inhabitants. Today you, with the same cynicism and arrogance are deleting its last memory.[148]

As in several other cases, this time the memory of the Vajont found its way to court, with a complaint of defamation and the request for compensation.

---

145. Francesco Patti, 'Sulla tragedia del Vajont dalla sinistra solo speculazioni politiche', *Il Giornale*, 9 October 2005.

146. See the special section on the Corona's polemic in *I Protagonisti* 205: 89.

147. Vastano 2008, p. 155.

148. Mario Pozzobon to the mayor of Logarone, 12 April 2003, quoted in Vastano 2008, pp. 254–55.

Epilogue

What is certain is that the memory of Vajont is still seeking its proper place in the history of the country.

Bibliography[1]

Printed Material

Anon. 1909. 'Gli sports della montagna'. *Rivista Mensile del TCI* 1.

Anon. 1911. 'Il Touring pel turismo invernale'. *Rivista mensile del TCI* 1.

Abba, Giuseppe Cesare. 1981 [1962]. *The Diary of One of Garibaldi's Thousand*. Trans. with an introduction by E. R. Vincent. (Westport, CT: Greenwood Press).

Acerbo, Giacomo. 1930. *Le direttive della politica forestale del governo fascista. Relazione presentata dal ministro dell'agricoltura e foreste del Regno d'Italia alla associazione dell'agricoltura nazionale ungherese. Budapest marzo 1930*. (Rome: Tip. Camera dei deputati).

Afan de Rivera, Carlo. 1833. *Considerazioni sui mezzi da restituire il valore proprio ai doni che la natura ha largamente conceduto al Regno delle Due Sicilie*. (Naples: Dalla Stamperia e Cartiera del Fibreno).

Agnew, John. 2011. 'Landscape and National Identity in Europe: England versus Italy in the Role of Landscape in Identity Formation', in Z. Roca, P. Claval and J. Agnew (eds.) *Landscape, Identities and Development*. (Aldershot: Ashgate).

Agnoloni, Veruska *et al.* 2008. *Siamo Passati. Luoghi della memoria e testimonianze sulla Grande Guerra a Vazzola, Visnà e Tezze*. (Vittorio Veneto: Dario De Bastiani Editore).

Agostini, Augusto. 1928. 'L'attività svolta dalla Milizia Nazionale Forestale dalla sua costituzione al 31 marzo 1928-VI'. *L'Alpe* 7.

Almagià, Roberto. 1937. 'Sguardo geografico-economico', in INEA, *Lo spopolamento montano in Italia vii l'Appennino abruzzese-laziale*. (Rome: Tip. Failli).

Altobelli, Dario. 2007. 'Il cibo del brigante. Una lettura metaforica del brigantaggio di fine Ottocento'. Etnoantropologia online 2 proceedings of the 10th National Congress AISEA on 'Cibo e alimentazione. Tradizione, simboli, saperi', Rome, 5–7 July. Available online at http://digilander.libero.it/aisea/atti_2006/saggio%20ALTOBELLI.pdf.

Altobello, Giuseppe. 1924. 'Un nemico da combattere: il lupo'. *Le Vie d'Italia* 8.

Aniasi, Aldo *et al.* 1997. *Ne valeva la pena. Dalla repubblica dell'Ossola alla costituzione italiana*. (Milan: M&B Publishing s.r.l.).

Ankarloo, Bengt and Stuart Clark (eds.) 1999. *Witchcraft and Magic in Europe. The Eighteenth and Nineteenth Centuries*. (Philadelphia: University of Pennsylvania Press).

Arbizzani, Luigi. 1981. *Habitat e partigiani in Emilia Romagna*. (Bologna: Brechtiana Editrice).

Argante Bocchio (Massimo). 1984. 'Il distaccamento di Gemisto nel dramma del primo inverno'. *L'impegno* 2.

---

1.   Note: all online sources were live at 2 April 2011.

Bibliography

Armiero, Marco and Nancy Peluso. 2008. 'Insurgent Natures and Nations: Unpacking Socio-Environmental Histories of Forest Conflict'. Paper presented at the international conference *Common Ground, Converging Gazes. Integrating the Social and Environmental in History*, Paris, 13 September 2008.

Armiero, Marco. 1999. *Il territorio come risorsa. Comunità, economie e istituzioni nei boschi abruzzesi (1806-1860)*. (Naples: Liguori).

Armiero, Marco. 2006. 'Italian Mountains', in M. Armiero (ed.) *Views from the South: Environmental Stories from the Mediterranean World (19th–20th Centuries)*. (Naples: ISSM-CNR).

Armiero, Marco. 2006. 'Montagne', in G. Massullo (ed.) *Storia del Molise*. (Rome: Donzelli).

Armiero, Marco. 2009. 'Seeing Like a Protester: Nature, Power, and Environmental Struggles'. *Left History* 13:1.

Armiero, Marco. 2010. 'Nationalizing the Mountains. Natural and Political Landscapes in World War I', in M. Armiero and M. Hall (eds.) *Nature and History in Modern Italy*. (Athens: Ohio University Press).

Armiero, Marco. 2011. 'Enclosing the Sea. Work and Leisure Spaces in the Remaking of the Naples Waterfront (1870–1900)'. *Radical History Review* 109.

Arnould, Paul and Simon Laurent. 1994. 'Forêt, guerre, après-guerre autour du Chemin-des-Dames', in A. Corvol and J.-P. Amat (eds.) *Forêt et guerre*. (Paris: L'Harmattan).

Ascari, Odorico. 1973. *Una arringa per Longarone*. (Feltre: Stab. Tipografico Panfilo Castaldi).

Associazione culturale Flaiano. 1986. *Il messia d'Abruzzo. Atti del convegno*. (Pescara: G. Fabiani).

Astarita, Tommaso. 2005. *Between Salt Water and Holy Water: A History of Southern Italy*. (New York: W.W. Norton & Company).

Azimonti, Eugenio. 1921. *Il Mezzogiorno agrario quale è*. (Bari: Laterza).

Bach, Maurice. 1994. 'La convalescence et la guérison des Forêt lorraines', in A. Corvol and J.-P. Amat (eds.) *Forêt et guerre*. (Paris: L'Harmattan).

Balbo, Adriano. 2005. *Quando inglesi arrivare noi tutti morti: cronache di lotta partigiana*. (Turin: Blu).

Ball, John. 1863. *A Guide to the Western Alps*. (London: Longman Roberts and Green).

Barbagallo, Francesco. 1984. *Nitti*. (Turin: Unione tipografico-editrice torinese).

Barbisan, Umberto. 2007. *Il crollo della diga di Pian del Gleno: un errore tecnico*. (Cavirana: Tecnologos).

Barca, Stefania. 2010. *Enclosing Water. Nature and Political Economy in a Mediterranean Valley, 1796–1916*. (Cambridge: White Horse Press).

Barca, Stefania. 2010. 'Pan y veneno. Reflexiones para una investigación sobre el 'ambientalismo del trabajo' en Italia, 1968–1998'. *Laboreal* 2.

Bardelli, Daniele. 2002. 'Alpinismo', in V. De Grazia and S. Luzzatto (eds.) *Dizionario del fascismo*. (Turin: Einaudi).

Bardelli, Francesco. 1977. *David Lazzaretti*. (Milan: Stampa Copte).

Bibliography

Barone, Giuseppe. 1986. *Mezzogiorno e modernizzazione: elettricità, irrigazione e bonifica nell'Italia contemporanea.* (Turin: Einaudi).

Barone, Giuseppe. 1993. 'Nitti e il dibattito sull'energia', in L. De Rosa (ed.) *Storia dell'industria elettrica in Italia. Il potenziamento tecnico e finanziario 1914–1925.* (Rome and Bari: Laterza).

Bartaletti, Fabrizio. 2004. *Geografia e cultura delle Alpi.* (Milan: Franco Angeli).

Bartolini, Carlo. 1897. *Il brigantaggio nello Stato Pontificio. Cenno storico-aneddotico dal 1860 al 1870.* (Rome: Stabilimento tipografico dell'opinione).

Barzellotti, Giacomo. 1885. *David Lazzaretti di Arcidosso detto il Santo: I suoi seguaci e la sua leggenda.* (Bologna: Nicola Zanichelli).

Barzini, Luigi. 1917. *Dal Trentino al Carso.* (Milan: Fratelli Treves).

Battilani, Patrizia. 2001. *Vacanze di pochi, vacanze di tutti. L'evoluzione del turismo europeo.* (Bologna: Il Mulino).

Battisti, Andrea. 1994. 'I boschi', in *Storia dell'altipiano dei Sette comuni.* (Vicenza: la grafica & stampa srl).

Battisti, Cesare. 1918. *Gli alpini.* (Milan: Fratelli Treves Editori).

Beattie, Andrew. 2006. *The Alps. A Cultural History.* (Oxford: Signal Books).

Belco, Victoria C. 2001. 'Mutineer Johnny? The Italian Partisan Movement as Mutiny', in J. Hathway (ed.) *Rebellion Repression Reinvention. Mutiny in Comparative Perspective.* (Westport: Praeger).

Ben-Ghiat, Ruth. 2001. *Fascist Modernities: Italy, 1922–1945.* (Berkeley: University of California Press).

Berardo, Livio (ed.). 2007. *I sentieri della libertà: Piemonte e Alpi occidentali 1938-1945: la guerra, la Resistenza, la persecuzione razziale.* (Milan: TCI).

Bertarelli, Luigi Vittorio. 1909. 'Come si mette in valore una montagna'. *Rivista mensile del TCI* 7.

Bertarelli, Luigi Vittorio. 1909. 'Per il bosco e per il pascolo. Appello ai volenterosi'. *Rivista mensile del TCI* 6.

Bertarelli, Luigi Vittorio. 1911. 'Il Mottarone'. *Rivista mensile del TCI* 9.

Bertarelli, Luigi Vittorio. 1915. 'Vent'anni di un sodalizio nazionale. Il Touring Club Italiano'. *Nuova Antologia* March: 37–8.

Bertarelli, Luigi Vittorio, 1926. 'La missione del Touring'. *Le Vie d'Italia* 3.

Bevilacqua, Piero. 1996. *Tra natura e storia. Ambiente, economie, risorse in Italia.* (Rome: Donzelli).

Blackbourn, David. 2006. *The Conquest of Nature. Water, Landscape and the Making of Modern Germany.* (New York: W. W. Norton & Co).

Bocca, Giorgio. 1995. *Storia dell'Italia partigiana.* (Milan: Mondadori).

Bocedi, R. and P.G. Bracchi. 2004. 'Evoluzione demografica del lupo (*Canis lupus*) in Italia: cause storiche del declino e della ripresa, nuove problematiche indotte e possibili soluzioni'. *Annali Facoltà Medicina Veterinaria di Parma* 24.

Bognetti, Giovanni. 1928. 'Per il parco nazionale d'Abruzzo'. *Le Vie d'Italia* 3.

Bibliography

Bollati, Giulio. 1983. *L'italiano. Il carattere nazionale come storia e come invenzione.* (Turin: Einaudi).

Bourelly, Giuseppe. 1865. *Brigantaggio nelle zone militari di Melfi e Lacedonia dal 1860 al 1865.* (Naples: Tip. Pasquale Mea).

Bramwell, Anna. 1989. *Ecology in the 20th Century. A History.* (New Haven: Yale University Press).

Brenna, Enrico. 1937. 'La vacca del povero e le capre dei ricchi'. *Il Bosco* 2.

Brocca, Giovanni. 1932. 'Valli ossolane', in INEA, *Lo spopolamento montano in Italia vol. I. Le Alpi liguri-piemontesi.* (Milan and Rome: Treves-Treccani-Tuminelli).

Brocca, Giovanni. 1934. 'Val Vigezzo e Valle Canobina', in INEA, *Lo spopolamento montano in Italia vol. I. Le Alpi liguri-piemontesi.* (Rome: Tip. Failli).

Brunello, Piero. 1981. *Ribelli, questuanti e banditi. Proteste contadine in Veneto e Friuli 1814-1866.* (Venice: Marsilio).

Bullard, Robert. 1990. *Dumping in Dixie. Race, Class, and Environmental Quality,* (Boulder: Westview Press).

Burat, Tavo. 2006. 'Dolcino, civiltà montanara e autonomia bioregionale', paper presented at the conference *Dolcino. Storia, pensiero, messaggio,* Varallo 4 November 2006. Available online at http://fradolcino.interfree.it/

Buratti, Gustavo. 1987. 'L'altra religione. L'obelisco per rivendicare Dolcino'. *L'impegno* 2.

Burckhardt, Jacob. 1929. *The Civilization of the Renaissance in Italy.* (London: G. G. Harrap & Co). Here quoted from Project Gutenberg Etext at http://www.paduan.dk/Kunsthistorie%202008/Tekster/The%20Civilization%20of%20the%20Renaissance%20in%20Italy%20-%20Burckhardt.pdf

Caloi, Pietro and Maria Cecilia Spadea. 1960. 'Serie di esperienze geosismiche eseguite in sponda sinistra a monte della diga del Vajont (Novembre 1959)'. Document in the *Proceedings of the Parliamentary Committee on the Vajont Disaster.*

Calvino, Floriano. 1974. 'Elementi tecnici di prevedibilita della catastrofe del Vajont'. *Sapere* January 768.

Calvino, Italo. 1972 [1964]. *Il sentiero dei nidi di ragno.* (Milan: Club degli Editori).

Calzone, Nicolino. 2001. *Briganti o partigiani, la rivolta contro l'unità d'Italia nel Sannio ed altre province del Sud.* (Benevento: Edizioni Realtà Sannita).

Camanni, Enrico. 2008. *Il Cervino è nudo.* (Courmayeur: Liaison).

Canestrini, Sandro. 2003. *Vajont: genocidio dei poveri.* (Verona: Cierre edizioni).

Caprettini, Gian Paolo (ed.) 2000. *Dizionario della fiaba italiana.* (Rome: Meltemi).

Caprin, Giulio. 1925. 'Il nostro Rosa'. *Le Vie d'Italia* 3.

Carmellini, Beatrice with Sara Maino. 2005. *Arco di storie: uno sguardo ravvicinato sul tempo dei sanatori ad Arco, 1945-1975.* (Trento: Museo storico in Trento).

Carullo, Francesco. 1929. 'La Piccola Sila'. *L'Alpe* 9.

Cattaneo, Carlo. 1925 [1844]. 'Notizie naturali e civili su la Lombardia', in C. Cattaneo, *Notizie su la Lombardia e altri scritti su l'agricoltura.* (Milan: Edizioni Risorgimento).

Bibliography

Cazzola, Franco. 1997. 'La ricchezza della terra. L'agricoltura emiliana fra tradizione e innovazione', in R. Finzi (ed.) *Storia d'Italia. Le regioni dall'Unità ad oggi, l'Emilia-Romagna.* (Turin: Einaudi).

Chiovini, Nino. 2006. 'Fuori legge??? Diario di un partigiano nel Verbano'. *I sentieri della ricerca. Rivista di storia contemporanea* 4.

Ciarlo, Pietro. 1993. 'Il testo unico del 1933 sulle acque e sugli impianti elettrici', in G. Galasso (ed.) *Storia dell'industria elettrica in Italia vol. 3. Espanzione e oligopolio. 1926–1945.* (Rome and Bari: Laterza).

Cibrario Luigi and Ugo Rondelli 1930. 'Lo spopolamento e i problemi della montagna' in *Atti del 1 congresso piemontese di economia montana.* (Turin: Tip. Barattini).

Claps, Tommaso. 1906. *A pie' del Carmine. Bozzetti e novelle basilicatesi.* (Rome and Turin: Roux and Viarengo).

Clary, David A. 1978. 'The Biggest Regiment in the Army'. *Journal of Forest History* 22:4.

Clementi, Alessandro, Stanislao Pietrostefani and Carlo Tobia. 1980. 'La nascita del rifugio', in *Il rifugio Garibaldi tra cronaca e storia.* (Bologna; Tamari).

Cognetti De Martiis, Luigi. 2001. 'Neve e Fiori nell'Alta Carnia', in M. and F. Michieli *Ricordi di guerra alpina: testimonianze dei combattenti sul fronte italiano 1915–1918.* (Trento: Casa Editrice Panorama).

Colamonico, Carmelo. 1928. 'Matese'. *Le Vie d'Italia* 7.

Colapietra, Raffaele. 1983. 'Il brigantaggio postunitario in Abruzzo, Molise e Capitanata nella crisi di trasformazione dal comunitarismo pastorale all'individualismo agrario'. *Archivio Storico per le province napoletane* CI, conference proceedings: *Il brigantaggio postunitario nel Mezzogiorno d'Italia.*

Colli, Luisa Martina. 1986. 'Il simbolismo della montagna cosmica e l'immagine delle Alpi', in M. Cucco and P. A. Rossi (eds.) *La strega il teologo lo scienziato.* (Genoa: Edizioni culturali internazionali).

Colombara, Filippo. 2006. 'Il fascino del leggendario. Moscatelli e Beltrami: miti resistenti'. *L'impegno* 1.

Coppola, Gauro. 1989. 'La montagna alpina. Vocazioni originarie e trasformazioni funzionali', in P. Bevilacqua (ed.) *Storia dell' agricoltura italiana in età contemporanea, vol.1, Spazi e Paesaggi.* (Venice: Marsilio).

Corona, Gabriella. 2004. 'Declino dei "commons" ed equilibri ambientali. Il caso italiano tra Otto e Novecento'. *Società e storia* 104.

Corona, Gabriella. 2010. 'The Decline of the Commons and the Environmental Balance in Early Modern Italy', in M. Armiero and M. Hall (eds.) *Nature and History in Modern Italy.* (Athens: Ohio University Press).

Corona, Giuseppe, Edoardo Pini, Vincenzo De Castro, Ercole Bassi, Rinaldo Bassi, Giovanni De Castro and Enrico Abbate. 1885. *Alpi e Appennini. Ascensioni, escursioni e descrizioni.* (Milan: Emilio Quadrio Editore).

Corpo volontari della libertà. 1945. *La vita per l'Italia. Brigata G. C. Puecher del raggruppamento divisioni patrioti Alfredo Di Dio.* (Milan: stab. tipografico Stefano Pinelli).

Bibliography

Cortese, Carmine. 1998. *Diario di guerra (1916–17)*, A. Pugliese (ed.) (Soveria Mannelli: Rubbettino).

Corvol, Andrée and Jean-Paul Amat (eds.) 1994. *Forêt et guerre*. (Paris: L'Harmattan).

Cotti, Alberto. 1994. *Il partigiano D'Artagnan: la lotta di liberazione nei ricordi di un partigiano di San Giovanni in Persiceto*. (San Giovanni in Persiceto: Comune di San Giovanni in Persiceto). Available online at http://it.wikisource.org/wiki/Il_Partigiano_D%27Artagnan

Cremonesi, Ernesto. 1937. 'Boschi dell'Impero'. *La conquista della terra. Rassegna dell'Opera Nazionale per i Combattenti* 5.

Crocco, Carmine. N.d. *Come divenni brigante. Autobiografia*. Ed. by Mario Proto, published online at http://www.brigantaggio.net/Brigantaggio/Briganti/Crocco.pdf

Croce, Benedetto. 1928. *Storia d'Italia dal 1871 al 1915*. (Bari: Laterza).

Cronon, William. 1997. 'The development of the aesthetic of the infinite', in Marjorie Hope Nicolson. [1959] *Mountain Gloom and Mountain Glory*. (Seattle and London: University of Washington Press).

Cuaz, Marco. 2005. *Le Alpi*. (Bologna: Il Mulino).

D'Agostino, Peter. 2002. 'Craniums, Criminals, and the "Cursed Race": Italian Anthropology in American Racial Thought, 1861–1924'. *Comparative Studies in Society and History* 44:2.

D'Amore, Fulvio. 1994. *Gli ultimi disperati. Sulle tracce dei briganti marsicani prima e dopo l'unità*. (L'Aquila: Amministrazione Provinciale).

D'Amore, Fulvio. 2004. *Viva Francesco II, morte a Vittorio Emanuele! Insorgenze popolari e briganti in Abruzzo, Lazio e Molise durante la conquista del Sud, 1860–1861*. (Naples: Controcorrente).

D'Antone, Leandra. 1979. 'Politica e cultura agraria: Arrigo Serpieri'. *Studi Storici* 3.

D'Onofrio, Andrea. 2007. *Razza, sangue e suolo. Utopie della razza e progetti eugenetici nel ruralismo nazista*. (Naples: ClioPress).

D'Urso, Donato. 1977. *Il brigantaggio ad Acerno dopo il 1860*. (Giffoni Valle Piana: Tip. Artistica).

Dal Piaz, Giorgio. 1960. 'Relazione riservata: esame delle condizioni geologiche del bacino del Vajont e della zona d'imposta della diga di sbarramento quali risultano allo stato attuale dei lavori (9 July 1960 with addendum December 1960)', copy sequestrated by the judicial authority xxxvi/5058-5049, in *Proceedings of the Parliamentary Committee on the Vajont Disaster*.

Datei, Claudio. 2005. *Vajont. La storia idraulica*. (Padua: Libreria Internazionale Cortina).

Davis, John. 2006. *Naples and Napoleon. Southern Italy and the European Revolutions (1780–1860)*. (Oxford and New York: Oxford University Press).

De Amicis, Edmondo. 1999. *Nel regno del Cervino: gli scritti del Giomein*. (Turin: Vivalda).

De Nino, Antonio. 1890. *Il Messia dell'Abruzzo: saggio biografico-critico*. (Lanciano: R. Carabba).

De' Franceschi, Franco. 2004. *Estate partigiana. In montagna con la Osoppo. Diario 1944-1945*, Lorenzo Rocca (ed.). (Sommacampagna: Cierre edizioni).

Bibliography

de' Sivo, Giacinto. 1863-64. *Storia delle due Sicilie dal 1847 al 1861*. (Rome: Tip. Salviucci).

Del Boca, Federico. 1966. *Il freddo, la paura e la fame. Ricordi di un partigiano semplice*. (Milan: Feltrinelli).

Della Porta, Donatella and Piazza, Gianni. 2008. *Le ragioni del no: le campagne contro la Tav in Val di Susa e il ponte sullo Stretto*. (Milan: Feltrinelli).

Di Tella, Giuseppe. 1912. *Il bosco contro il torrente: la redenzione delle terre povere. (*Milan: tipografia il Capriolo e Massimo).

Divisi, Ferdinando. 1929. 'Rendiamo ai colli l'ombra perduta'. *L'Alpe* 3.

Dogliani, Patrizia. 1996. 'Redipuglia', in M. Isnenghi (ed.) *I luoghi della memoria. Simboli e miti dell'Italia unita. (*Rome: Laterza).

Dogliani, Patrizia. 1999. *L'Italia fascista 1922–1940*. (Milan: RCS).

Dolino, Gianni. 1989. *Partigiani in Val di Lanzo*. (Milan: Franco Angeli).

Domenichelli, Piero. 1937. 'La mostra forestale e montana "Arnaldo Mussolini" alla Fiera del Levante'. *L'Alpe* 10.

Domenico Rinaldi, Domenico. 1937. 'Il Terminillo "Montagna di Roma"'. *Rivista mensile del CAI* 56.

Don Berto. 1982. *Sulla montagna con i partigiani*. (Genoa: Sagep editore).

Dunnage, Jonathan. 2002. *Twentieth-Century Italy: A Social History*. (London: Pearson Education Limited).

Engel, Claire Éliane. 1950. *A History of Mountaineering in the Alps*. (New York: Scribner).

Etna, Donato. 1930. 'Conseguenze dello spopolamento della montagna sulla efficienza delle truppe alpine e sulla difesa della frontiera montana', in *Atti del 1 congresso piemontese di economia montana. (*Turin: Tip. Barattini).

Evola, Julius. 1998. *Meditations on the Peaks: Mountain Climbing as Metaphor for the Spiritual Quest*. (Rochester, VT : Inner Traditions).

Faber, Daniel (ed.) 1998. *The Struggle for Ecological Democracy. Environmental Justice Movements in the United States* (New York: Guilford Press).

Fagioli, Simone. 1999. 'Un eroe perturbante nel mondo dei carbonai. Un'analisi strutturale del mito di Ciapino Ciampi'. *QF, Periodico dell'Istituto Storico Provinciale della Resistenza di Pistoia* 4.

Fenoglio, Beppe. 1994. *Il partigiano Johnny*. (Turin: Einaudi).

Ferguson, Kathy E. and Phyllis Turnbull. 1996. 'Narratives of History, Nature, and Death at the National Memorial Cemetery'. *Frontiers: A Journal of Women Studies* 16: 2–3.

Ferrazza, Marco. 2006. *Grigna assassina: Eugenio Fasana e l'alpinismo milanese*. (Turin: CDA & Vivalda).

Filippin Lazzeris, Felice. 1983. *Leggende, storie, cronache*. (Milan: Cavallotti editori).

Fiore, Adelio and Fausta Fiore. 2005. *Memorie di un ribelle*. (Foligno: Editoriale Umbra).

Flaiano, Ennio. 1982. *Il Messia. (*Milano: all'insegna del pesce d'oro).

Fleming, Fergus. 2000. *Killing Dragons, The Conquest of the Alps*. (New York: Grove).

Fontana, Vincenzo. 1981. *Il nuovo paesaggio dell'Italia giolittiana*. (Rome: Laterza).

Bibliography

Fortunato, Giustino. 1884. *L'Appennino della Campania*. (Naples: CAI).

Fottivento [Mino Maccari]. 1927. 'Italia paesana'. *Il Selvaggio* 11–15 June.

Fottivento [Mino Maccari]. 1928. 'Campagna'. *Il Selvaggio* 30 August.

Franzina, Emilio. 2005. *Storia dell'emigrazione veneta: dall'unità al fascismo*. (Sommacampagna: Cierre).

Freshfield W. Douglas. 1875. *Italian Alps*. (London: Longman, Green and Co.).

Friedly Isaak. 1984. *Quattro mesi tra i briganti in Sud Italia (1865–66)*, in A. Caiazza (ed.) *La banda Manzo*. (Naples: Tempi Moderni).

Friedmann, Giovanni. 1929. 'Innalzando i pascoli i boschi si estendono'. *L'Alpe* 12.

Fumian, Carlo. 1979. 'Modernizzazione tecnocrazia, ruralismo: Arrigo Serpieri'. *Italia Contemporanea* 137.

Gabaccia, Donna R. 1999. 'Is Everywhere Nowhere? Nomads, Nations, and the Immigrant Paradigm of United States History'. *Journal of American History* 3:86.

Gabaccia, Donna. 1997. 'Per una storia italiana dell'emigrazione'. *Altreitalie* 16.

Gabbrielli, Antonio. 1994. 'La prima guerra mondiale e i nostri boschi'. *Linea ecologica* 26:5.

Gaifas, Enrico junior. 1937. 'I littoriali della neve e del ghiaccio'. *Rivista Mensile del CAI* 56.

Gaspari, Oscar. 1994. *Il segretariato per la montagna (1919–1965). Ruini, Serpieri e Sturzo per la bonifica d'alta quota*. (Rome: Presidenza del Consiglio dei Ministri, Dipartimento per l'informazione e l'editoria).

Gaspari, Oscar. 1999. 'Studi e tradizioni: il padre della questione montanara'. *Montagna oggi* 4 July/August.

Gaspari, Oscar. 2000. 'Luzzatti, Le Play e la "Questione sociale in montagna". Politica forestale e per la montagna dall'Unità alla costituzione repubblicana'. *Ricerche di storia sociale e religiosa* 58.

Gaudemard, Francis. 1994. '*Les bois mitraillés dans le département de la Marne*', in A. Corvol and J.P. Amat (eds.) *Forêt et guerre*. (Paris: L'Harmattan).

Gautieri, Giuseppe. 1817. *Dello influsso de' boschi sullo stato fisico de' paesi e la prosperità delle nazioni*. (Milan: Giovanni Pirotta).

Gervasoni, Armando. 1969. *Il Vajont e le responsabilità dei manager*. (Milan: Bramante).

Ghilardi, Guido. 1932. 'Valli Locana e Soana', in INEA, *Lo spopolamento montano in Italia: indagine geografico-economico-agraria*, vol. 1 (Milan and Rome: Soc. Treves-Treccani-Tumminelli).

Gibelli, Antonio. 1998. *La grande guerra degli italiani*. (Milan: RCS libri).

Gillette, Aaron. 2002. *Racial Theories in Fascist Italy*. (New York: Routledge).

Ginzburg, Carlo. 1985 [1966]. *The Night Battles: Witchcraft and Agrarian Cults in the Sixteenth and Seventeenth Centuries*. (New York: Penguin Books).

Giovana, Mario. 1988. *Guerriglia e mondo contadino. I garibaldini nelle Langhe 1943–1945*. (Bologna: Cappelli).

Giudici, Franco and Semenza, Edoardo. 1960. 'Studio geologico sul serbatoio del Vajont', in G. Masè, M. Semenza, P. Semenza and M. C. Turrini (eds.) *Le foto della frana*. (Fondazione Vajont, K-flash).

Bibliography

Giura Longo, Raffaele. 1992. *La Basilicata moderna e contemporanea*. (Naples: Edizioni del Sole).

Giussani, Aurelio. N.d. *Diario clandestino (appunti di vita partigiana)*. (Milan: Collegio San Carlo).

Gobetti, Ada. 1996. *Diario partigiano*. (Turin: Einaudi).

Gouch, Paul. 2000. 'From Heroes' Grove to Parks of Peace: Landscapes of Remembrance, Protest and Peace'. *Landscape Research* 25:2.

Gramsci, Antonio. 1949. *Il Risorgimento*. (Turin: Einaudi).

Gribble, Francis. 1904. *The Story of Alpine Climbing*. (London: George Newnes).

Grossi, Paolo. 1977. *Un altro modo di possedere. L'emersione di forme alternative di proprietà alla coscienza giuridica postunitaria*. (Milan: Giuffrè).

Guarnieri, Emilio. 1937. 'Ruralità di Arnaldo'. *Il Bosco* 23.

Guillaume, Pierre. 1986. *Du desespoir au salut: les tuberculeux au 19. et 20. siecles*. (Paris: Aubier).

Hall, Marcus. 2005. *Earth Repair: A Transatlantic History of Environmental Restoration*. (Charlottesville: University of Virginia Press).

Herzen A.1890. 'Rimboschimenti e inondazioni'. *Nuova Rivista Forestale*, 107.

High, Holly. 2007. 'Violent Landscape: Global Explosions and Lao Life-Worlds'. *Global Environment* 1:1.

Hobsbawm Eric. 1959. *Primitive Rebels. Studies in Archaic Forms of Social Movements in the 19th and 20th Centuries*. (New York: Frederick A. Praeger).

Hurley, Andrew. 1995. *Environmental Inequalities. Class, Race, and Industrial Pollution in Gary, Indiana, 1945–1980*. (Chapel Hill: University of North Carolina Press).

Isnardi, Giuseppe. 1927. 'La Sila'. *Le Vie d'Italia* 7.

Isnenghi, Mario and Rochat, Giorgio. 2000. *La grande guerra 1914–1918*. (Milan: RCS libri).

Izzo, Fulvio. 2002. *I guerriglieri di Dio: vandeani, legittimisti, briganti*. (Naples: Controcorrente).

Jacini, Stefano. 1883. *Frammenti dell'inchiesta agraria relazione sulle condizioni dell'agricoltura e degli agricoltori in Lombardia*. (Rome: Forzani).

Jahier, Pietro. 1934. *Con me e con gli alpini*. (Turin: Einaudi).

Johnson, Matthew. 2007. *Ideas of Landscape*. (Malden, MA: Blackwell Publishing).

Kalaora, Bernard and Savoye, Antoine. 1986. *La forêt pacifiée: les forestiers de l'école de Le Play, experts des sociétés pastorales*. (Paris: L'Harmattan).

Kelly, C. Michael. 2005. 'Italy Rejects Her Past: Revisionists and the Anti-Fascist Foundations of the Italian Republic'. *CESAA Review* 33.

Korherr, Richard. 1928. *Regresso delle nascite: morte dei popoli*. (Rome: Libreria del Littorio).

Labollita, Giacchino. 1863. *Monografia del Bosco Monticchio del già Ordine Costantiniano dell'ex reame di Napoli: con alcune osservazioni sul nuovo governo economico di quella foresta*. (Perugia: Martiniand Boncompagni).

Labriola, Antonio. 1906. *Socialism and Philosophy*. (Chicago: C. H. Kerr).

Bibliography

Lanaro, Silvio. 1991. 'Da contadini a italiani', in P. Bevilacqua (ed.) *Storia dell'agricoltura italiana in età contemporanea* vol. 3. *Mercati e istituzioni*. (Venice: Marsilio).

Lazzarini, Antonio. 1991. 'Degrado ambientale e isolamento economico: elementi di crisi nella montagna bellunese nell'Ottocento', in A. Lazzarini and F. Vendramini (eds.) *La montagna veneta in età contemporanea. Storia e ambiente. Uomini e risorse*. (Rome: Edizioni di Storia e Letteratura).

Le cento città di Italia illustrate, Biella Oropa, Graglia, Andorno. 1930. (Milan: Sozogno).

Lekan, Thomas and Thomas Zeller. 2005. 'The Landscape of German Environmental History', in T. Lekan and T. Zeller (eds.) *Germany's Nature. Cultural Landscapes and Environmental History*. (New Brunswick and London: Rutgers University Press).

Lekan, Thomas. 2004. *Imagining the Nation in Nature. Landscape Preservation and German Identity 1885–1945*. (Cambridge and London: Harvard University Press).

Lekan, Thomas. 2005. 'It Shall Be the Whole Landscape. The Reich Nature Protection Law and Regional Planning in the Third Reich', in F-J. Brüggemeier, M. Cioc and T. Zeller (eds.) *How Green Were the Nazis? Nature, Environment, and Nation in the Third Reich*. (Athens: Ohio UP).

Leslie, Stephen. 1871. *The Playground of Europe*. (London: Longmans, Green and Co.).

Levi, Carlo. 1963 [1947]. *Christ Stopped at Eboli; The Story of a Year*. (New York: Farrar, Straus and Company).

Lichtensteiger, Johann Jakob. 1984. *Quattro mesi fra i briganti (1865–66)*, Ugo Di Pace (ed.) (Cava dei Tirreni: Avagliano).

Lioy, Paolo.1889. *In alto*. (Milan: Giuseppe Galli).

Lowenthal, David. 2000. *George Perkins Marsh, Prophet of Conservation*. (Seattle: University of Washington Press).

Lunn, Arnold. 1914. *The Exploration of the Alps*. (New York: Henry Holt and Co.).

Lupo, Salvatore. 1988. 'Tra centro e periferia. Sui modi dell'aggregazione politica nel Mezzogiorno contemporaneo'. *Meridiana. Rivista di storia e scienze sociali* 2.

Maccari, Mino. 1926. 'Così sia'. *Il Selvaggio* 1–14 April 1926.

Macry, Paolo. 1997. *Giocare la vita. Storia del lotto a Napoli tra Sette e Ottocento*. (Rome: Donzelli).

Maffei, A[ndrea?], Count. 1865. *Brigand Life in Italy: A History of Bourbonist Reaction*. (London: Hurst and Blackett).

Malinverni, Angelo. 2000 [1942]. 'O Luna, o luna tu me lo dicevi…', in M. Balbi and L. Viazzi. *Spunta l'alba del sedici giugno*. (Milan: Mursia).

Mammone, Andrea. 2006. 'A Daily Revision of the Past: Fascism, Anti-Fascism, and Memory in Contemporary Italy'. *Modern Italy* 11:2.

Manaresi, Angelo. 1934. 'Tenere d'occhio il Cervino'. *Rivista Mensile del CAI* 12.

Manaresi, Angelo. 1936. 'Alpinismo guerriero'. *Rivista Mensile del CAI* 5.

Manaresi, Angelo. 1937. 'Mussolini sciatore'. *Rivista mensile del CAI* 56.

Manaresi, Angelo. 1938. 'Alpini e alpinisti'. *Rivista mensile del CAI* 57.

Manaresi, Angelo. 1938. 'Mostra della montagna'. *Rivista mensile del CAI* 57.

Bibliography

Manaresi, Angelo. 1938. 'Universitari all'assalto dei monti. Il rostro d'oro'. *Rivista mensile del CAI* 57.

Mann, Thomas. 1927. *The Magic Mountain*. (New York, A. A. Knopf).

Marescalchi, Arturo. 1938. 'Bonifica umana per l'avvenire d'Italia'. *La conquista della terra* 12.

Mariani, Mario. 1915. *Sulle Alpi e sull'Isonzo*. (Milan: Società Editrice Italiana).

Marinelli, Olinto. 1926. 'Le vicende di un laghetto alpino'. *Le Vie d'Italia* 12.

Marini, Nicola. 1888. *Tra le foreste di Monticchio*. (Milan: Zanichelli).

Marro, Giovani. 1940. *Primato della razza italiana*. (Milan and Messina: Casa Editrice Giuseppe Principato).

Marsh, George Perkins. 1864. *Man and Nature; or Physical Geography as Modified by Human Action*. (New York: Charles Scribner).

Martinez Alier, Joan. 2005. *The Environmentalism of the Poor: A Study of Ecological Conflicts and Valuation*. (New Delhi and New York: Oxford University Press).

Marzio, Angelo. 1934. 'Nel Gran Sasso d'Italia'. *Rivista mensile del CAI* 8.

Masera, Diana. 1971. *Langa partigiana 43–45*. (Parma: Guanda, 1971).

Massard-Guilbaud, Geneviève and Richard Rodger (eds.) 2011. *Environmental and Social Justice in the City: Historical Perspectives*. (Cambridge: The White Horse Press).

Mathieu, Jon. 2009 [2000]. *History of the Alps, 1500–1900*. (Morgantown: West Virginia University Press). Quoted here from the 2000 Italian edition, *Storia delle Alpi 1500–1900*. (Bellinzona: Casagrande).

Mattei, T. 1928. 'Salvare il monte!' *L'Alpe* 6.

Mazzini Giuseppe. 1862. 'Della guerra di insurrezione', in *Scritti editi e inediti di Giuseppe Mazzini*. (Milan: Daelli editore).

McNeill John. 1992. *The Mountains of the Mediterranean World*. (Cambridge and New York: Cambridge University Press).

McNeill, John. 2002. 'Tragedy of Privatization: Land, Liberty and Environmental Change in Spain and Italy, 1800-1910', in J. F. Richards (ed.) *Land, Property, and the Environment*. (Oakland, California: Institute for Contemporary Studies).

McNeill, John R. 2004. 'Woods and Warfare in World History'. *Environmental History* 9:3.

Medici, Giuseppe. 1935. 'Montagna lombarda occidentale', in INEA, *Lo spopolamento montano in Italia vol. II. Le Alpi lombarde*. (Rome: Tip. Failli).

Melosi, Martin. 2000. 'Equity, Eco-Racism and Environmental Justice Movement', in J. Donald Hughes (ed.) *The Face of the Earth. Environment and World History* (New York, London: Armonk-M.E. Sharpe).

Merendi, Ariberto. 1935. 'Il Duce visita la selva del Circeo'. *L'Alpe* 1.

Merlin, Tina. 2001. *Sulla pelle viva. Come si costruisce una catastrofe. Il caso Vajont*. (Sommacampagna: Cierre).

Merlin, Tina. 2004. *La rabbia e la speranza: la montagna, l'emigrazione, il Vajont*. (Verona: Cierre 2004).

Merlin, Tina. 1993. *Vajont 1963. La costruzione di una catastrofe*. (Venice: Il Cardo).

Meyer, Edgar. 1995. *I pionieri dell'ambiente*. (Milan: Carabà).

Bibliography

Milizia Forestale dal V al XV anno dell'Era Fascista. 1938. (Bergamo: Officine dell'Istituto di arti grafiche).

Milli, Ervino. 1954. 'Sondaggi geologici per accertamento roccia in sponda destra del bacino del Vajont in prossimità dell'abitato di Erto', document seized by the judicial authority, doc. xiv/2100, in *Proceedings of the Parliamentary Committee on the Vajont Disaster.*

Misasi, Nicola. 1881. *Racconti calabresi.* (Naples: Morano).

Moe, Nelson. 2002. *The View from Vesuvius: Italian Culture and the Southern Question.* (Berkeley: University of California Press).

Molfese, Franco. 1964. *Storia del brigantaggio dopo l'Unità.* (Milan: Feltrinelli).

Momigliano Levi, Paolo. 2005. 'Aosta "Carrefour"', in E. Alessandrone Perona and A. Cavaglion. *I luoghi della memoria, la memoria dei luoghi nelle regioni alpine occidentali.* (Turin: Blu).

Mondo, Lorenzo. 2000. *Il messia è stanco.* (Milan: Garzanti).

Monnier, Marc. 1862. *Notizie storiche documentate sul brigantaggio nelle provincie napoletane dai tempi di fra Diavolo sino ai giorni nostri.* (Florence: G. Barbera).

Monti, Mario. 2005 [1959]. *I briganti italiani.* (Naples: edizioni Partagées).

Mornese, Corrado. 2002. *Eresia dolciniana e resistenza montanara.* (Rome: DeriveApprodi).

Mornese, Corrado. 2006. 'Dolcino: novità storiografiche negli ultimi vent'anni', paper presented at the conference *Dolcino. Storia, pensiero, messaggio,* Varallo 4 November 2006. Available online at http://fradolcino.interfree.it/

Moscatelli, Cino. 1982. 'Là, sul Briasco ... Le origini del movimento partigiano in Valsesia'. *L'impegno* 3.

Moscato, Antonio. 1978. *Davide Lazzaretti: il Messia dell'Amiata. L'ultima delle eresie popolari agli albori del movimento operaio e contadino.* (Rome: Savelli).

Mosse, George L. 1979. 'National Cemeteries and National Revival: The Cult of the Fallen Soldiers in Germany'. *Journal of Contemporary History* 14:1.

Mosse, George L. 1990. *Fallen Soldiers: Reshaping the Memory of the World Wars.* (New York and Oxford: Oxford University Press).

Motta, Renzo, Roberta Berretti, Emanuele Lingua and Pietro Piussi. 2006. 'Coarse Woody Debris, Forest Structure and Regeneration in the Valbona Forest Riserve, Panaveggio, Italian Alps'. *Forest and Ecology Management* 235.

Motta, Renzo, P. Nola and Pietro Piussi. 2002. 'Long-Term Investigations in a Strict Forest Reserve in the Eastern Italian Alps: Spatio-Temporal Origin and Development in Two Multi-Layered Subalpine Stands'. *Journal of Ecology* 90:3.

Müller, Leopold. 1959. 'Rapporto geologico per conto della SADE', document seized by the judicial authority, doc. xxxix/1729, in *Proceedings of the Parliamentary Committee on the Vajont Disaster.*

Müller, Leopold. 1961. 'Rapporto geologico preparato per conto della SADE', document seized by the judicial authority, doc. xxxix/1729, in *Proceedings of the Parliamentary Committee on the Vajont Disaster.*

Mumford, Lewis. 1934. *Technics and Civilization.* (New York: Harcourt, Brace and Co.).

Bibliography

Mussolini, Arnaldo. 1934 [1928]. 'Discorso di Asiago. Per la giornata forestale dell'8 settembre 1928', in *Scritti e discorsi di Arnaldo Mussolini*. (Milan: Urlico Hoepli).

Mussolini, Arnaldo. 1934 [1928]. 'L'agricoltura nella vita italiana, discorso alla fiera di Milano 25 maggio 1928', in *Scritti e discorsi di Arnaldo Mussolini*. (Milano: Urlico Hoepli).

Mussolini, Benito. 1932. *Vita di Arnaldo*. (Milan: Tipografia del Popolo d'Italia).

Nash, Linda. 2006. *Inescapable Ecologies. A History of Environment, Disease, and Knowledge*. (Berkeley: University of California Press).

Nebbia, Alessio. 1930. *Guida turistica di Courmayeur*. (Courmayeur: Bottega d'arte alpina).

Negri, Gaetano. 1905. 'Alla caccia dei briganti', in *Opere di Gaetano Negri*. (Milano, Urlico Hoepli).

Neri Serneri, Simone. 1995. 'A Past to be Thrown Away? Politics and History in the Italian Resistance'. *Contemporary European History* 4.

Nigro, Raffaele. N.d. *Il brigantaggio nella letteratura*. Published online at http://www.paroladi-donna.net/TestiAcrobat/Briganti%20e%20Letteratura.pdf

Nitti, Francesco Saverio. 1905. *La conquista della forza*. (Turin and Rome: Roux-Viarengo).

Nitti, Francesco Saverio. 1946. *Eroi e briganti*. (Rome: Longanesi).

Oliva, Gianni. 1985. *Storia degli Alpini*. (Milan: Rizzoli).

Omodeo, Angelo. 1916. *Nuovi orizzonti dell'idraulica italiana in gruppo nazionale di azione economica, il problema idraulico e la legislazione delle acque*. (Rome: Bertero).

Oreste Del Buono (ed.) 1971. *Eia, eia, eia alalà. La stampa italiana sotto il fascismo 1919–1943*. (Milan: Feltrinelli).

Ortolani, Mario. 1942. *Il massiccio del Gran Sasso d'Italia*. (Rome: Società Italiana Arti Grafiche).

Ottolini, Giammaria. 2006. '*Fuori legge???* di Nino Chiovini. Note su un diario partigiano'. *I sentieri della ricerca* 4.

Padula, Vincenzo 1974. *Cronache del brigantaggio in Calabria: 1864–65*, A. Piromalli and D. Scafoglio (eds.). (Naples: Athena stampa).

Pais, Andrea. 1963. 'Longarone'. *Antincendio e Protezione Civile Rivista Mensile* 59.

Pallotta, Francesco. 1930. 'Reggente della sezione per le trasformazioni fondiare e agrarie della cattedra di agricoltura di Campobasso'. *Apicoltura italiana* 7.

Pansa, Giampaolo. 2003. *Il sangue dei vinti: quello che accadde in Italia dopo il 25 aprile*. (Milan: Sperling & Kupfer).

Paolini, Marco and Gabriele Vacis. 2006. *Vajont 9 ottobre 1963: orazione civile*. (Rome: Rai Trade-Medialia).

Parpagliolo, Luigi. 1926. 'Le acque'. *Le Vie d'Italia* 2.

Parpagliolo, Luigi. 1927. 'L'albero'. *Le Vie d'Italia* 5.

Passi, Mario. 1968. *Morire sul Vajont. Storia di una tragedia italiana*. (Venice: Marsilio).

Pastore, Alessandro. 2003. *Alpinismo e storia d'Italia*. (Bologna: Il Mulino).

Patriarca, Pierluigi. 2001. *La valle incantata: storia della tubercolosi e della lotta antitubercolare in Valtellina*. (Sondrio: L'officina del libro).

Bibliography

Pavari, Aldo. 1934. 'The Fascist Government and the Restoration of Italian Forests'. *Forestry* 8:1.

Pavari, Aldo.1930. 'Genesi e sviluppo della bonifica in Italia'. *Le Vie d'Italia* 8.

Pavia, Rosario (ed.) 1998. *Paesaggi elettrici : territori, architetture, culture.* (Venice: Marsilio and ENEL).

PCI [Italian Comunist Party]. 1965. *Le cause e le responsabilità della catastrofe del Vajont, Relazione di minoranza per la commissione di inchiesta parlamentare.* (Rome: n. p.).

PCI. 1963. *Libro bianco sulla tragedia del Vajont. Prima documentazione presentata dalla delegazione parlamentare del P.C.I. al Presidente della Repubblica, Antonio Segni. Belluno, 13 ottobre 1963.* (Rome: Stabilimento Tipografico SETI).

Pedersoli, Giacomo Sebastiano. 2006. *Il disastro del Gleno: 1923, un Vajont dimenticato.* (Verona: Cierre).

Pedio, Tommaso. 1983. *Inchiesta Massari sul brigantaggio.* (Manduria: Pietro Lacaita).

Peli, Santo. 2004. *La Resistenza in Italia: storia e critica.* (Turin: Einaudi).

Perona, Gianni. 'Cultura urbana, resistenza e territorio', in E. Alessandrone Perona and A. Cavaglion. *I luoghi della memoria, la memoria dei luoghi nelle regioni alpine occidentali.* (Turin: Blu).

Pesce, Giovanni. 1929. 'La montagna all'adunata di Roma'. *L'Alpe* 2 .

Petraccone, Claudia. 2005. *Le due Italie: la questione meridionale tra realtà e rappresentazione.* (Rome and Bari: Laterza).

Petrakis Marina. 2006. *The Metaxas Myth. Dictatorship and Propaganda in Greece.* (London and New York: I.B.Tauris & Co.).

Petrusewicz, Marta. 1998. *Come il Meridione divenne una questione: rappresentazioni del Sud prima e dopo il Quarantotto.* (Soveria Mannelli: Rubbettino).

Piccioni, Luigi. 1999. *Il volto amato della Patria.* (Camerino: Università degli Studi di Camerino).

Piccioni, Luigi. 2000. 'La natura come posta in gioco. La dialettica tutela ambientale-sviluppo turistico nella storia della "regione dei parchi"', in C. Felice and M. Costantini (eds.) *Storia d'Italia. Le regioni dall'Unità ad oggi. L'Abruzzo.* (Turin: Einaudi).

Piccioni, Luigi. 2010. 'Nature Preservation and Protection in Nineteenth and Twentieth-Century Italy, 1880–1950', in M. Armiero and M. Hall (eds.) *Nature and History in Modern Italy.* (Athens: Ohio University Press).

Piromalli, Antonio and Domenico Scafoglio. 1977. *Terre e briganti. Il brigantaggio cantato dalle classi subalterne.* (Messina and Florence: G. D'Anna).

Piromalli, Antonio. 1996. *La letteratura calabrese.* (Cosenza: Luigi Pellegrino Editore).

Pittoni, G. 1938. 'Montagna vicentina', in INEA, *Lo spopolamento montano in Italia vol. IV. Alpi Venete.* (Rome: Tip. Failli).

Pollano, Marco. 2006–2007. *La 17a brigata Garibaldi 'Felice Cima' storia di una formazione partigiana.* Dissertation at the University of Torino, School of the Humanities–History.

Pratesi, Fulco. 1978. 'Il Lupo', in *Esclusi dall'arca - Animali estinti e in via di estinzione in Italia.* (Milan: Arnoldo Mondadori).

Bibliography

Pratesi, Fulco. 2001. *Storia della natura d'Italia.* (Rome: Editori Riuniti).

Proceedings of the Royal Commission for Commons in the provinces of the South. 1902. (Rome: G. Bertero).

Pulido, Laura. 1996. *Environmentalism and Economic Justice: Two Chicano Struggles in the Southwest.* (Tucson: University of Arizona Press).

Rabbeno, Aronne. 1883. *Legge forestale (20 giugno 1877, n. 3917) e relativo regolamento 10 febbraio 1878.* (Turin: Unione Tipografico Editrice).

Radice, Benedetto. 1963. *Nino Bixio a Bronte.* (Caltanisetta and Rome: Edizioni Sciacca).

Raiteri, Erminio, 1977. 'I giorni del diluvio'. *Sapere* 797 January and February.

Ratschiller, Ludwig Karl. 2004. *Il compagno Ludi. Autobiografia di un partigiano.* G. De Donà and G. Mezzalira (eds.) (Bolzano: Circolo Culturale ANPI, quaderni della memoria 3).

Reberschack, Maurizio (ed.) 2003. *Il Grande Vajont.* (Sommacampagna: Cierre).

Reberschak, Maurizio and Ivo Mattozzi (eds.) 2009. *Il Vajont dopo il Vajont: 1963–2000.* (Venice: Marsilio.)

Recarli, Riccardo. 2004. 'Lo sci sulle Alpi orientali', in 'Sport e fascism', ed. by C. Ambrosi and W. Weber – special issue of *Geschichte und Region/storia e regione* 1.

Relazione presentata dal ministro dell'agricoltura e foreste del regno d'Italia alla associazione dell'agricoltura nazionale ungherese. (Rome: Tip. Camera dei Deputati).

Revelli, Nuto. 2003. *Le due guerre. Guerra fascista e guerra partigiana.* (Turin: Einaudi).

Rey, Guido. 1904. *Il Monte Cervino.* (Milan: Ulrico Hoepli).

Riall, Lucy. 1994. *The Italian Risorgimento: State, Society, and National Unification.* (London and New York: Routledge).

Rigoni Stern, Mario. 1994. 'La ricostruzione (1919–21)', in *Storia dell'altipiano dei Sette Comuni.* (Vicenza: la grafica & stampa srl).

Rinaldi, Antonio. 2002. 'Un presidente in Basilicata. Cento anni fa il viaggio di Giuseppe Zanardelli'. *Incontri* 74.

Ring, Jim. 2000. *How the English Made the Alps.* (London: John Murray).

Roshwald, Aviel and Richard Stites (eds.) 1999. *European Culture in the Great War: The Arts, Entertainment, and Propaganda, 1914–1918.* (Cambridge and New York: Cambridge University Press).

Rudatis, Domenico. 1934. 'Il campanile di Brabante'. *Rivista Mensile del CAI* 2.

Rudatis, Domenico. 1938. 'Il sentimento delle vette'. *Rivista mensile del CAI* 57.

Rudaz, Gilles. 2009. 'The Poetics and Politics of Local Knowledge in the Valaisan Alps', in D. Cosgrove and V. della Dora (eds.) *High Places. Cultural Geographies of Mountains, Ice, and Science.* (New York: I.B.Tauris).

Ruini, Meuccio. 1918. *La montagna in guerra e dopo la guerra.* (Rome: Athenaeum).

Rumiz, Paolo. 2007. 'Il ritorno di Dolcino ribelle per sempre'. *La domenica di Repubblica*, 6 May.

Saba, Andrea Filippo. 2004. *Angelo Omodeo: vita, progetti, opere per la modernizzazione : una raccolta di scritti.* (Rome: Laterza and ENEL).

Bibliography

Sacchi, Edoardo. 2002. *La mia guerra 1942–1945*. (ANPI, available online at http://www.passolento.it/storie/dado.pdf)

Sala, G. 1935. 'Val Camonica', in INEA, *Lo spopolamento montano in Italia vol. II. Le Alpi lombarde*. (Rome: Tip. Failli).

Sangiuolo, Luisa. 1975. *Il brigantaggio nella provincia di Benevento*. (Benevento: De Martini).

Savastano, Luigi. 1899. 'Alpinisti e rimboschimenti'. *L'Appennino meridionale* 4:109.

Savi Lopez, Maria. 1889. *Leggende delle Alpi*. (Turin: Loescher).

Sbordone, Giovanni. 2005. 'Veneziani in montagna', in G. Albanese and N. Borghi (eds.) *Memoria resistente: la lotta partigiana a Venezia e provincia nel ricordo dei protagonisti*. (Portogruaro: Nuova Dimensione).

Scarpino, Salvatore. 1985. *La mala unità. Scene di brigantaggio nel Sud*. (Cosenza: Effesette).

Schama, Simon. 1995. *Landscape and Memory*. (New York: Knopf).

Schubert, Frank N. 1978. 'All Wooden on the Western Front'. *Journal of Forest History* 22:4.

Scotto di Luzio, Adolfo. 1999. *Il liceo classico*. (Bologna: Il Mulino).

Secchia Pietro and Moscatelli, Cino. 1958 *Il monte Rosa è sceso a Milano. La Resistenza nel Biellese, nella Valsesia e nella Valdossola*. (Turin: Einaudi).

Secchia, Pietro and Moscatelli, Cino. 1958. 'Dove combatté Dolcino', in P. Secchia and C. Moscatelli. *Il Monte Rosa è sceso a Milano*. (Turin: Einaudi).

Semenza, Carlo. 1934. 'Nelle Alpi Noriche'. *Rivista mensile del CAI* 7.

Semenza, Carlo. 1950. 'Le utilizzazioni idroelettriche ed irrigue nel bacino del Piave', in *Guide dei monti d'Italia. Le Dolomiti orientali* vol. I. Third edition. (Milan: Cai).

Semenza, Edoardo. 2001. *La storia del Vajont raccontata dal geologo che ha scoperto la frana*. (Ferrara: K-flash editore).

Serafin, Roberto and Matteo Serafin. 2002. *Scarpone e moschetto. Alpinismo in camicia nera*. (Turin: centro documentazione alpina).

Serafini, Gino. 1981. *I ribelli della montagna: Amiata 1948: anatomia di una rivolta*. (Montepulciano: del Grifo).

Serpieri, Arrigo, Eugenio Azimonti, Giuseppe Di Tella *et al*. 1911. *Il bosco, il pascolo, il monte*. (Milan: Capriolo e Massimo).

Serpieri, Arrigo. 1928. 'Per la montagna e per i montanari'. *L'Alpe* 3.

Serpieri, Arrigo. 1929. 'Il problema montano e forestale al parlamento'. *L'Alpe* 8.

Serpieri, Arrigo. 1931. *La legge sulla bonifica integrale nel primo anno di applicazione*. Rome: Istituto poligrafico dello Stato

Serpieri, Arrigo. 1932. 'Discorso al congresso della montagna a Sondrio (13–14 December 1931 per iniziativa dei sindacati fascista dell'agricoltura)'. *L'Alpe* 1.

Siddel, Felix. 1998. 'Sette volte volte bosco, sette volte prato. An interview with Mario Rigoni Stern'. *MNL* 113.

Sievert, James, 2000. *The Origins of Nature Conservation in Italy*. (Bern and New York: Peter Lang).

Silone, Ignazio. 1967 [1933]. *Fontamara*. (Milan: A. Mondadori, 1967).

Bibliography

Snowden, Frank M. 2006. *The Conquest of Malaria. Italy, 1900–1962*. (New Haven: Yale University Press).

Soffici, Ardengo. 1928. *Kobilek : giornale di battaglia*. (Florence: Vallecchi).

Soldati, Mario. 1925. 'Il nuovo gioiello del villaggio'. *Le Vie d'Italia* 9.

Sori, Ercole. 1973. 'Assetto e redistribuzione della popolazione italiana 1861–1961', in G. Toniolo (ed.) *Lo sviluppo economico italiano 1861–1940*. (Bari and Rome: Laterza, 1973).

Stampacchia, Mauro. 2000. *Ruralizzare l'Italia. Agricoltura e bonifiche tra Mussolini e Serpieri (1928–1943)*. (Milan: Franco Angeli).

Stoppani, Antonio. 1915. *Il Bel Paese*. (Milan: Cogliati).

Sulli, Mario and Alessandra Zanzi Sulli. 2002. 'La commissione nazionale di propaganda per il bosco e per il pascolo del Touring Club Italiano', in A. Lazzarini (ed.) *Diboscamento montano e politiche territoriali. Alpi e Appennini dal Settecento al Duemila*. (Milan: Franco Angeli).

Tassinari, Giuseppe. 1940. *Autarchia e bonifica*. (Bologna: Nicola Zanichelli).

Tedeschi, Enrica. 1989. *Per una sociologia del millennio. David Lazzaretti: carisma e mutamento sociale*. (Venice: Marsilio).

Tedeschi, Mario. 1928. 'La colonia invernale al villaggio alpino del Touring'. *Le Vie d'Italia* 5.

Tegani, Ulderico. 1931. 'Il bosco della Coroncina e la tenuta delle Cottede'. *L'Alpe* 9.

Thirgood, J. V. 1981. *Man and the Mediterranean Forest: A History of Resource Depletion*. (London and New York: Academic Press).

Thompson, Edward Palmer. 1975. *Whigs and Hunters* (London: Allen Lane).

Tino, Pietro. 1989. 'La montagna meridionale: Boschi, uomini, economie tra Otto e Novecento', in P. Bevilacqua (ed.) *Storia dell'agricoltura italiana in età contemporanea*, vol. 1, *Spazi e paesaggi*. (Venice: Marsilio).

Tosi, Giorgio. 2009. *Vajont. Mors inimica venit*. (Padua: Cooperativa libraria Editrice Università di Padova).

Touring Club Italiano (TCI). 1928. *Sui Campi di Battaglia. Il Monte Grappa*. (Milan: presso il TCI).

Treves, Anna. 1976. *Le migrazioni interne nell'Italia fascista*. (Turin: Einaudi).

Triglia, Caterina. 1986. 'A morte la strega!' in M. Cuccu and P. A. Rossi (eds.) *La strega il teologo lo scienziato*. (Genoa: Edizioni Culturali Internazionali).

Trotter, Alessandro. 1923. 'Alcune premesse relative al miglioramento dei pascoli montani dell'Appennino, specialmente meridionale'. *Bollettino del comitato tecnico per l'agricoltura* 2.

Troyansky, David G. 1987. 'Monumental Politics: National History and Local Memory'. *French Historical Studies* 15:1.

Vaccari, Lino. 1932. *Difendiamo i nostri boschi*. (Milan: Tipografia del Popolo d'Italia).

Valente, Luca and Giorgio Dall'Igna (eds.) 2002. *La tutela del patrimonio storico della Grande Guerra*. (Schio: Tipografia Operaia Menin).

Valenti, Ghino. 1911. *L'Italia agricola dal 1861 al 1911*. (Rome: Tip. della R. Accademia dei Lincei).

Bibliography

Valsesia, William. 1984. 'Sui combattimenti di Rassa'. *L'impegno* 1.

Vastano, Lucia. 2008. *Vajont, l'onda lunga : quarantacinque anni di truffe e soprusi contro chi sopravvisse alla notte piu crudele della Repubblica.* (Milan: Ponte alle Grazie).

Vecchio, Bruno, Pietro Piussi and Marco Armiero. 2003. 'L'uso dei boschi e degli incolti', in *L'Italia agricola dalle origini ad oggi.* (Florence: Polistampa).

Vecchio, Bruno. 1974. *Il bosco negli scrittori italiani del Settecento e dell'età napoleonica.* (Turin: Einaudi).

Vecchio, Bruno. 1981. 'Resistenze locali e iniziativa pubblica nella fondazione post-unitaria di una normativa forestale: il caso dell'Amiata senese', in R. Pazzagli (ed.) *Davide Lazzaretti e il monte Amiata. Protesta sociale e rinnovamento religioso.* (Florence: Nuova Guaraldi editrice).

Vecchio, Bruno. 2010. 'Forest Visions in Early Modern Italy', in M. Armiero and M. Hall (eds.) *Nature and History in Modern Italy.* (Athens: Ohio University Press).

Verga, Giovanni. 1984 [1882]. 'Freedom', in *Short Sicilian Novels.* Trans. from the Italian by D.H. Lawrence, with an introduction and chronology by Eric Lane. (London: Dedalus).

Verger, Amedeo. 1934. 'La milizia forestale alla fiera del Levante di Bari'. *L'Alpe* 10.

Vescovi, Giulio. 1994. 'Dal fascismo alla resistenza' in *Storia dell'altipiano dei sette comuni.* (Vicenza: la grafica & stampa srl).

Vidulich, Tullio and Corrado Pasquali. 2000. *Alpini in guerra. Storie di uomini atti di leggenda.* (Bolzano: Società Storica della Grande Guerra).

Villani, Pasquale. 1964. *La vendita dei beni dello Stato nel Regno di Napoli : 1806–1815.* (Milan: Banca Commerciale Italiana).

Virgilio, Attilio. 1929. *A fil di cielo, impressioni di vita e ambiente alpini.* (Turin: Alfredo Fornica).

Weber, Eugene. 1989. *Da contadini a francesi : la modernizzazione della Francia rurale, 1870–1914* (Bologna: Il Mulino).

White, Richard. 1999. 'The Problem with Purity', in *The Tanner Lectures on Human Values* delivered at University of California, Davis.

Whited, Tamara L. 2000. *Forests and Peasant Politics in Modern France.* (New Haven and London: Yale University Press).

Williams, Raymond. 1983. *The Year 2000.* (New York: Pantheon).

Winter, Jay. 1995. *Sites of Memory, Sites of Mourning. The Great War in European Cultural History.* (Cambridge and New York: Cambridge University Press).

Worster, Donald. 1989. 'Doing Environmental History', in D. Worster (ed.) *The Ends of the Earth.* (Cambridge and New York: Cambridge University Press).

Zavattari, Eduardo. 1938. 'Ambiente naturale e caratteri biopsichici della razza italiana', *La Difesa della Razza* 1.

Bibliography

Documentaries from the Istituto Luce

'Belvedere in Cortina d'Ampezzo' 02/1929-A0272

'Scalatori CAI alla prese con le Dolomiti', 1930s- n.n.

'Nuova funivia a Chamonix' A0/60-04/1931

'Scuola Rocciatori', 31/4/41-Co114

'La festa degli alberi a Montemorello presso Firenze' 04/1931- A0768

'Colonie montane', October 1931, A0848

'Ascensione sulle Alpi dolomitiche' October 1931-A0866

'Campeggio internazionale SUCAI' sulle Dolomiti', 1932-B0050

'Ascensione ai ghiacciai del Monte Rosa', 1932- n.n.

'Capranica Prenestina. La festa degli alberi'03/1932- A0943

'Chamonix, La più alta teleferica del mondo. Come si sale senza fatica sul Monte Bianco a 3480 metri' B0144-30/09/1932

'Nava Arma di Taggio', 1933, B0342

'Dopolavoro Vicentino', 1934-B0516

'Esercitazioni alpini sui monti coperti di neve', 1934, B0401

'Il trofeo "Stoppani" per la gara di ski è stato vinto da Battisti dello "Sci club" reatino' 1934-B0408

'Esercitazioni alpini sui monti coperti di neve', 1934, B0401

'Esercitazioni Alpini sui monti coperti di neve', 1934-B0401

'La funivia del Gran Sasso' B0475-05/1934

'Milizia Alpina, giovani fascisti di Belluno', 1935, n.n.

'Marcia alpina. Giovani fascisti di Belluno', 1935, n.n.

'Lo sci sul Terminillo'2/1935-B0622

'Varallo. Inaugurazione della funevia per il santuario del Sacro Monte' B0737-28/08/1935

'Partenza da Roma', 4 October 1935, B0743

'Ciquencento Bambini partono da Roma', 10 July 1935, B0708

'Dolomiti', 12 February 1936-B0831

'Mareson Belluno Colonia Alpina Generale Giurati', 1936, B0924

'Una gita sul Terminillo' 25/03/1936- B0856

'Campeggio Balilla Moschettieri Romani a Colalbo', 12 August 1936, B0937

'Santa Cristina', 19 August 1936, B0938

'L'aspra meta', 1937- n.n.

'Il vice segretario del PNF Morigi e il vice presidente della Società Sportiva Parioli di Roma Vittorio Mussolini inaugurano il rifugio realizzato dalla Società Parioli in meno di un mese' 13/01/1937- B1025

'Alpi di Siusi' 20 January 1937-B1027

'I campi di neve della montagna di Roma' 10/02/1937- B1041

Bibliography

'Alpini a Roma', 22/4/1937-B1080

'Colonia figli Marittimi ad Aquila', 4 August 1937, B1141

'Esercitazioni Cervino', 1938-B1254

'L'inaugurazione di una nuova moderna funivia' 26/01/1938- B1242

'Sestriere. Inaugurazione della funivia del Fraiteve' B1241-26/1/1938

'Terminillo, Inaugurazione della moderna funivia' B1242-26/01/1938

'Pianaccio, colonia montana dell'ONC' 10 August 1938, B1354

'Le esercitazioni annuali della Milizia Forestale', 31/08/1938, B 1366

'Oro Bianco', 1939, without reference number

'Fiamme Verdi', 1939, n.n.

'Cortina d'Ampezzo. Il panorama delle Dolomiti alla nuova funivia del Monte Faloria' B1445-18/01/1939

'Viaggio del Duce in Piemonte', Maggio 1939.

'Raduno Cervino' 19 July 1939-B1548

'Scuola Militare Duca d'Abruzzo', 9/8/1939-B1560

'Alpi Giulie, Batteria Conegliano', 9/8/1939-B1561

'Sondrio Pizzo Plaù. Simulazione militare', 08/09/1939-B1571

'Strada per il Museo degli Alpini', 29/11/1940-C0096

'Sul Cervino. La funivia più alta del mondo' C0105-31/12/1940

'2500 dopolavoristi milanesi partecipano alla Festa degli Alberi' 23/11/1942- C0299

'Ai sacri confini della Patria', n.d., no reference number

'Milizia Forestale in Albania', n.d., n.n.

Index

Asti 59
Austrian Empire; Austro-Hungarian Empire
    7, 51, 92 n., 100, 103
avalanches 13, 31, 164
Avio Valley 106 n.
AZ Vajont 1971 (documentary for the Italian
    Public Television) 189 n.
Azimonti, Eugenio 24, 30 n.

B

Baccelli, Guido 123
Bach, Maurice 103 n.
Balbi, Marco 95 n.
Balbo, Adriano 158, 166, 171
Balilla Youth Organisation 125
Ball, John 27
bandite (see also common property) 79
bandits 7, 67
Barbagallo, Francesco 37 n.
Barbisan, Umberto 41 n.
Barca, Stefania xii, xv, 22, 80, 174 n.
Bardelli, Daniele 152 n.
Bardelli, Francesco 61 n.
Bari 78, 113, 115,
Barone, Giuseppe 35 n., 36–7
Bartaletti, Fabrizio 14 n., 15
Bartolini, Carlo 72 n.
Barzellotti, Giacomo 59 n.
Barzini, Luigi 100
Basilicata (Lucania) 16, 36, 37, 64, 65, 69,
    70, 75,
Bassi, Ercole 28 n.
Bassi, Rinaldo 28 n.
Batigiati 164
Battilani, Patrizia 52 n.
Battisti, Andrea 103 n.
Battisti, Cesare 98 n., 99
Beattie, Andrew 15 n.
Belco, Victoria C. 158 n.
Belforte 159
Belluno 153 n., 186
Beltrame, Achille 25, 97
Berlusconi, Silvio; Berlusconi family 65 n.,
    192
Bertani, Agostino 82
Bertarelli, Luigi Vittorio 30, 44 n., 50

Berti, Antonio 92, 169
Bes, Celestino 151
Bettiol, Giorgio 182, 186
Bevilacqua, Piero xii, 21 n., 82 n.
Bianco, Monte 5, 15, 27, 51 n.
Biella 15 n., 57 162 n., 164
Bill Lane Center for the Study of the Ameri-
    can West – Stanford University xii,
    xiii
Blackbourn David 3, 4, 5 n., 138, 140 n.
Blackshirt 142
Bobbio 161
Bocca, Giorgio 170, 171 n., 172 n., 190
Bocchio, Argante ('Massimo') 162 n., 164
Bocedi, R. 20 n.
Bognetti, Giovanni 39 n.
Boite-Piave-Vajont basin 179
Bollati, Giulio 74 n., 98 n.
Bologna 141, 158, 161
Bonaria, Vittorio 43
Bosco, Il [The Forest] 110 n., 121 n., 123,
    124, 125, 131, 132, 140–2, 143
    n., 144
Bosco contro il torrente, Il [The Forest Against
    the Stream] 30
Bosco, il pascolo, il monte, Il [The Forest, the
    Pasture, the Mountain] 30, 34
Bourbon Kingdom; Kingdom of Two Sicilies
    63, 76
Bourelly, Giuseppe 71 n.
Bourrit, Marc Theodore 27
Boves 170
Bracchi, Pier Giovanni 20 n.
Bramwell, Anna 8
Brenna, Enrico 132
Brescia 31, 78 n., 144
Breuil Valley 49
Bridge of the Devil 15
Bridges and Roads Corps (Kingdom of
    Naples) 82
British Alpine Club 12, 27
British Navy 63
Brocca, Giovanni 83 n., 130 n., 133 n.,
    134 n.
Broccoli, Armide 158
Bronte 76
Brunello, Piero 84 n.

Index

Index

Index

Index

Index

Index

Index

Index

www.ingramcontent.com/pod-product-compliance
Lightning Source LLC
Chambersburg PA
CBHW021814270326
41932CB00007B/177